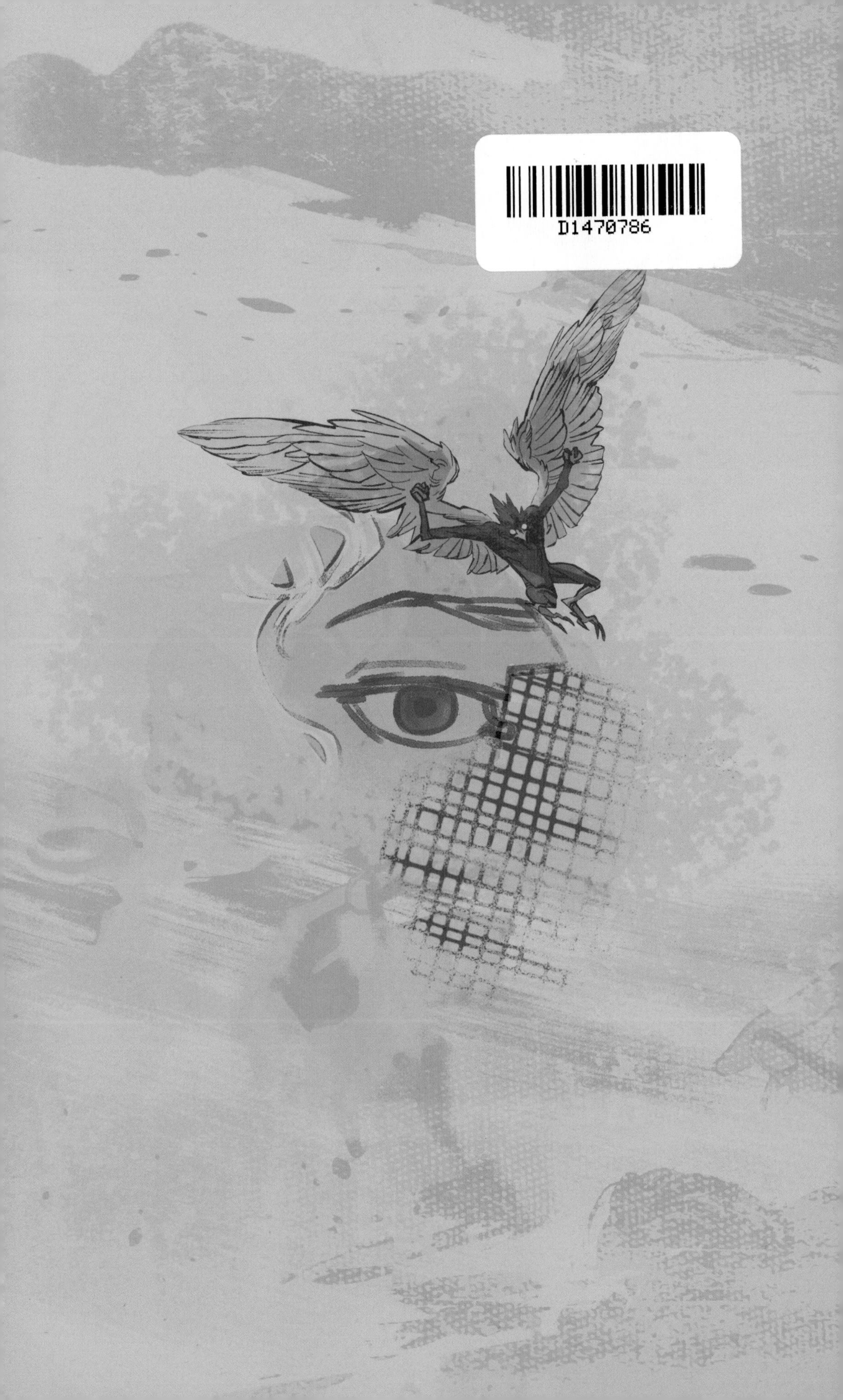

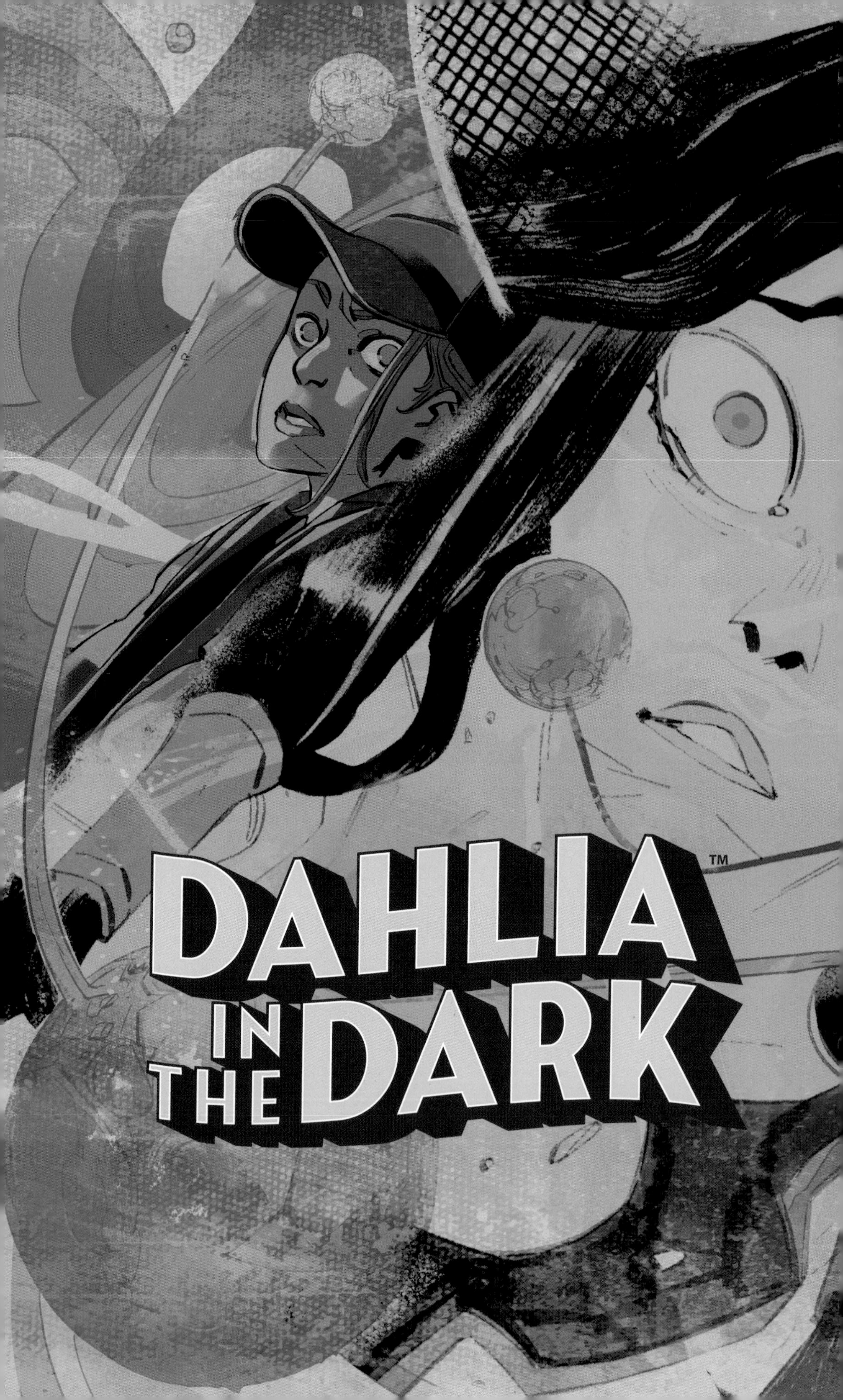
DAHLIA IN THE DARK™

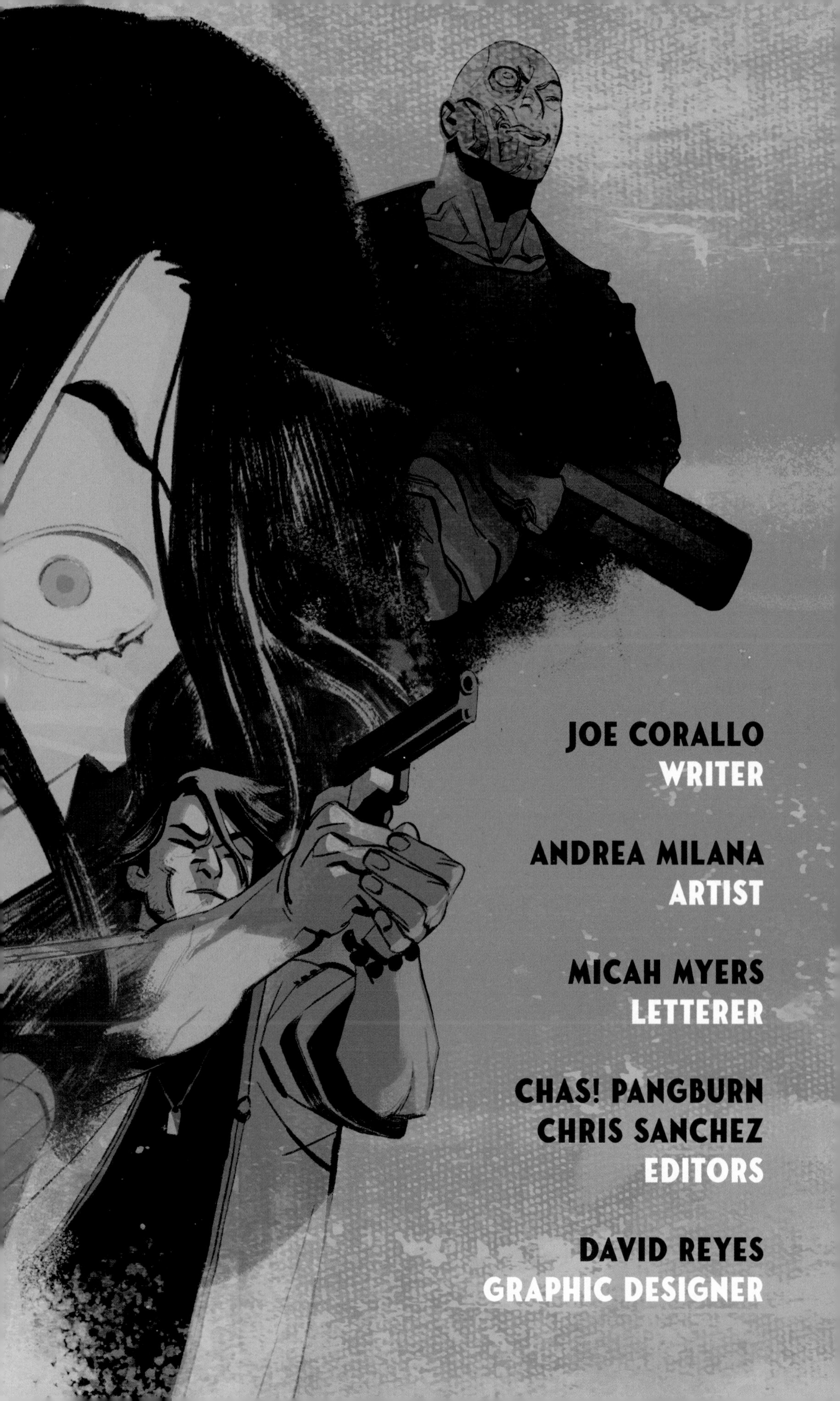

JOE CORALLO
WRITER

ANDREA MILANA
ARTIST

MICAH MYERS
LETTERER

CHAS! PANGBURN
CHRIS SANCHEZ
EDITORS

DAVID REYES
GRAPHIC DESIGNER

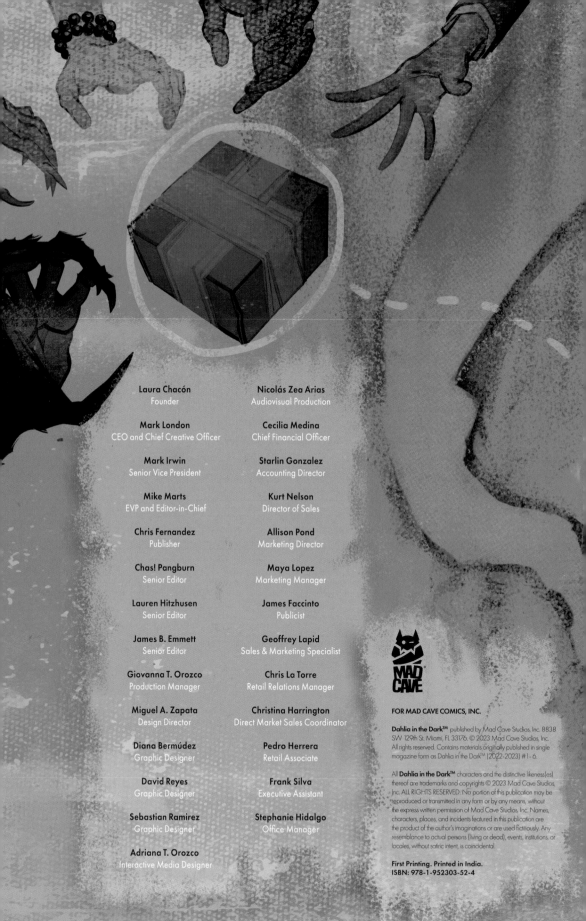

Laura Chacón
Founder

Mark London
CEO and Chief Creative Officer

Mark Irwin
Senior Vice President

Mike Marts
EVP and Editor-in-Chief

Chris Fernandez
Publisher

Chas! Pangburn
Senior Editor

Lauren Hitzhusen
Senior Editor

James B. Emmett
Senior Editor

Giovanna T. Orozco
Production Manager

Miguel A. Zapata
Design Director

Diana Bermúdez
Graphic Designer

David Reyes
Graphic Designer

Sebastian Ramirez
Graphic Designer

Adriana T. Orozco
Interactive Media Designer

Nicolás Zea Arias
Audiovisual Production

Cecilia Medina
Chief Financial Officer

Starlin Gonzalez
Accounting Director

Kurt Nelson
Director of Sales

Allison Pond
Marketing Director

Maya Lopez
Marketing Manager

James Faccinto
Publicist

Geoffrey Lapid
Sales & Marketing Specialist

Chris La Torre
Retail Relations Manager

Christina Harrington
Direct Market Sales Coordinator

Pedro Herrera
Retail Associate

Frank Silva
Executive Assistant

Stephanie Hidalgo
Office Manager

FOR MAD CAVE COMICS, INC.

Dahlia in the Dark™ published by Mad Cave Studios, Inc. 8838 SW 129th St. Miami, FL 33176. © 2023 Mad Cave Studios, Inc. All rights reserved. Contains materials originally published in single magazine form as Dahlia in the Dark™ (2022-2023) #1- 6.

First Printing. Printed in India.
ISBN: 978-1-952303-52-4

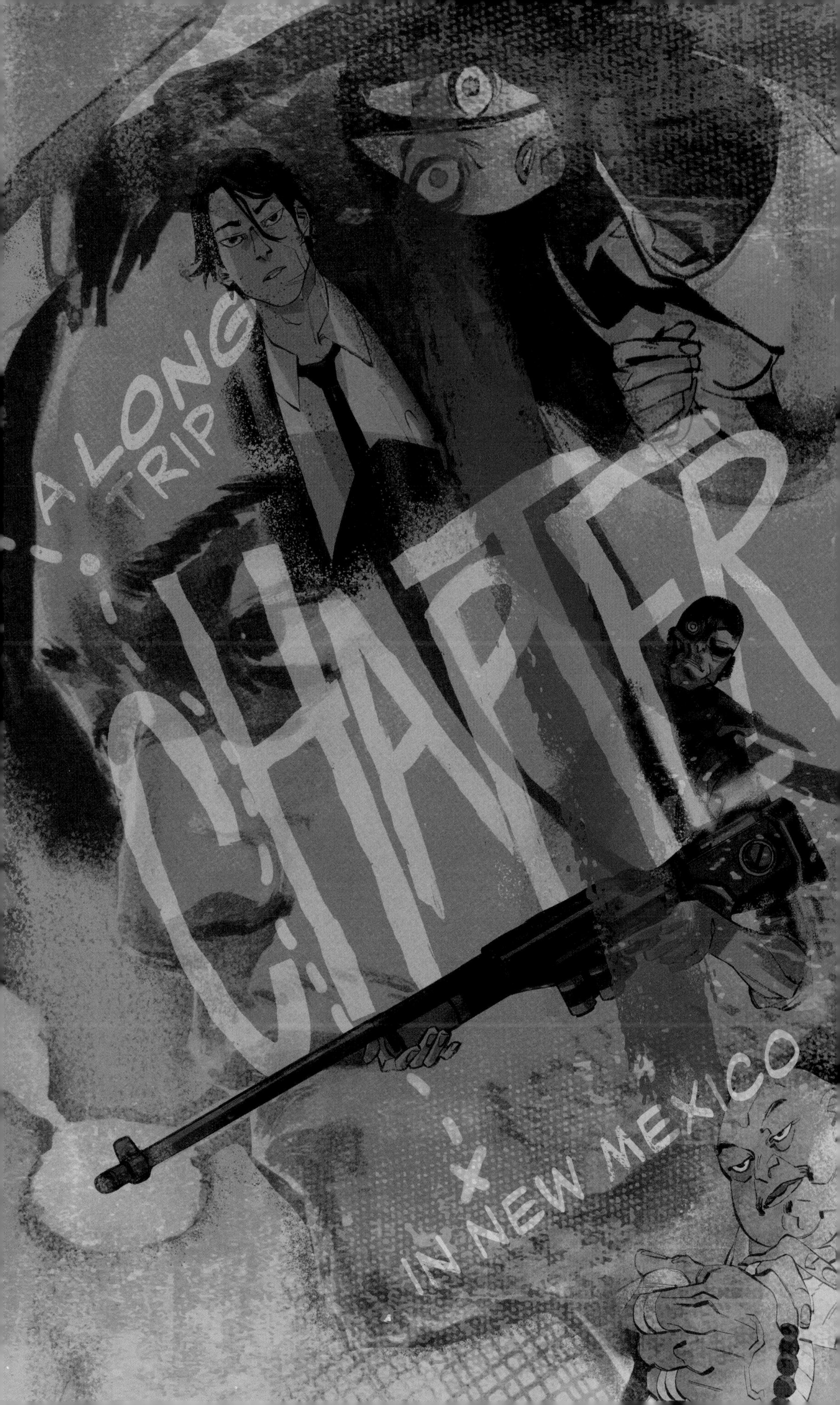
A LONG TRIP
CHAPTER 1
IN NEW MEXICO

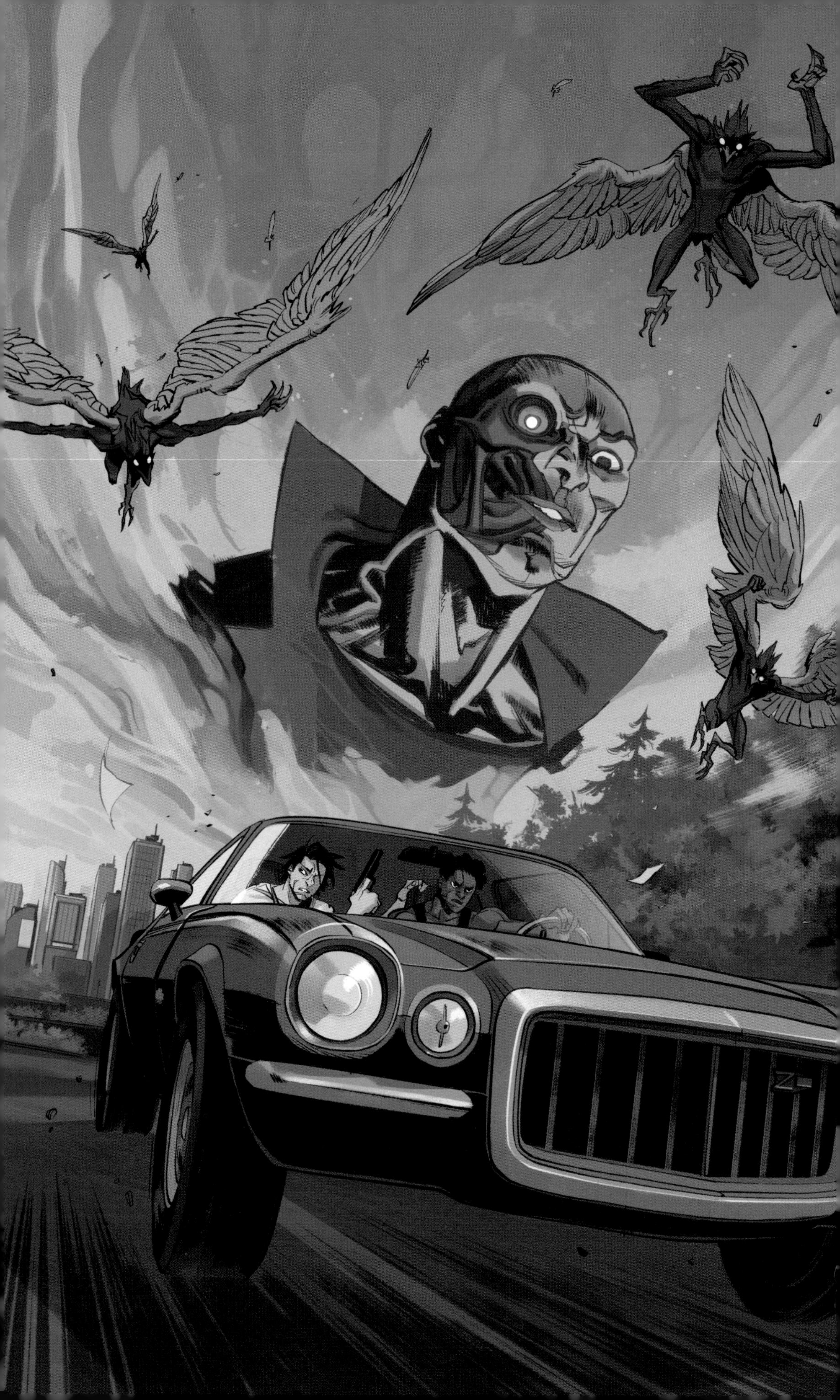

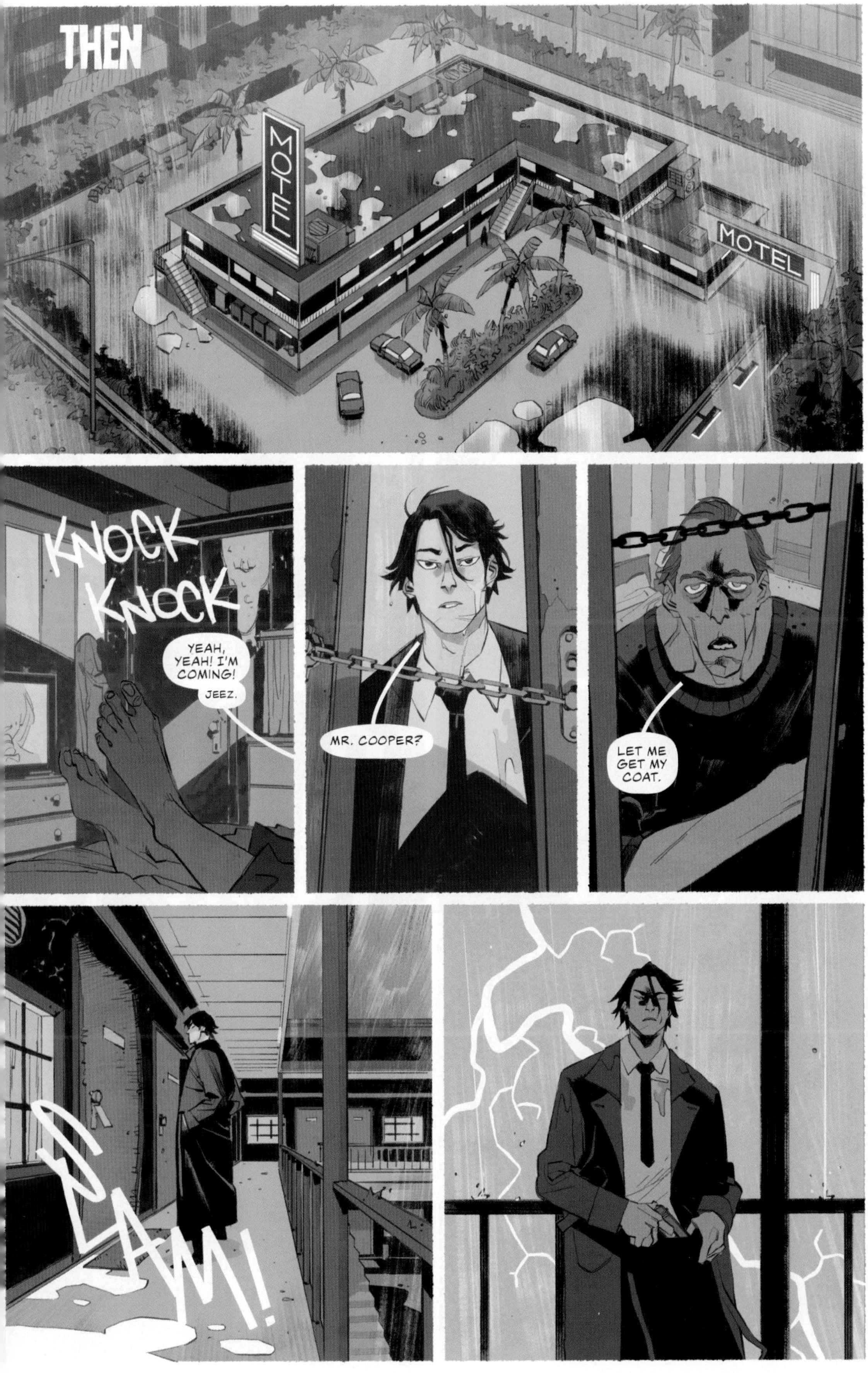
THEN
MOTEL
MOTEL
KNOCK
KNOCK
YEAH, YEAH! I'M COMING!
JEEZ.
MR. COOPER?
LET ME GET MY COAT.
SLAM!

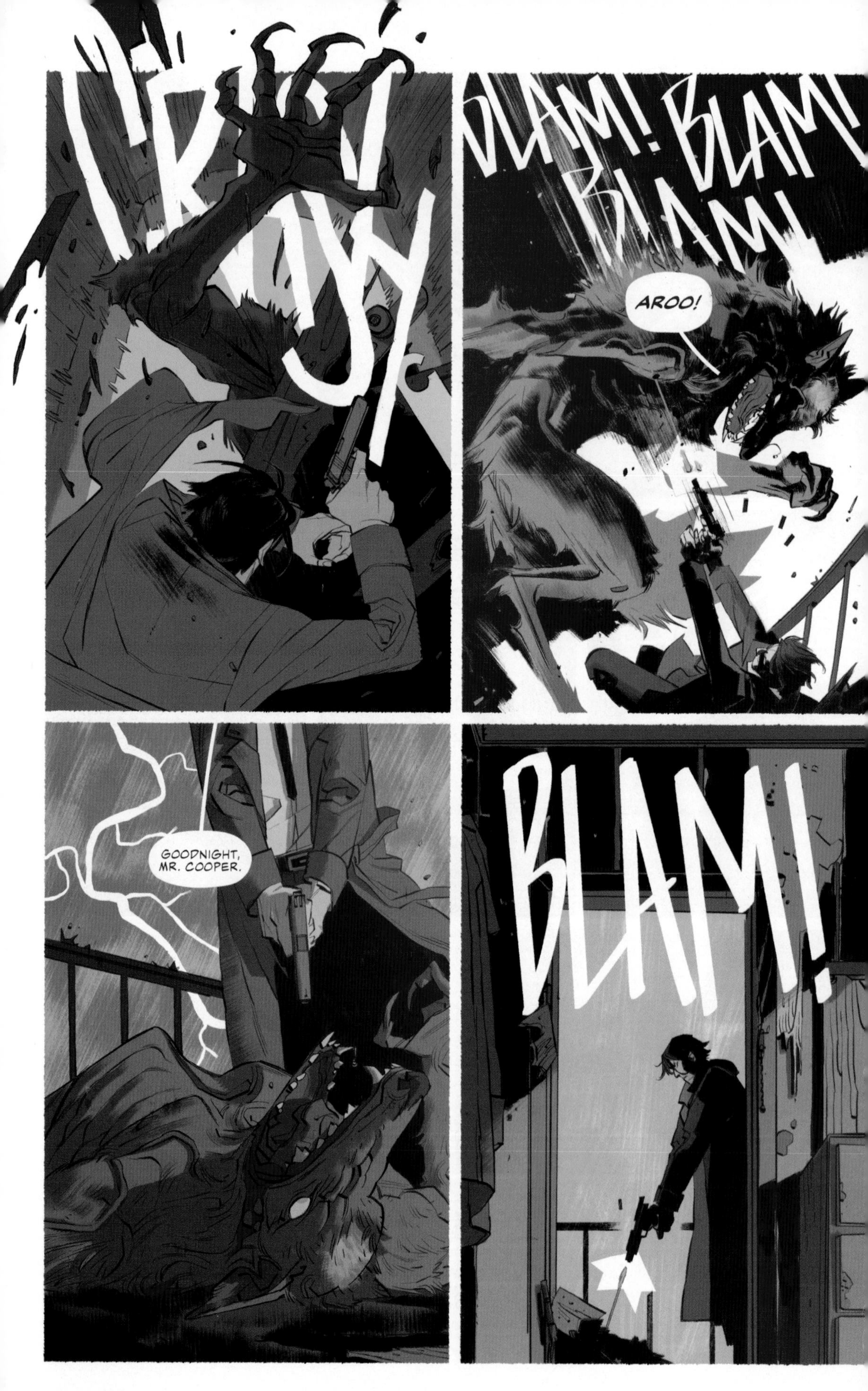
BLAM! BLAM!
BLAM!
AROO!
GOODNIGHT, MR. COOPER.
BLAM!

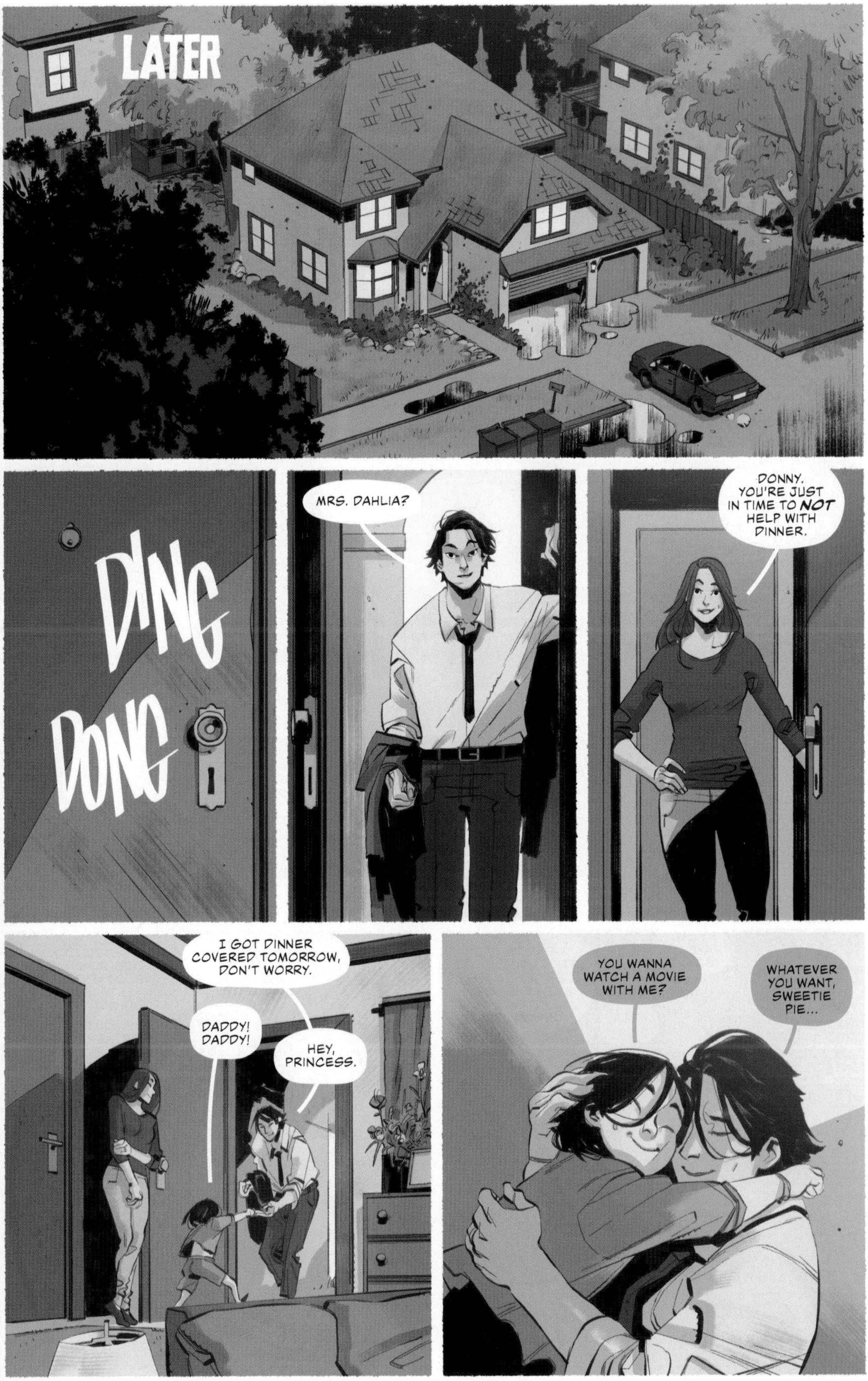
LATER
DING
DONG
MRS. DAHLIA?
DONNY. YOU'RE JUST IN TIME TO NOT HELP WITH DINNER.
I GOT DINNER COVERED TOMORROW, DON'T WORRY.
DADDY! DADDY!
HEY, PRINCESS.
YOU WANNA WATCH A MOVIE WITH ME?
WHATEVER YOU WANT, SWEETIE PIE...

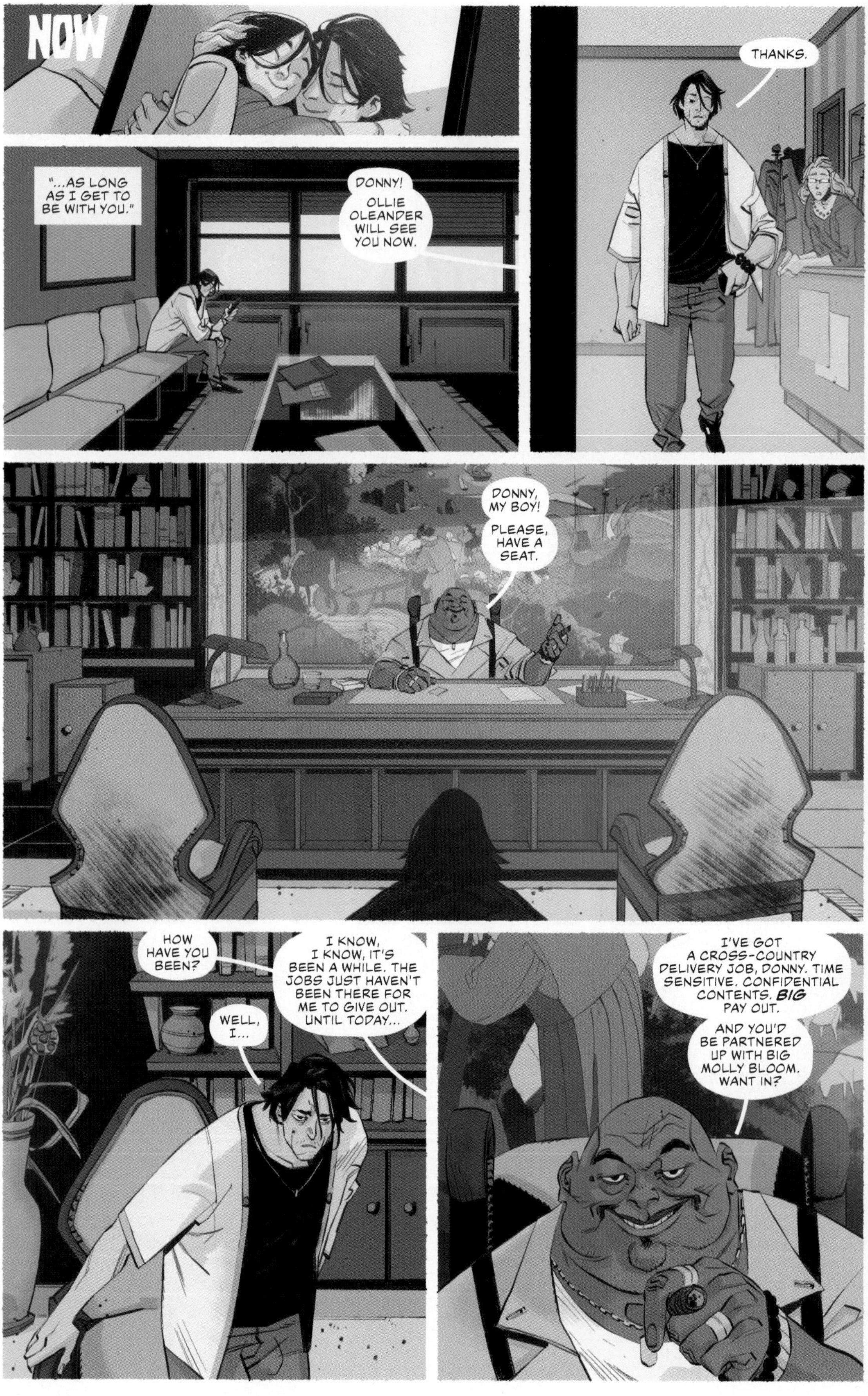
NOW
THANKS.
"...AS LONG AS I GET TO BE WITH YOU."
DONNY!
OLLIE OLEANDER WILL SEE YOU NOW.
DONNY, MY BOY!
PLEASE, HAVE A SEAT.
HOW HAVE YOU BEEN?
WELL, I...
I KNOW, I KNOW, IT'S BEEN A WHILE. THE JOBS JUST HAVEN'T BEEN THERE FOR ME TO GIVE OUT. UNTIL TODAY...
I'VE GOT A CROSS-COUNTRY DELIVERY JOB, DONNY. TIME SENSITIVE. CONFIDENTIAL CONTENTS. BIG PAY OUT.
AND YOU'D BE PARTNERED UP WITH BIG MOLLY BLOOM. WANT IN?

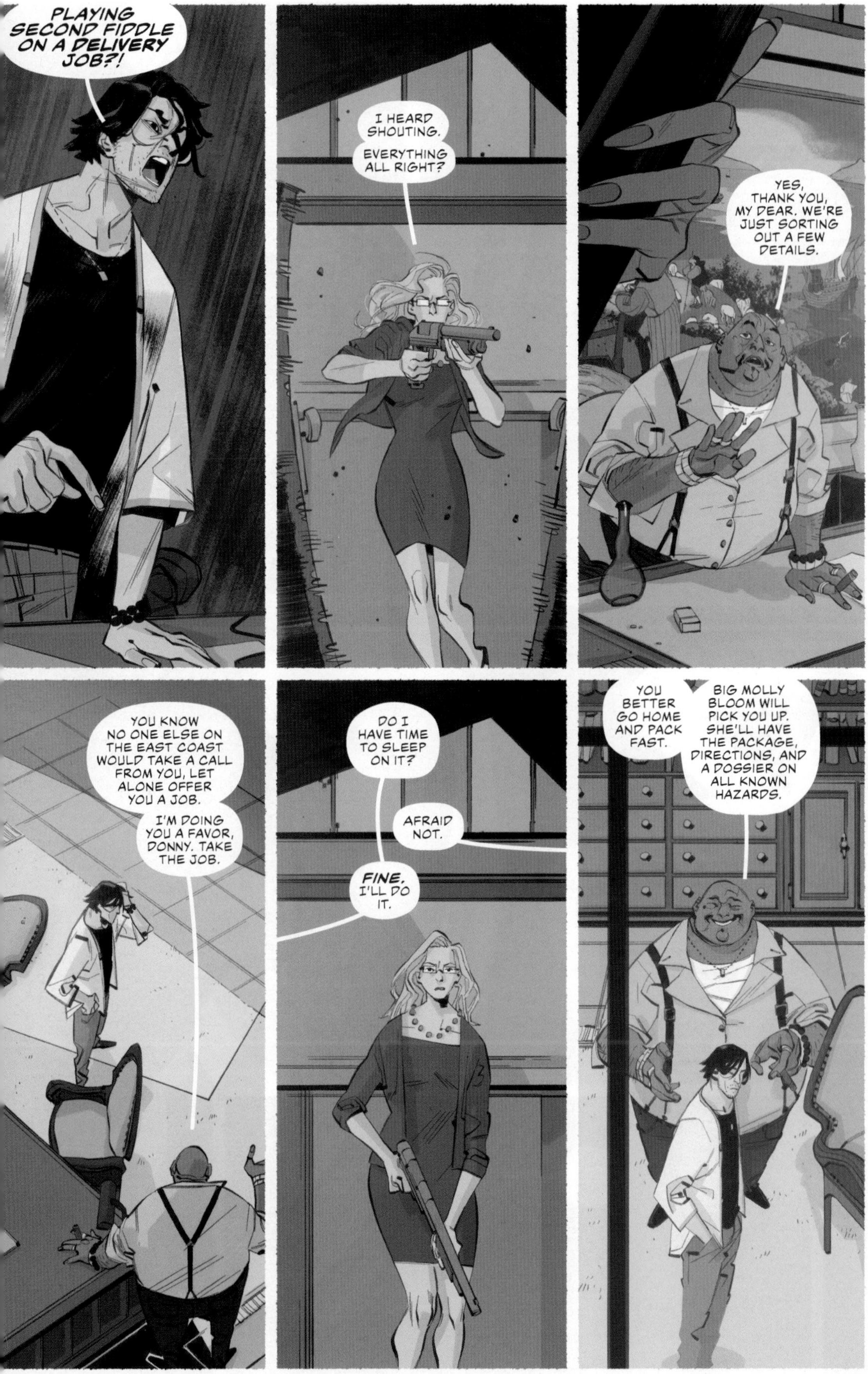
PLAYING SECOND FIDDLE ON A DELIVERY JOB?!
I HEARD SHOUTING.
EVERYTHING ALL RIGHT?
YES, THANK YOU, MY DEAR. WE'RE JUST SORTING OUT A FEW DETAILS.
YOU KNOW NO ONE ELSE ON THE EAST COAST WOULD TAKE A CALL FROM YOU, LET ALONE OFFER YOU A JOB.
I'M DOING YOU A FAVOR, DONNY. TAKE THE JOB.
DO I HAVE TIME TO SLEEP ON IT?
AFRAID NOT.
FINE. I'LL DO IT.
YOU BETTER GO HOME AND PACK FAST.
BIG MOLLY BLOOM WILL PICK YOU UP. SHE'LL HAVE THE PACKAGE, DIRECTIONS, AND A DOSSIER ON ALL KNOWN HAZARDS.

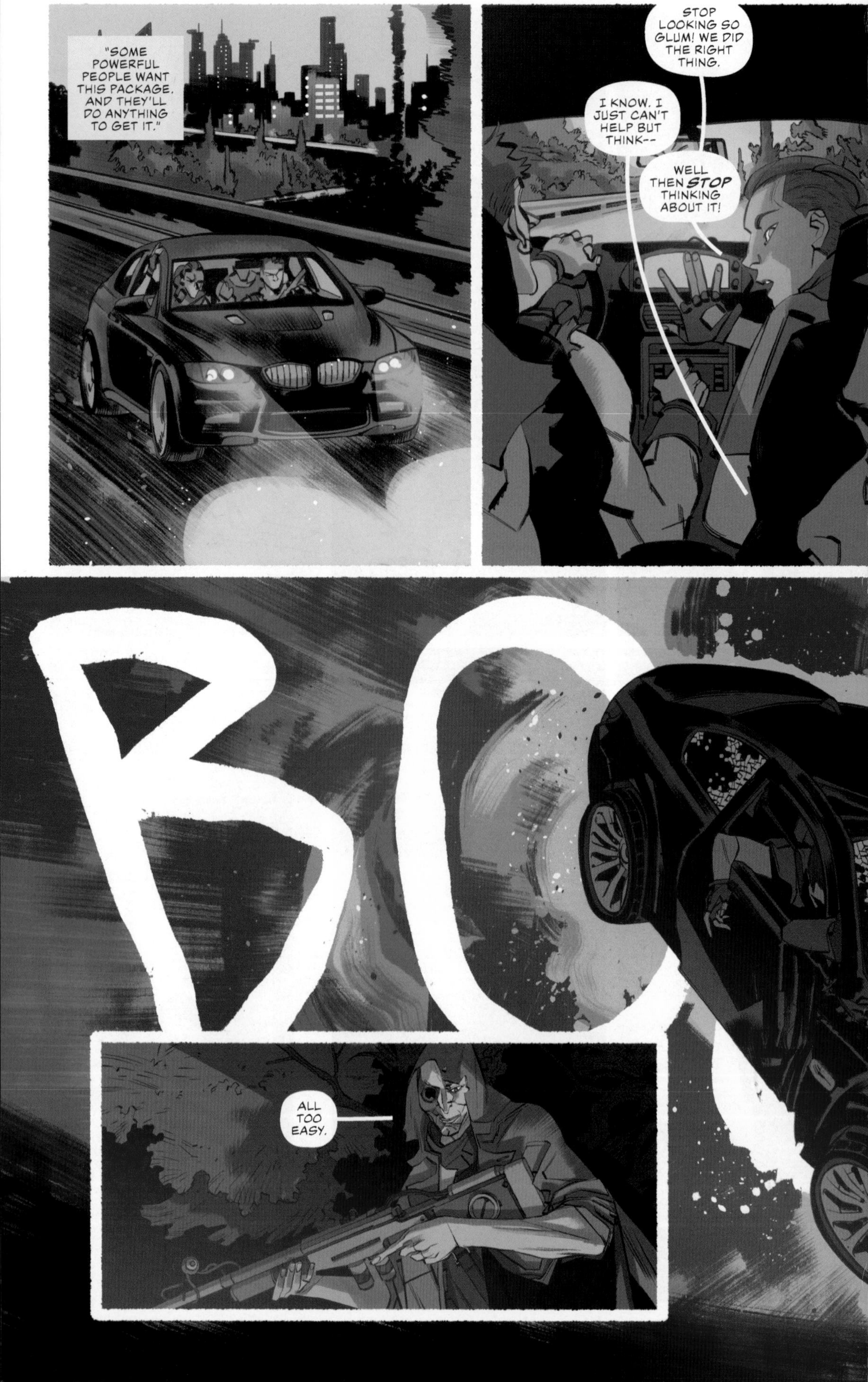
"SOME POWERFUL PEOPLE WANT THIS PACKAGE. AND THEY'LL DO ANYTHING TO GET IT."
STOP LOOKING SO GLUM! WE DID THE RIGHT THING.
I KNOW. I JUST CAN'T HELP BUT THINK--
WELL THEN STOP THINKING ABOUT IT!
BO
ALL TOO EASY.

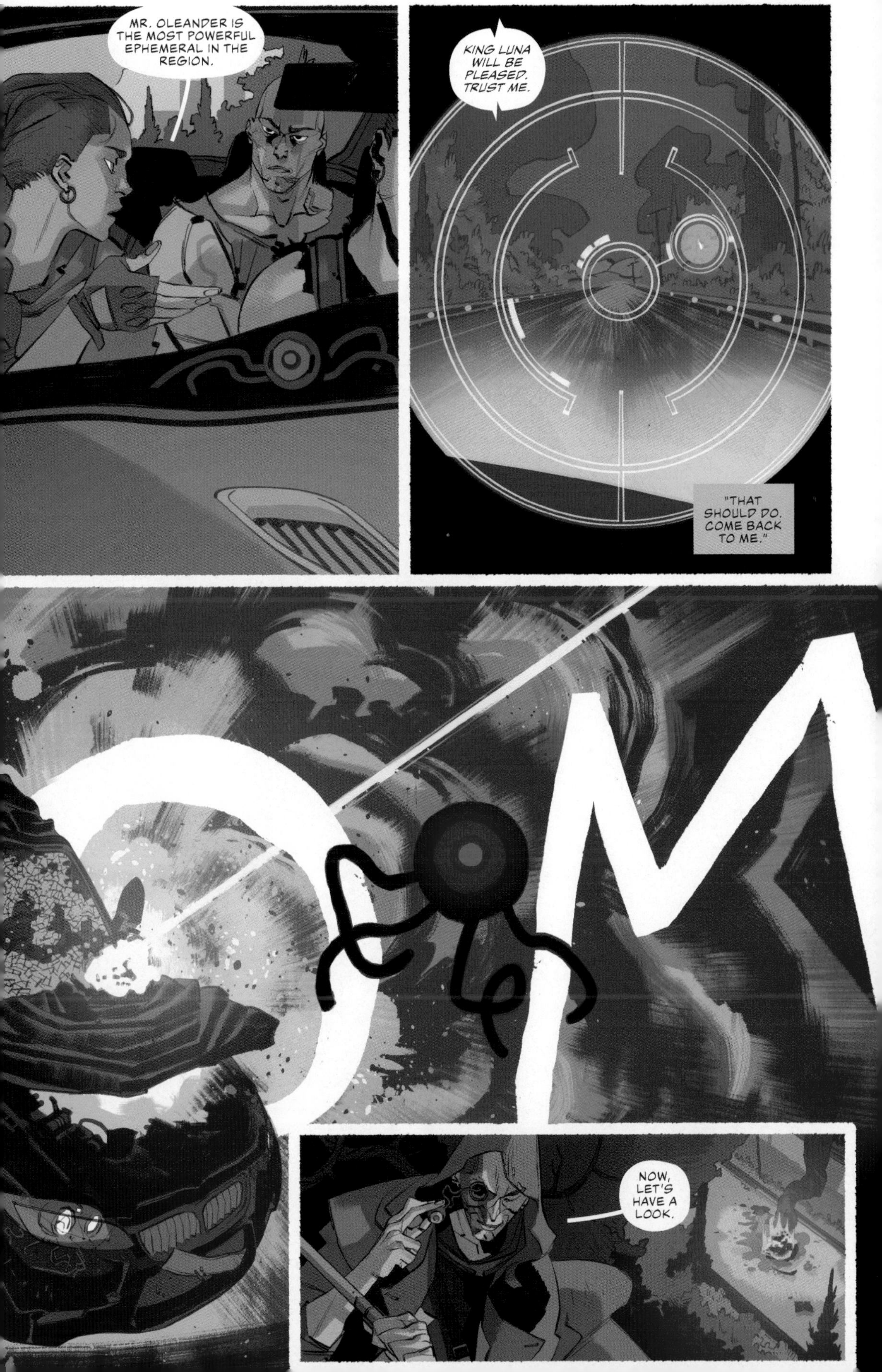
MR. OLEANDER IS THE MOST POWERFUL EPHEMERAL IN THE REGION.
KING LUNA WILL BE PLEASED. TRUST ME.
"THAT SHOULD DO. COME BACK TO ME."
NOW, LET'S HAVE A LOOK.

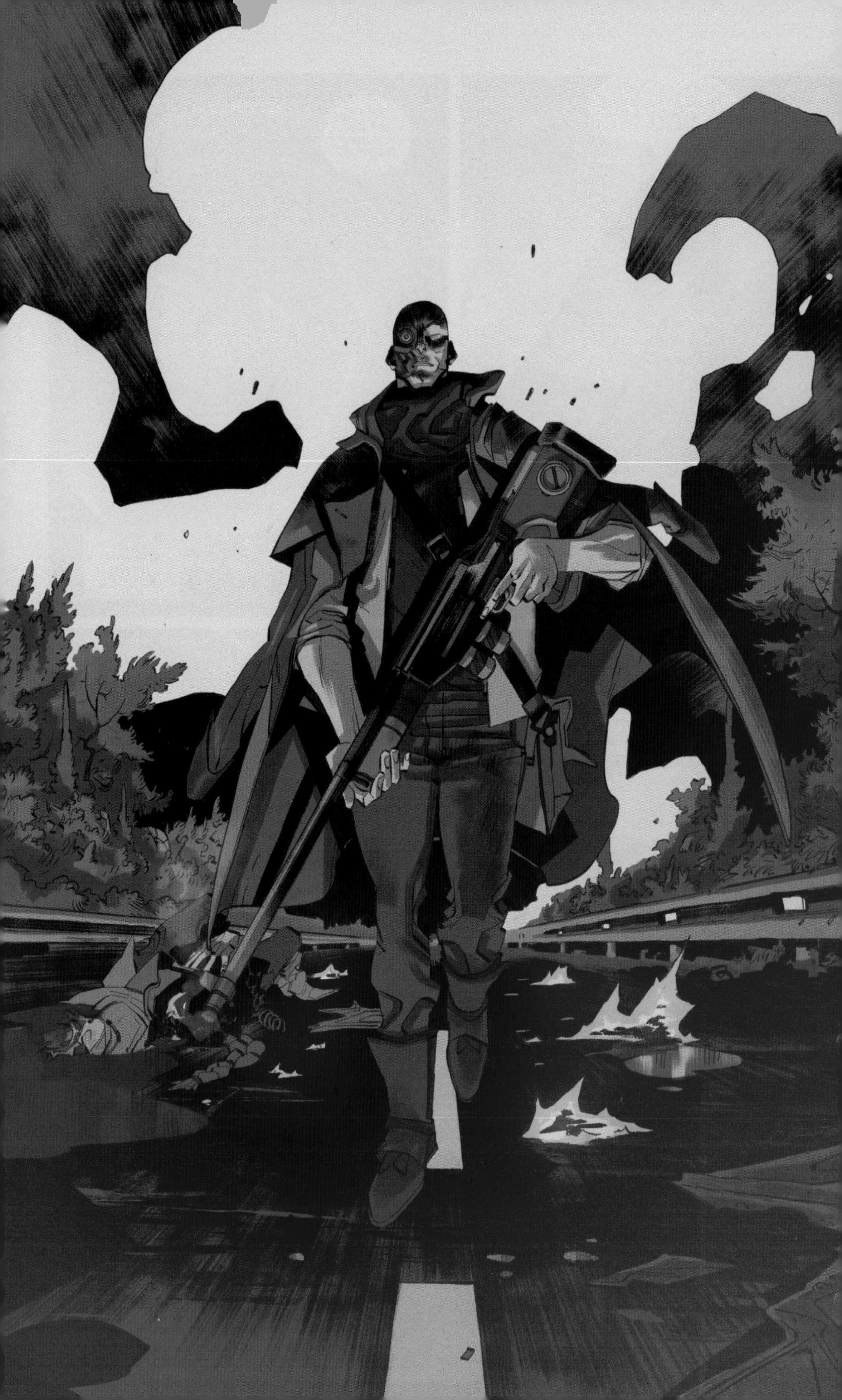

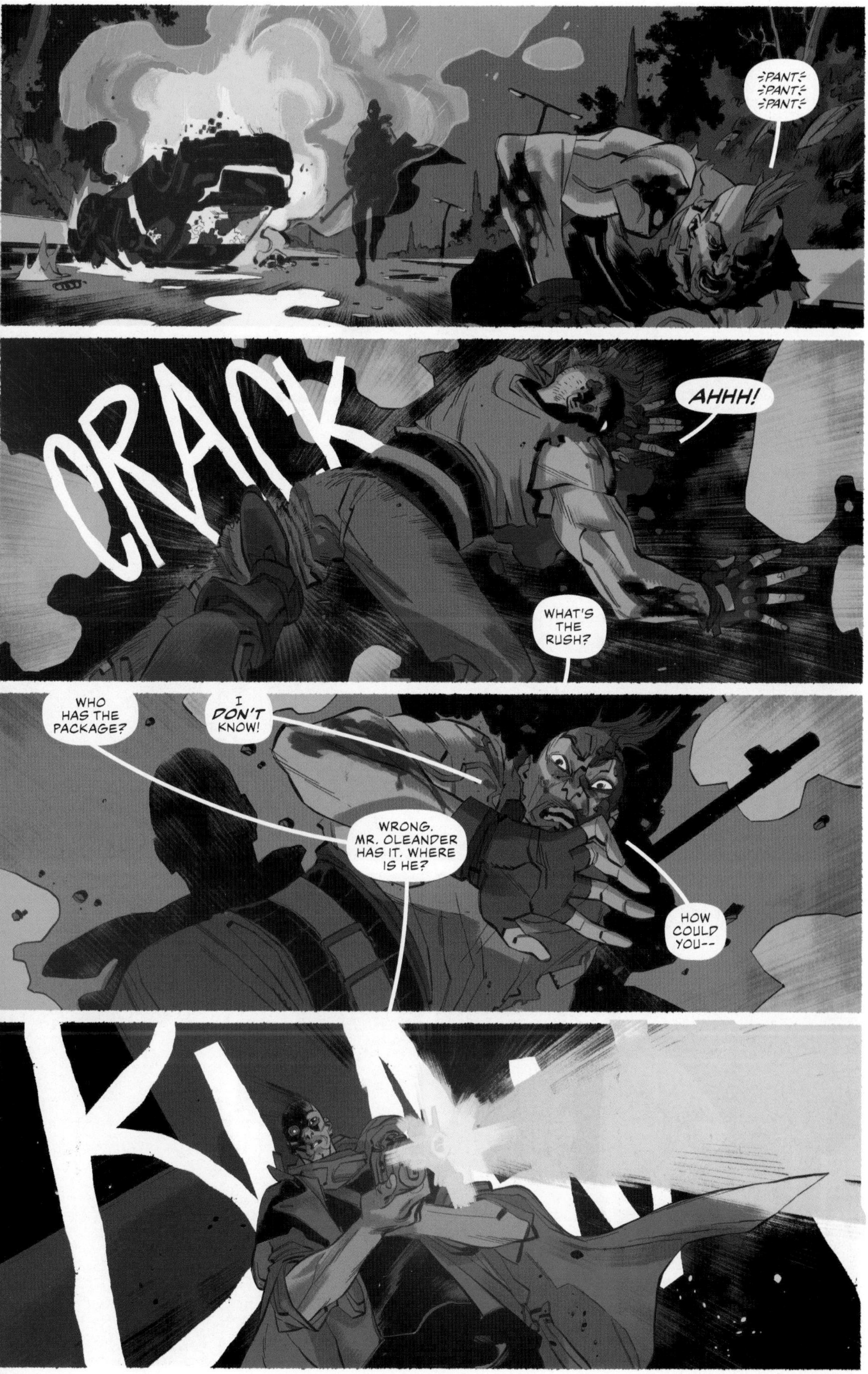
PANT PANT PANT
CRACK
AHHH!
WHAT'S THE RUSH?
WHO HAS THE PACKAGE?
I DON'T KNOW!
WRONG. MR. OLEANDER HAS IT. WHERE IS HE?
HOW COULD YOU--

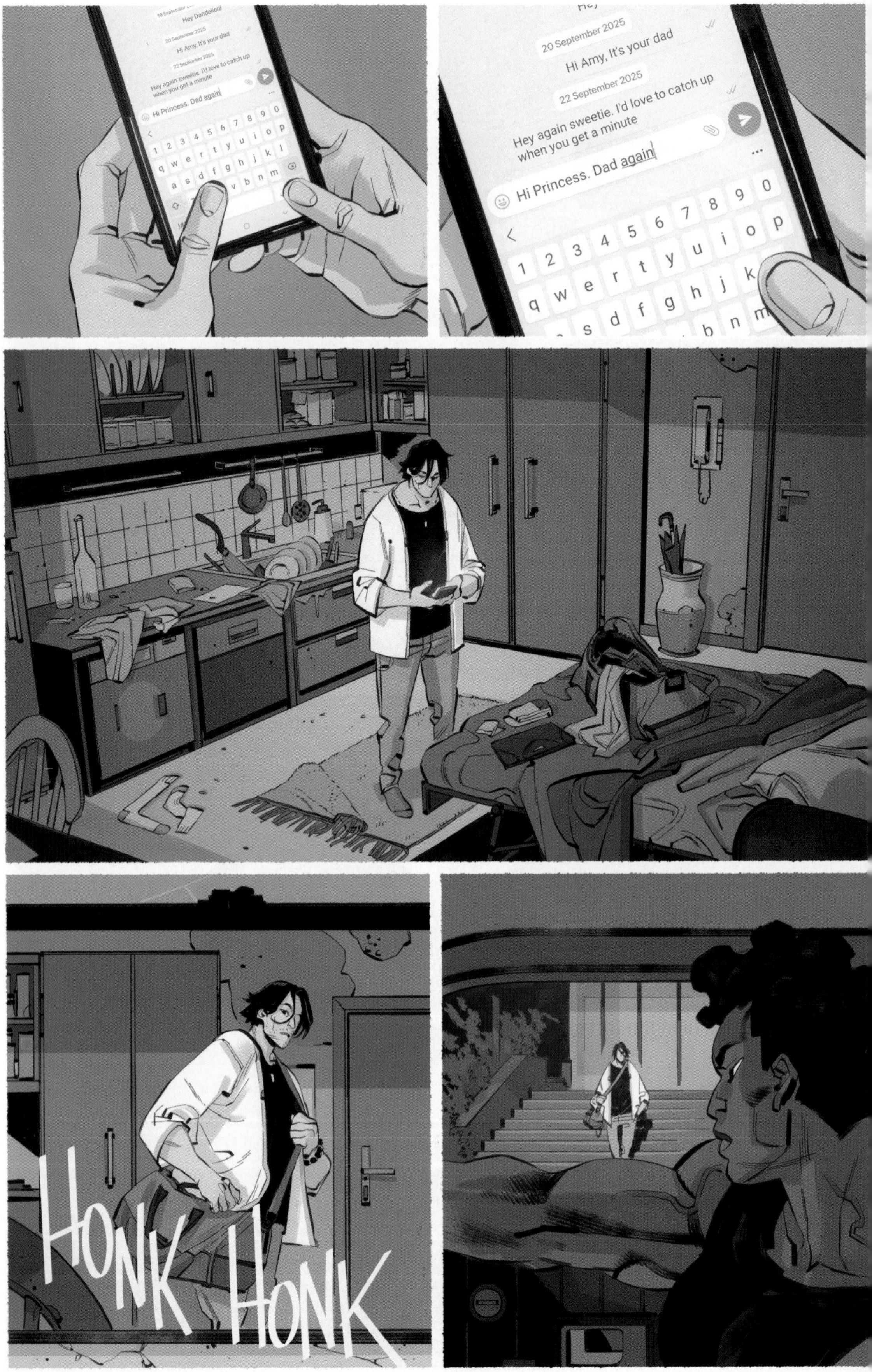
Hey Dandelion!
20 September 2025
Hi Amy, It's your dad
22 September 2025
Hey again sweetie. I'd love to catch up when you get a minute
Hi Princess. Dad again
20 September 2025
Hi Amy, It's your dad
22 September 2025
Hey again sweetie. I'd love to catch up when you get a minute
Hi Princess. Dad again
HONK HONK

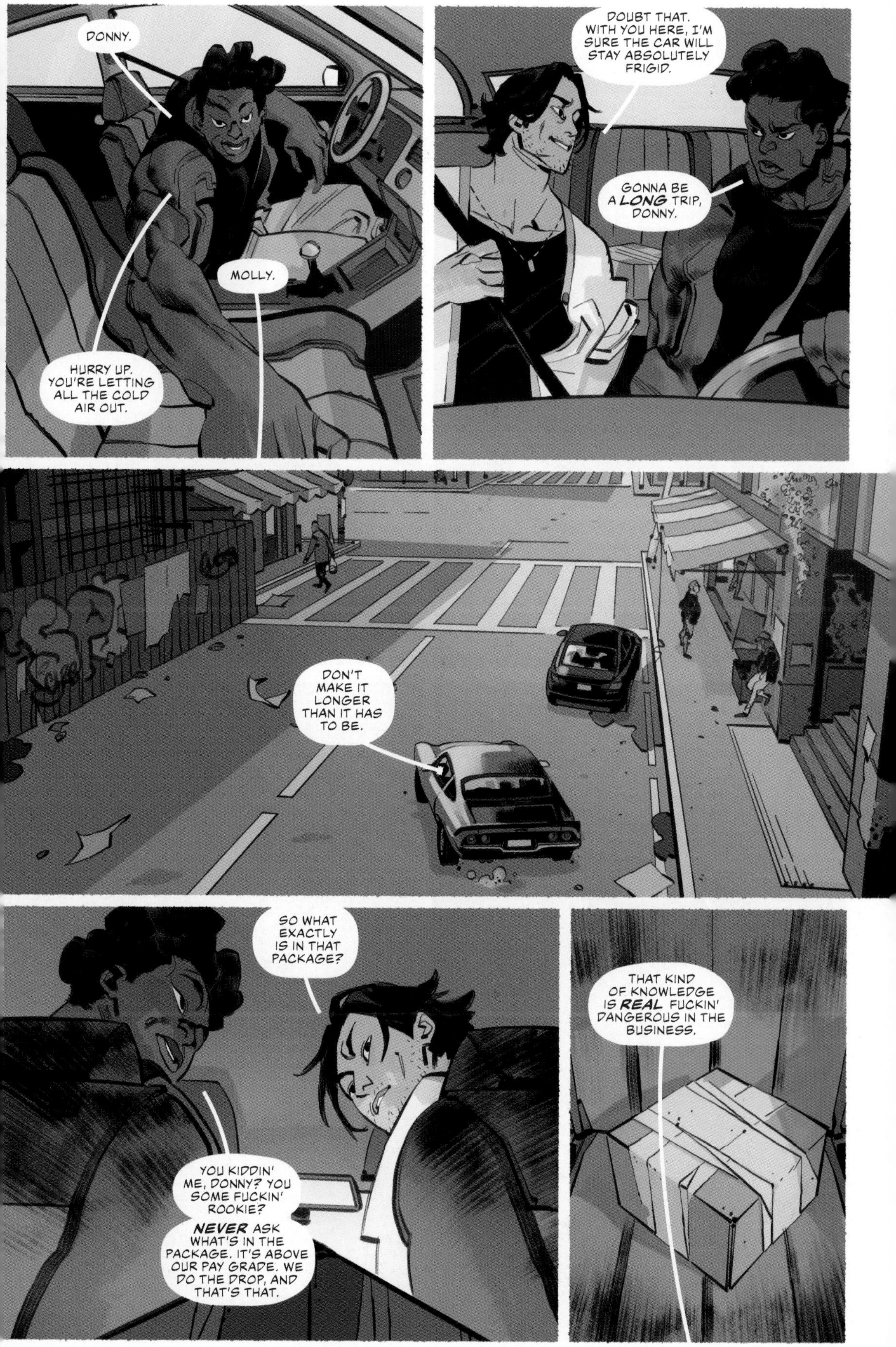
DONNY.
HURRY UP. YOU'RE LETTING ALL THE COLD AIR OUT.
MOLLY.
DOUBT THAT. WITH YOU HERE, I'M SURE THE CAR WILL STAY ABSOLUTELY FRIGID.
GONNA BE A LONG TRIP, DONNY.
DON'T MAKE IT LONGER THAN IT HAS TO BE.
SO WHAT EXACTLY IS IN THAT PACKAGE?
YOU KIDDIN' ME, DONNY? YOU SOME FUCKIN' ROOKIE?
NEVER ASK WHAT'S IN THE PACKAGE. IT'S ABOVE OUR PAY GRADE. WE DO THE DROP, AND THAT'S THAT.
THAT KIND OF KNOWLEDGE IS REAL FUCKIN' DANGEROUS IN THE BUSINESS.

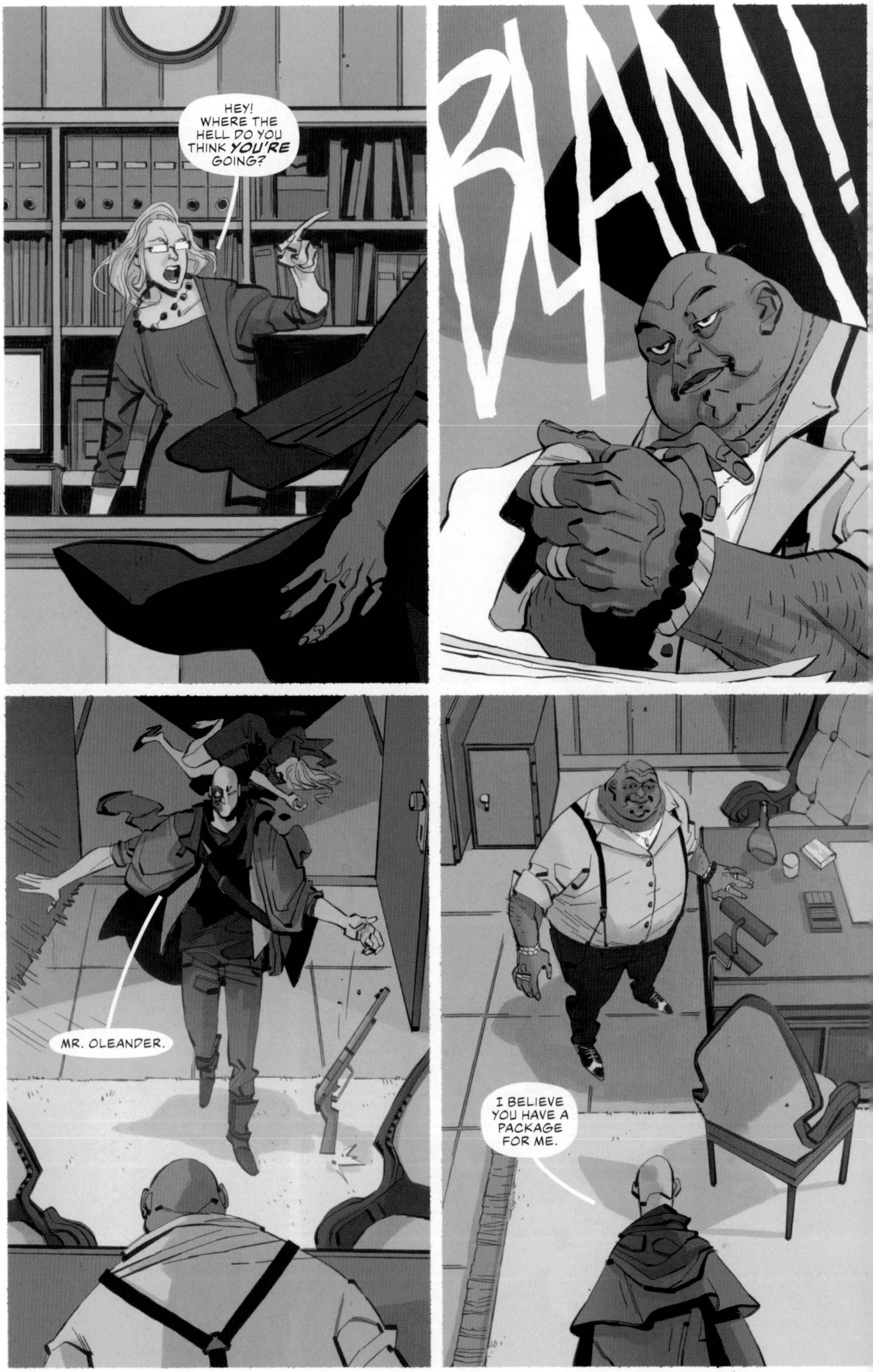
HEY! WHERE THE HELL DO YOU THINK *YOU'RE* GOING?
BLAM!
MR. OLEANDER.
I BELIEVE YOU HAVE A PACKAGE FOR ME.

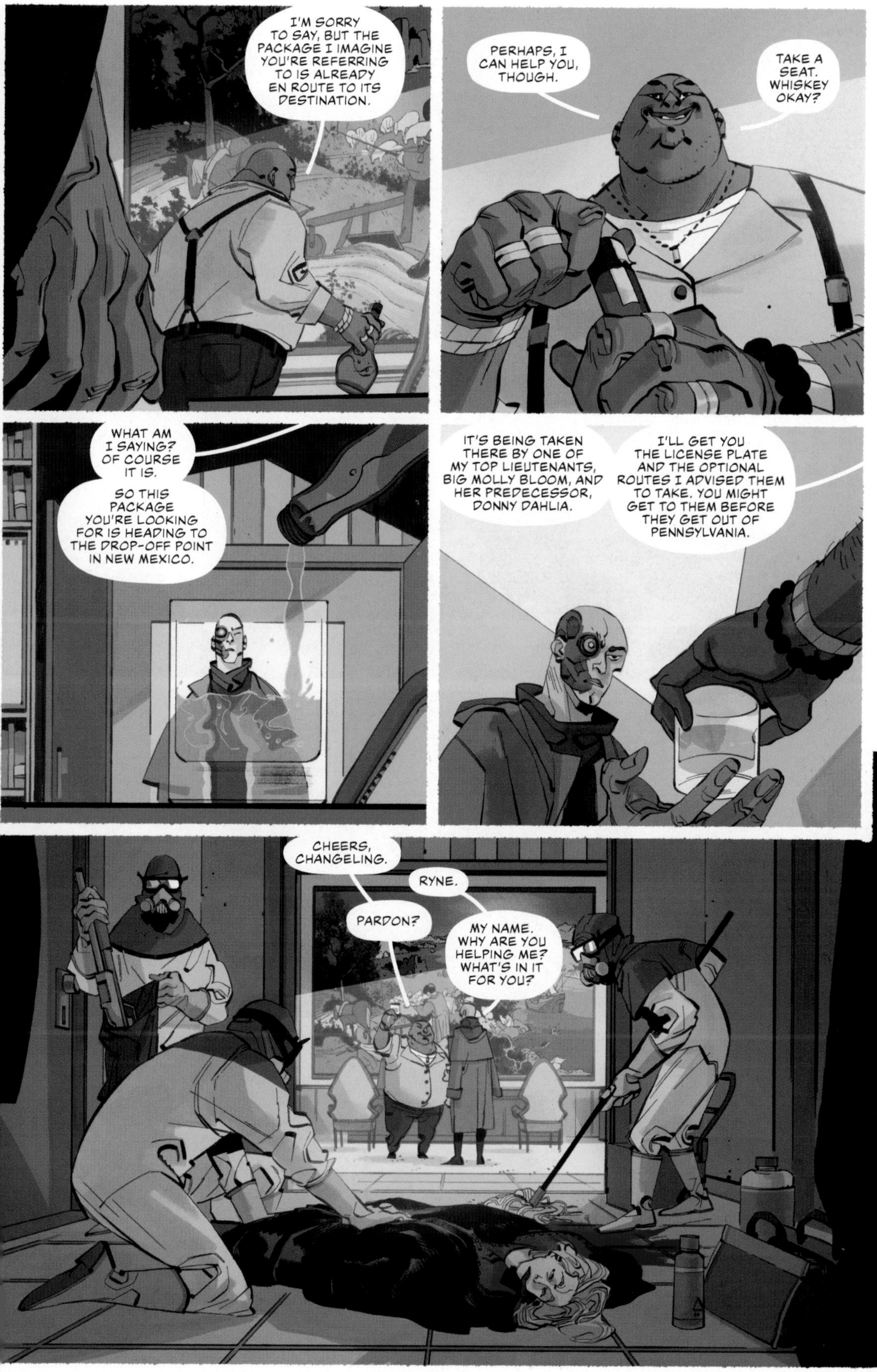
I'M SORRY TO SAY, BUT THE PACKAGE I IMAGINE YOU'RE REFERRING TO IS ALREADY EN ROUTE TO ITS DESTINATION.
PERHAPS, I CAN HELP YOU, THOUGH.
TAKE A SEAT. WHISKEY OKAY?
WHAT AM I SAYING? OF COURSE IT IS.
SO THIS PACKAGE YOU'RE LOOKING FOR IS HEADING TO THE DROP-OFF POINT IN NEW MEXICO.
IT'S BEING TAKEN THERE BY ONE OF MY TOP LIEUTENANTS, BIG MOLLY BLOOM, AND HER PREDECESSOR, DONNY DAHLIA.
I'LL GET YOU THE LICENSE PLATE AND THE OPTIONAL ROUTES I ADVISED THEM TO TAKE. YOU MIGHT GET TO THEM BEFORE THEY GET OUT OF PENNSYLVANIA.
CHEERS, CHANGELING.
RYNE.
PARDON?
MY NAME. WHY ARE YOU HELPING ME? WHAT'S IN IT FOR YOU?

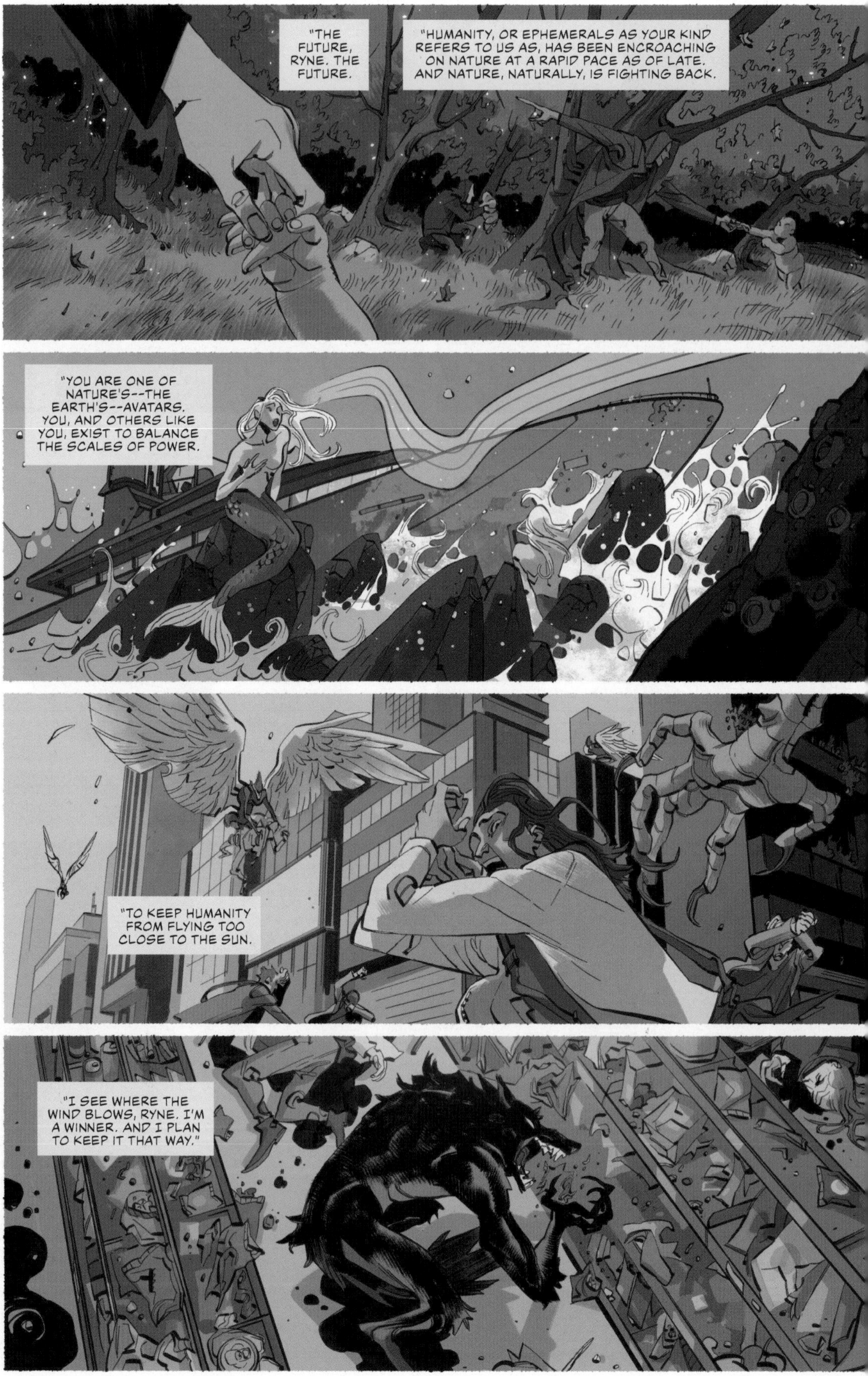
"THE FUTURE, RYNE. THE FUTURE.
"HUMANITY, OR EPHEMERALS AS YOUR KIND REFERS TO US AS, HAS BEEN ENCROACHING ON NATURE AT A RAPID PACE AS OF LATE. AND NATURE, NATURALLY, IS FIGHTING BACK.
"YOU ARE ONE OF NATURE'S--THE EARTH'S--AVATARS. YOU, AND OTHERS LIKE YOU, EXIST TO BALANCE THE SCALES OF POWER.
"TO KEEP HUMANITY FROM FLYING TOO CLOSE TO THE SUN.
"I SEE WHERE THE WIND BLOWS, RYNE. I'M A WINNER. AND I PLAN TO KEEP IT THAT WAY."

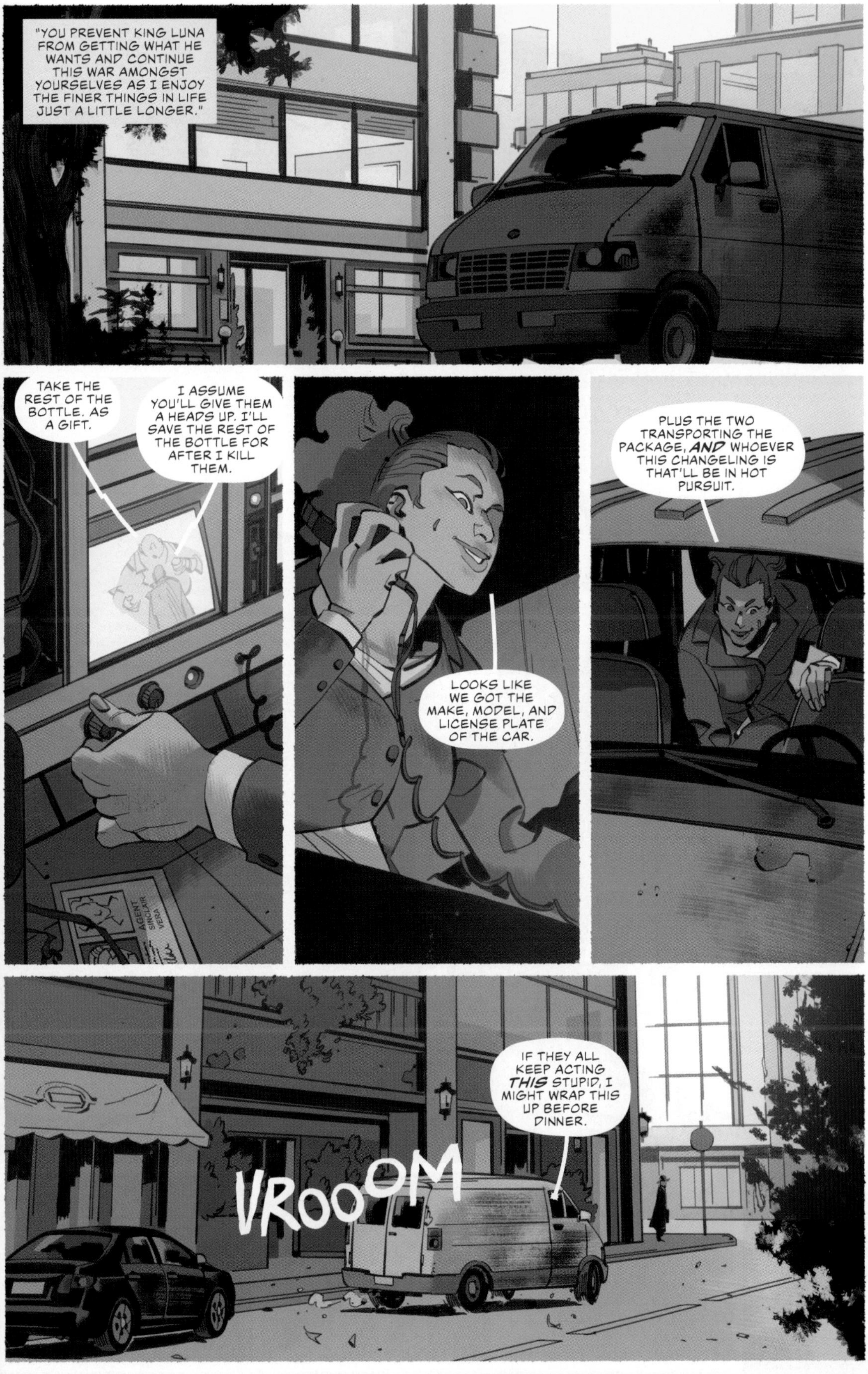
"YOU PREVENT KING LUNA FROM GETTING WHAT HE WANTS AND CONTINUE THIS WAR AMONGST YOURSELVES AS I ENJOY THE FINER THINGS IN LIFE JUST A LITTLE LONGER."
TAKE THE REST OF THE BOTTLE. AS A GIFT.
I ASSUME YOU'LL GIVE THEM A HEADS UP. I'LL SAVE THE REST OF THE BOTTLE FOR AFTER I KILL THEM.
AGENT SINCLAIR VERA
LOOKS LIKE WE GOT THE MAKE, MODEL, AND LICENSE PLATE OF THE CAR.
PLUS THE TWO TRANSPORTING THE PACKAGE, AND WHOEVER THIS CHANGELING IS THAT'LL BE IN HOT PURSUIT.
IF THEY ALL KEEP ACTING THIS STUPID, I MIGHT WRAP THIS UP BEFORE DINNER.
VROOOM

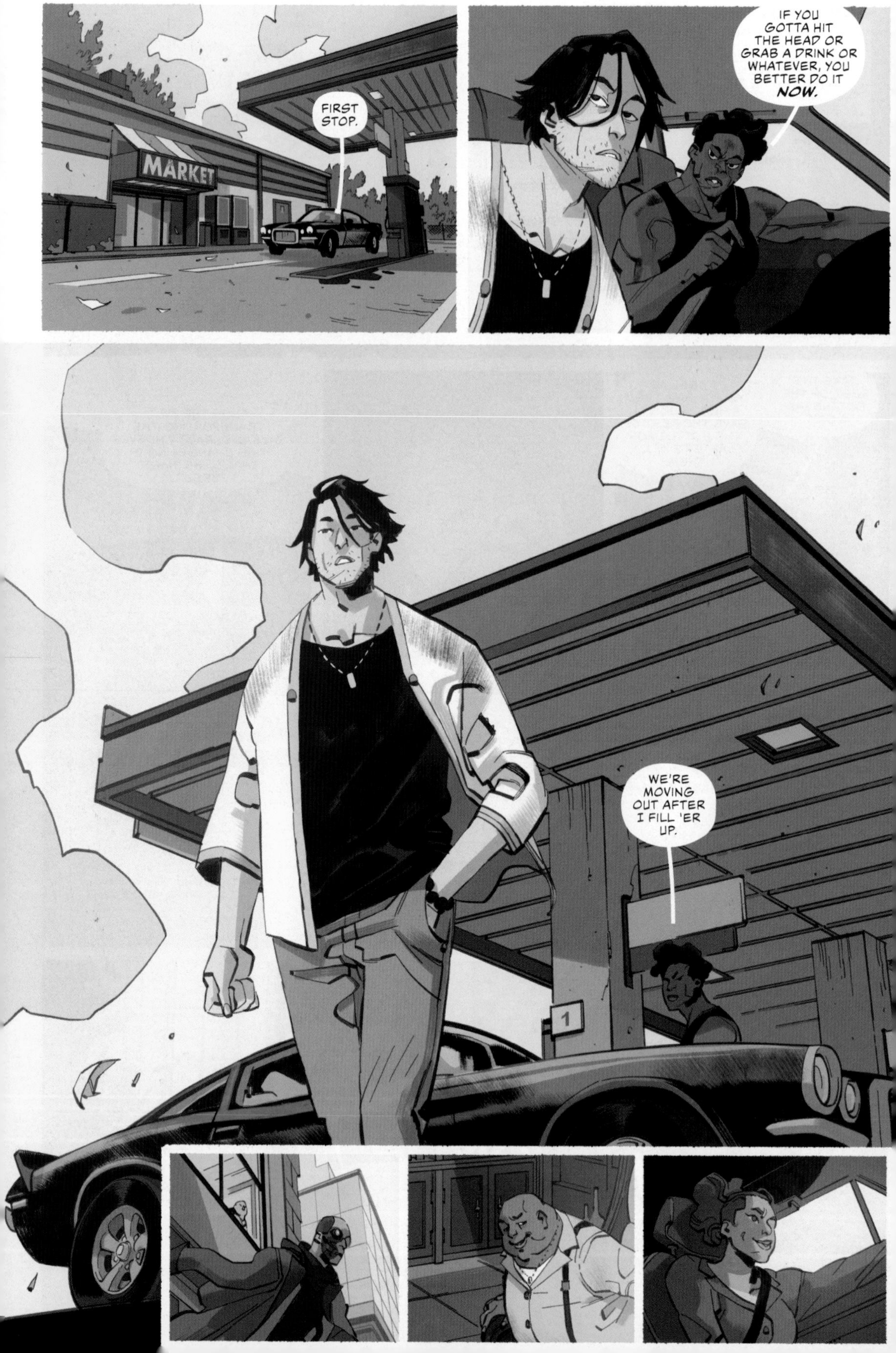
FIRST STOP.
IF YOU GOTTA HIT THE HEAD OR GRAB A DRINK OR WHATEVER, YOU BETTER DO IT ***NOW.***
WE'RE MOVING OUT AFTER I FILL 'ER UP.

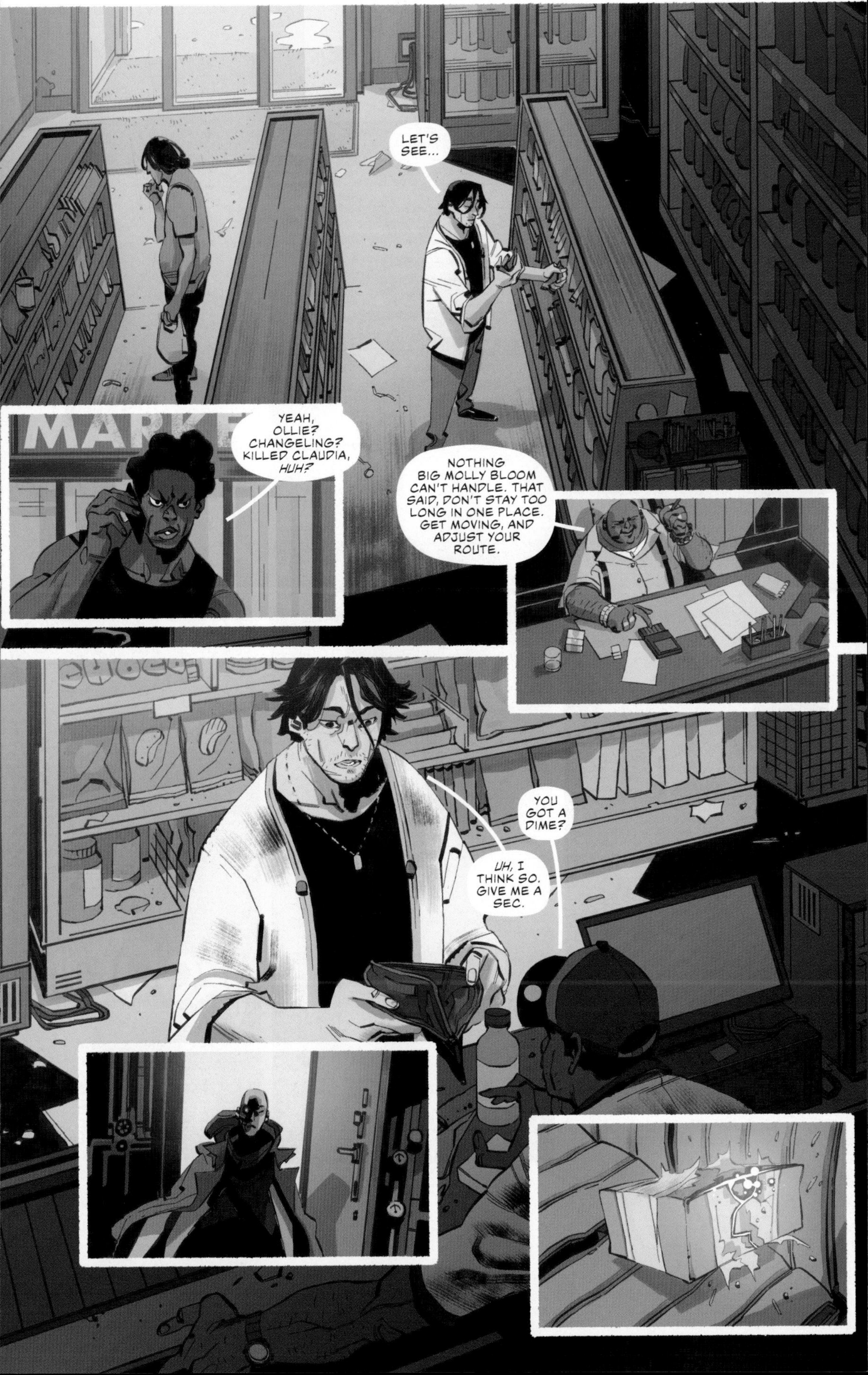
LET'S SEE...
MARKE
YEAH, OLLIE? CHANGELING? KILLED CLAUDIA, HUH?
NOTHING BIG MOLLY BLOOM CAN'T HANDLE. THAT SAID, DON'T STAY TOO LONG IN ONE PLACE. GET MOVING, AND ADJUST YOUR ROUTE.
YOU GOT A DIME?
UH, I THINK SO. GIVE ME A SEC.

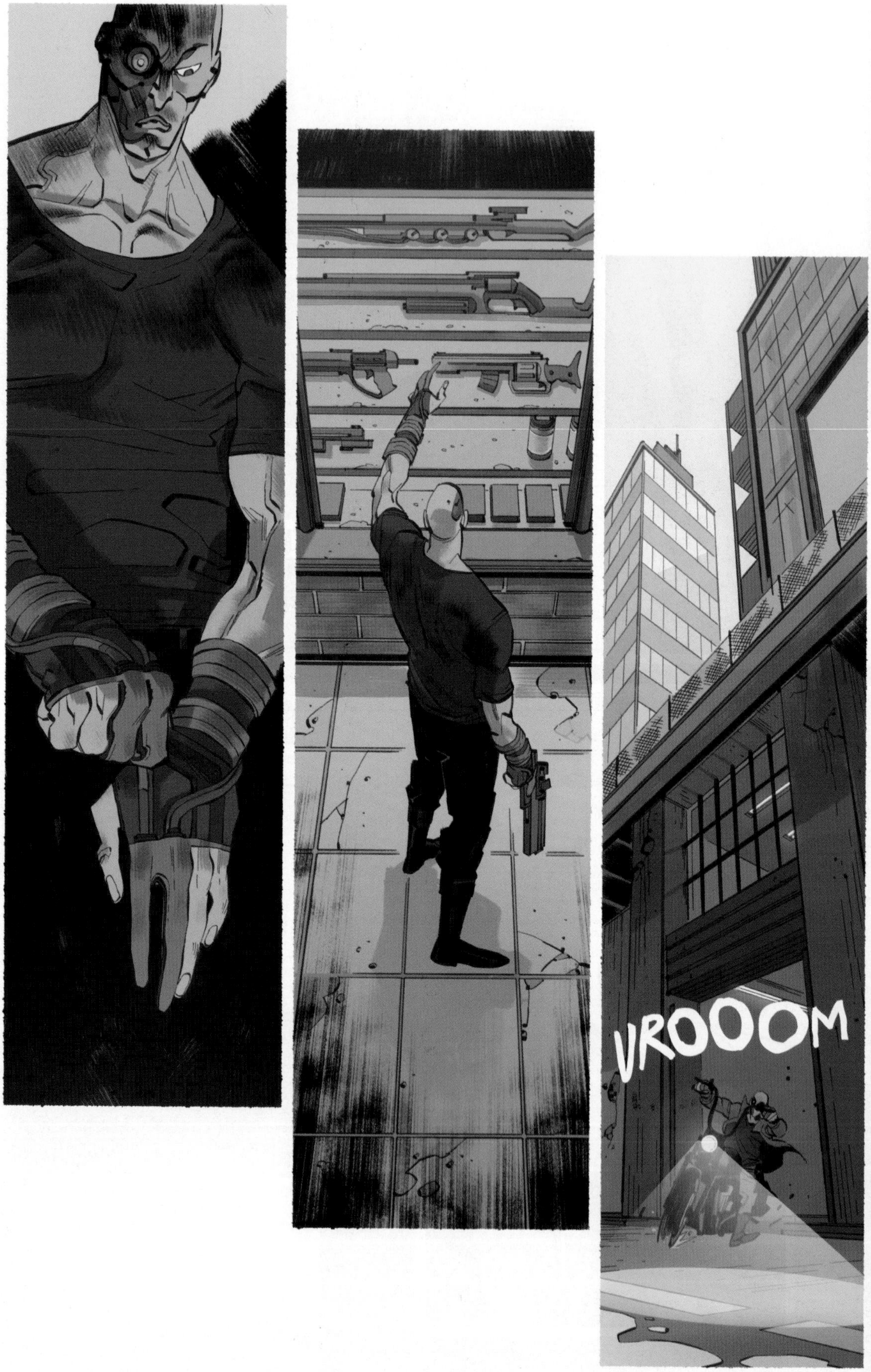
VROOOM

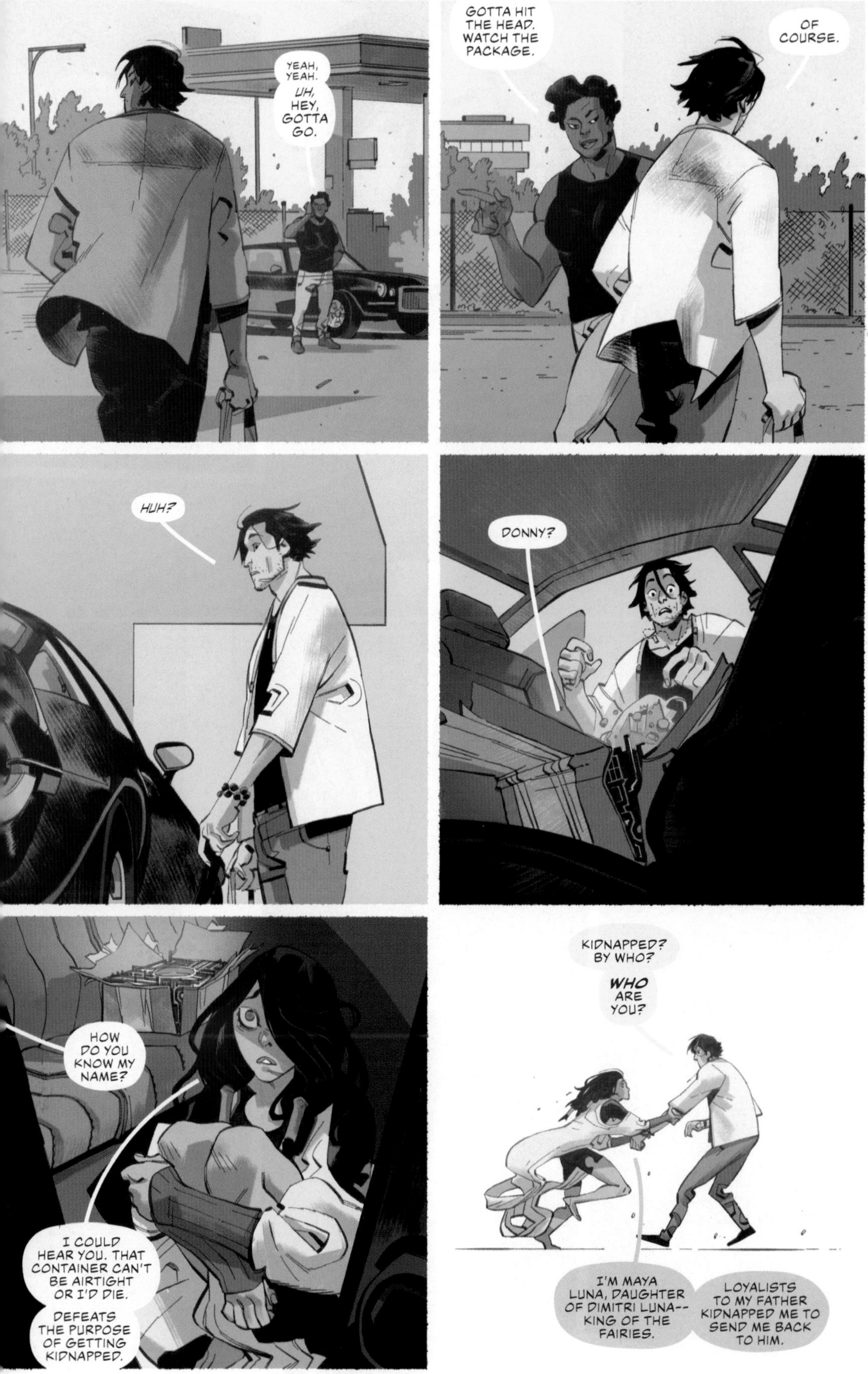
YEAH, YEAH.
UH, HEY, GOTTA GO.
GOTTA HIT THE HEAD. WATCH THE PACKAGE.
OF COURSE.
HUH?
DONNY?
HOW DO YOU KNOW MY NAME?
I COULD HEAR YOU. THAT CONTAINER CAN'T BE AIRTIGHT OR I'D DIE.
DEFEATS THE PURPOSE OF GETTING KIDNAPPED.
KIDNAPPED? BY WHO?
WHO ARE YOU?
I'M MAYA LUNA, DAUGHTER OF DIMITRI LUNA-- KING OF THE FAIRIES.
LOYALISTS TO MY FATHER KIDNAPPED ME TO SEND ME BACK TO HIM.

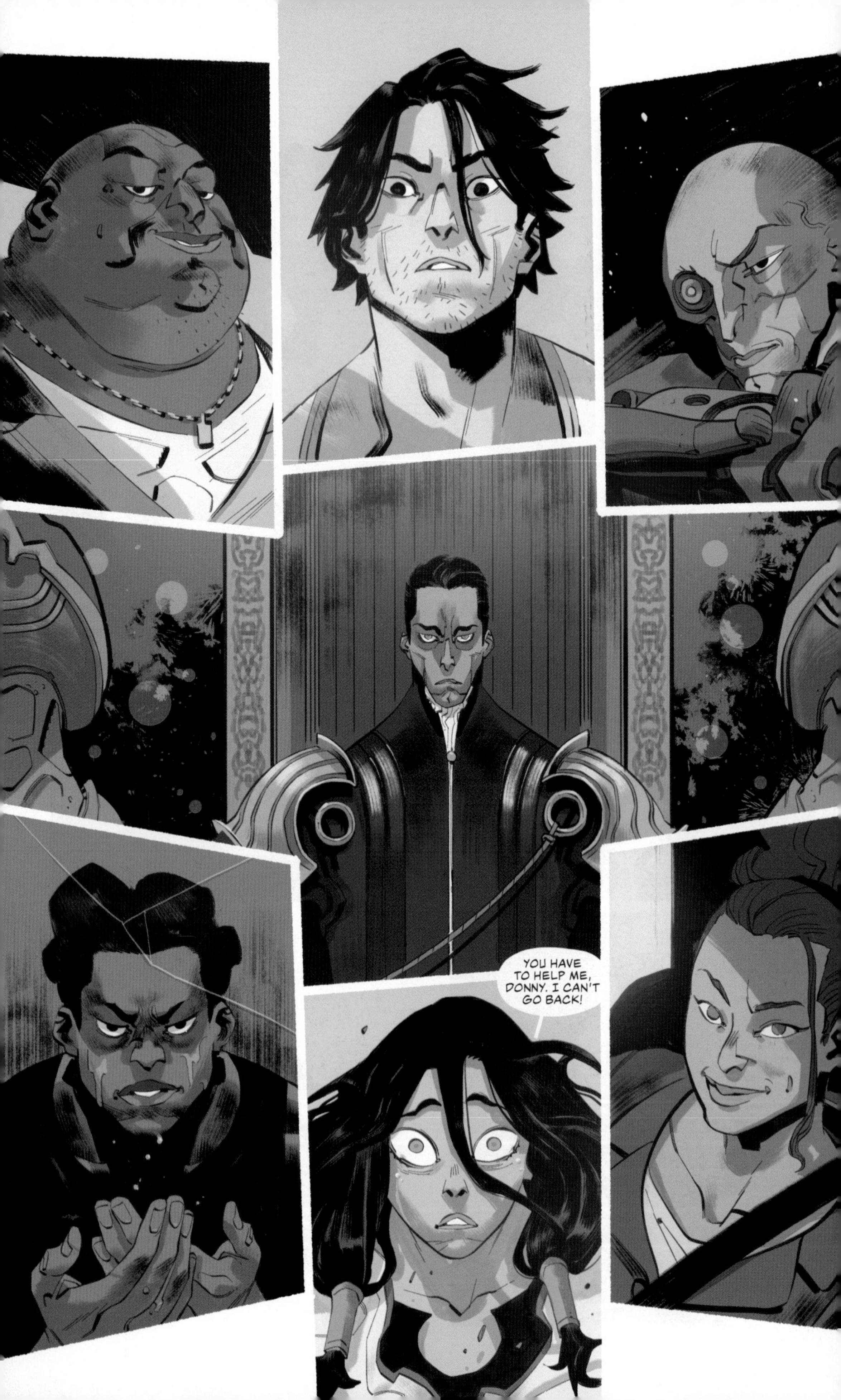
YOU HAVE TO HELP ME, DONNY. I CAN'T GO BACK!

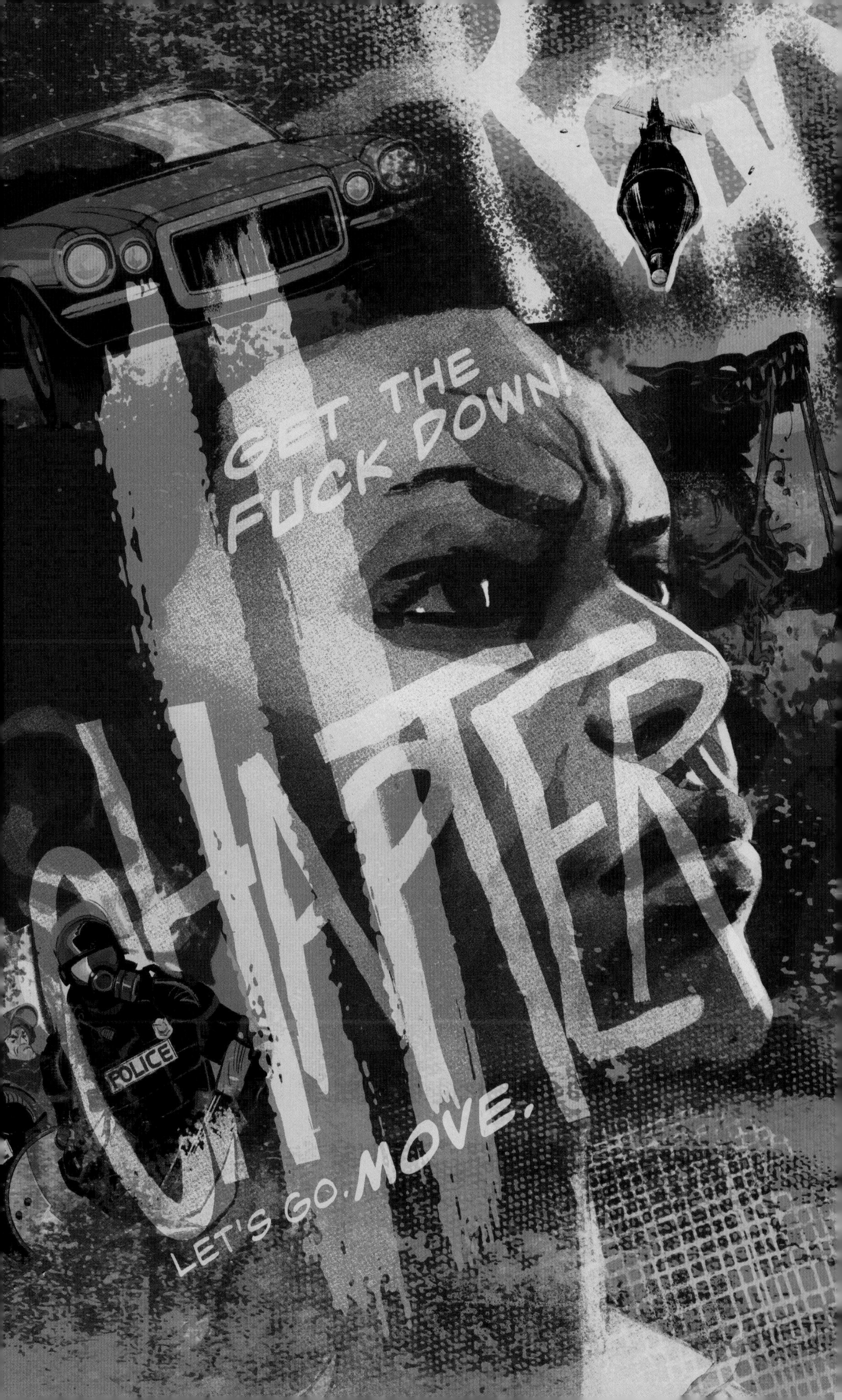
GET THE FUCK DOWN!
CHAPTER
POLICE
LET'S GO. MOVE.

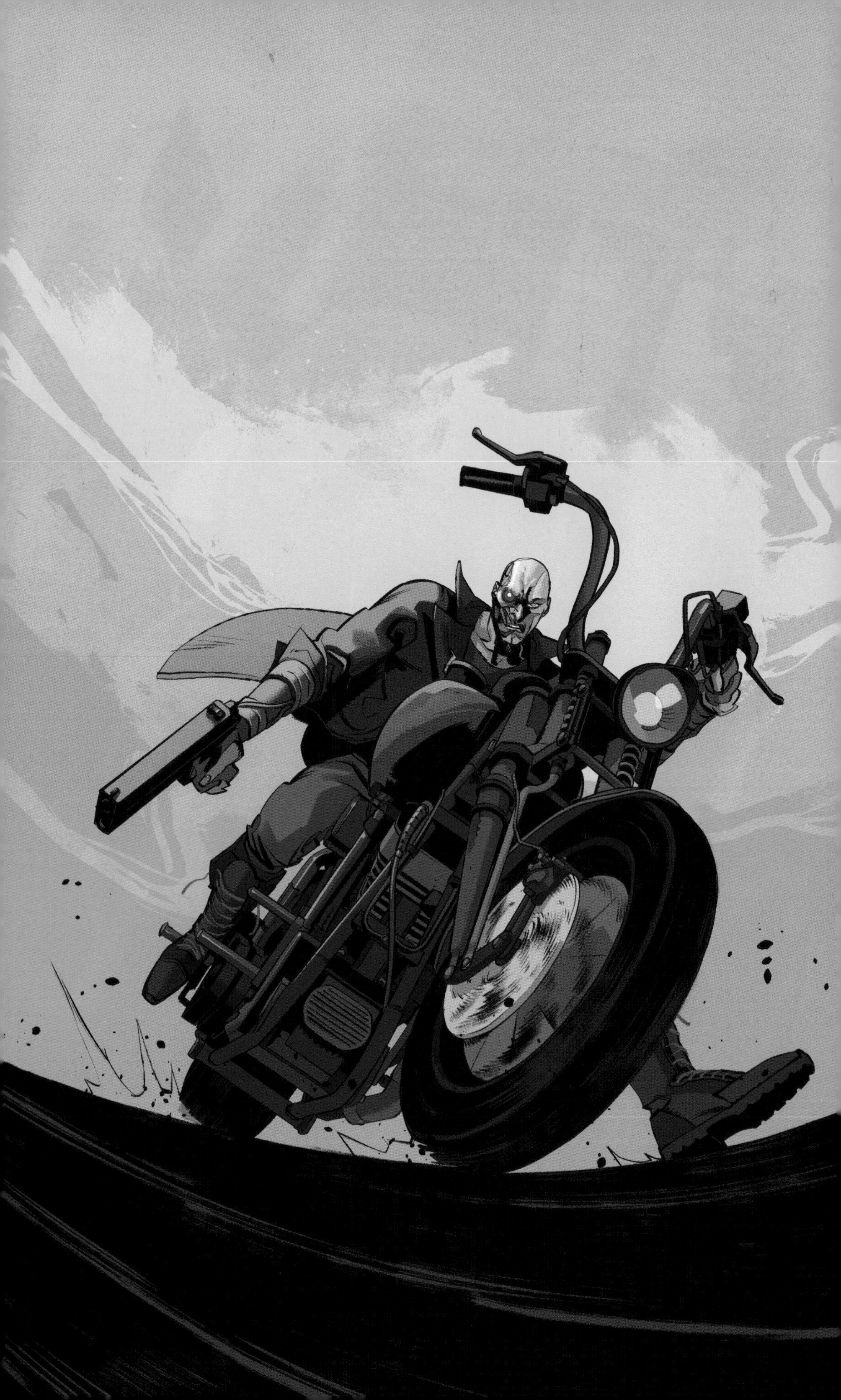

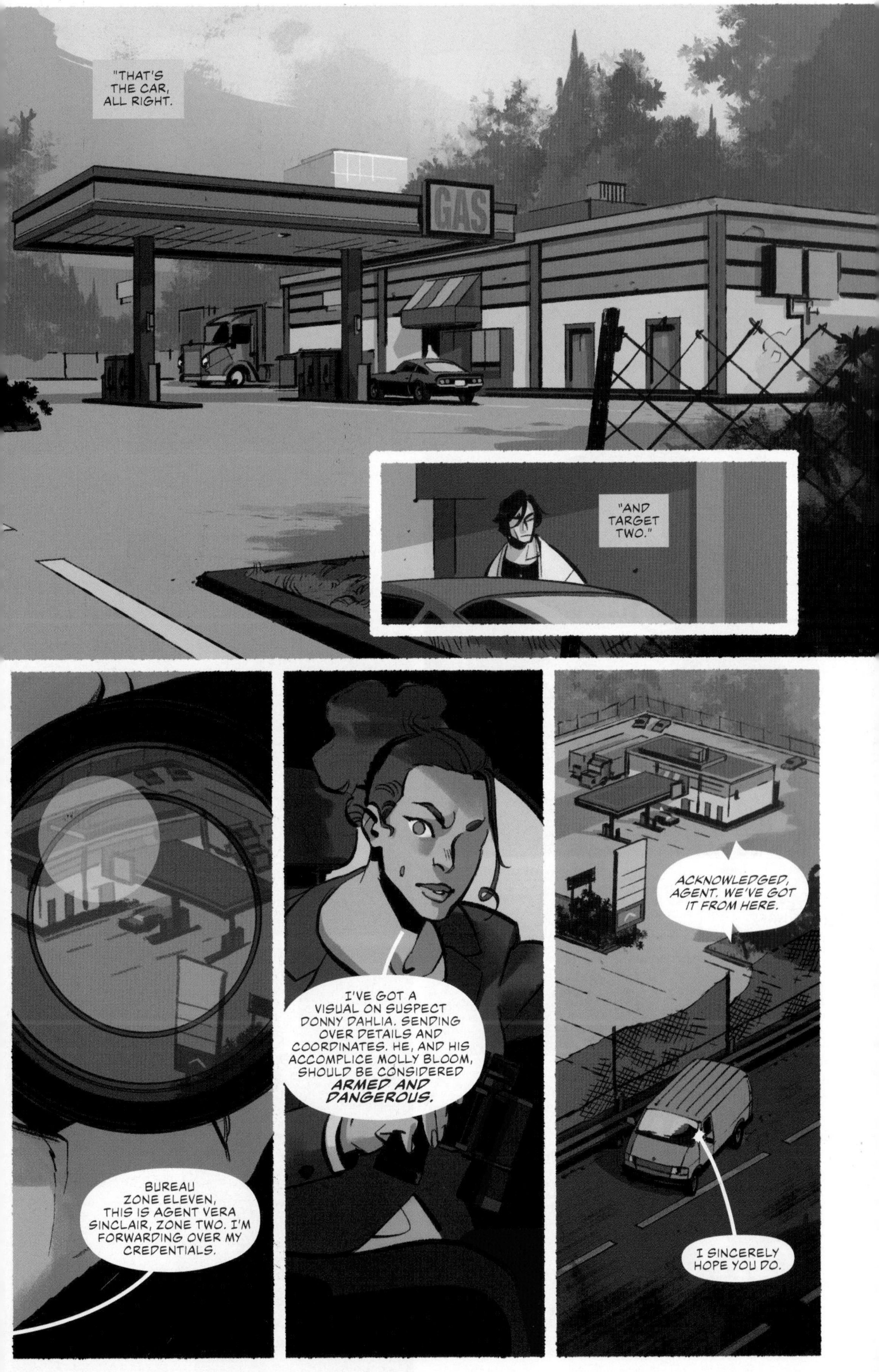
"THAT'S THE CAR, ALL RIGHT.
GAS
"AND TARGET TWO."
BUREAU ZONE ELEVEN, THIS IS AGENT VERA SINCLAIR, ZONE TWO. I'M FORWARDING OVER MY CREDENTIALS.
I'VE GOT A VISUAL ON SUSPECT DONNY DAHLIA. SENDING OVER DETAILS AND COORDINATES. HE, AND HIS ACCOMPLICE MOLLY BLOOM, SHOULD BE CONSIDERED ARMED AND DANGEROUS.
ACKNOWLEDGED, AGENT. WE'VE GOT IT FROM HERE.
I SINCERELY HOPE YOU DO.

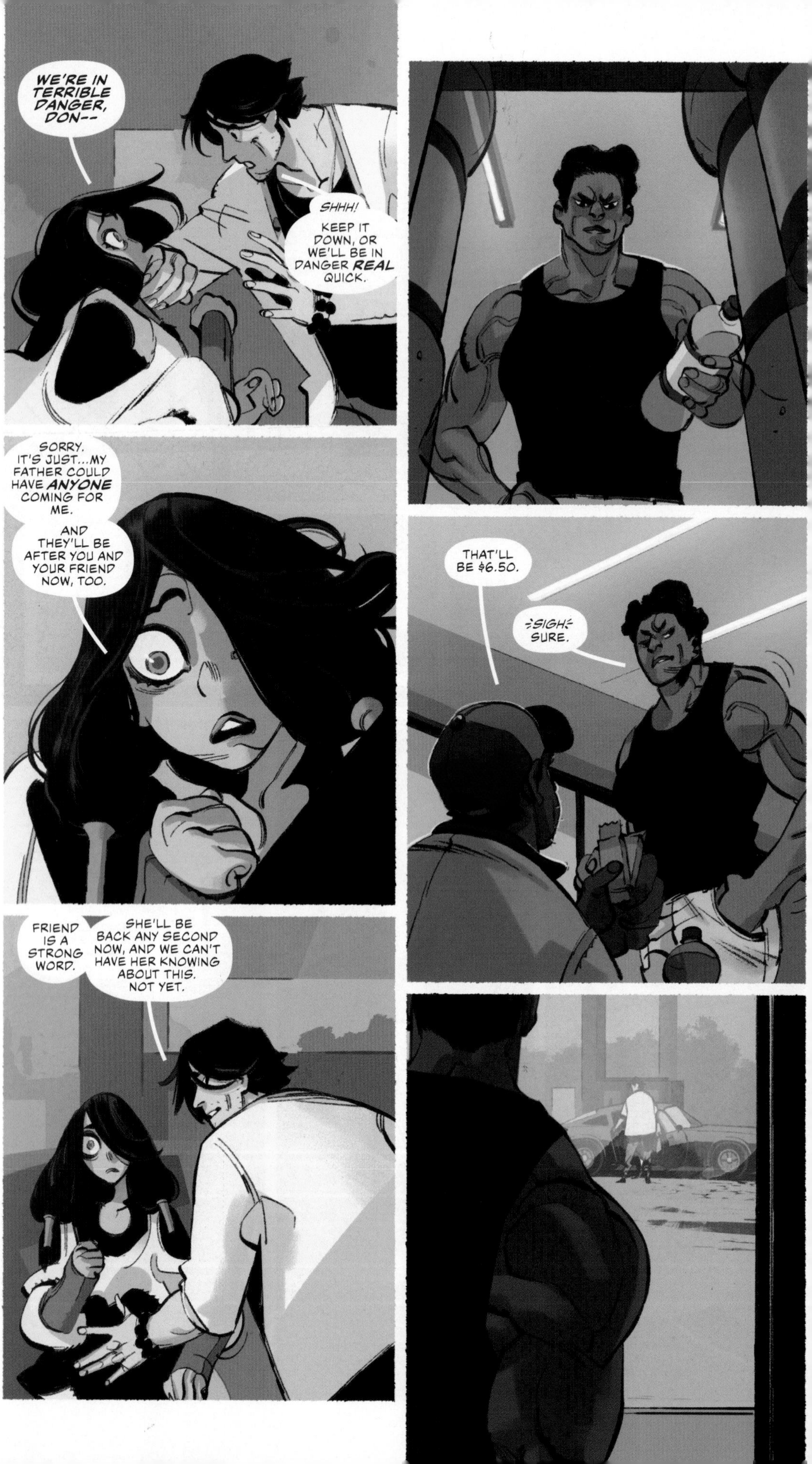
WE'RE IN TERRIBLE DANGER, DON--
SHHH!
KEEP IT DOWN, OR WE'LL BE IN DANGER REAL QUICK.
SORRY. IT'S JUST...MY FATHER COULD HAVE ANYONE COMING FOR ME.
AND THEY'LL BE AFTER YOU AND YOUR FRIEND NOW, TOO.
FRIEND IS A STRONG WORD.
SHE'LL BE BACK ANY SECOND NOW, AND WE CAN'T HAVE HER KNOWING ABOUT THIS. NOT YET.
THAT'LL BE $6.50.
SIGH SURE.

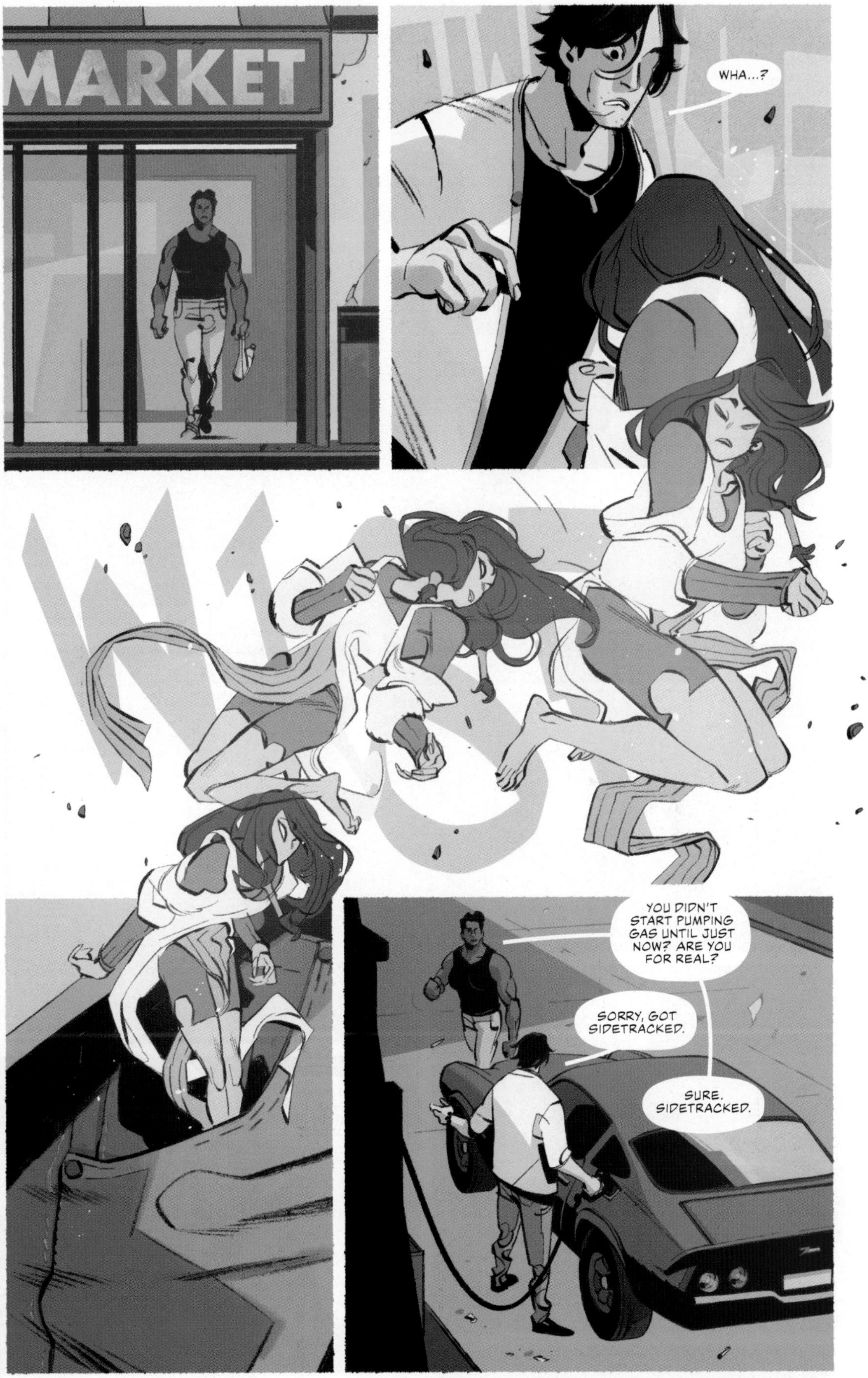
MARKET
WHA...?
YOU DIDN'T START PUMPING GAS UNTIL JUST NOW? ARE YOU FOR REAL?
SORRY, GOT SIDETRACKED.
SURE. SIDETRACKED.

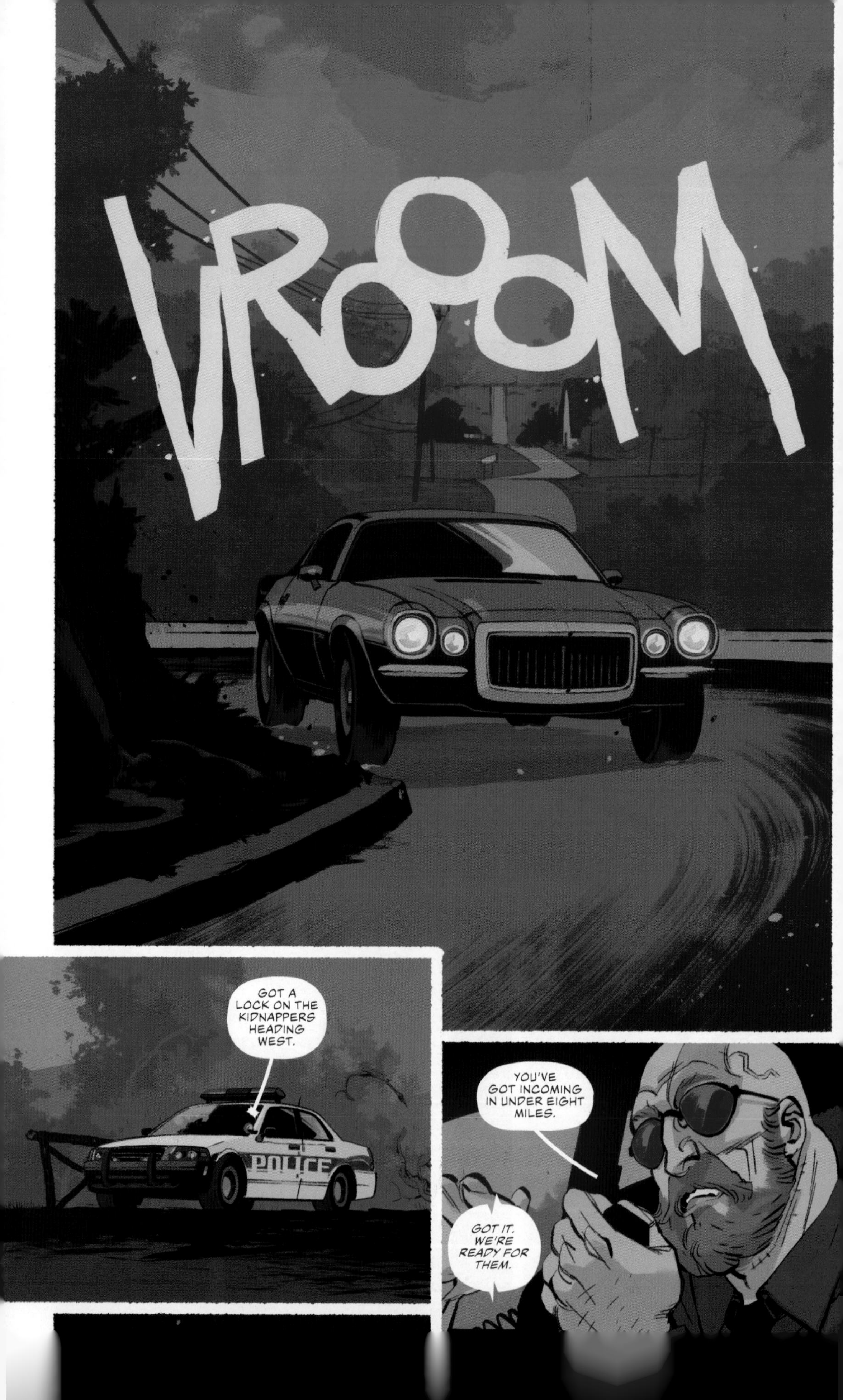
VROOOM
GOT A LOCK ON THE KIDNAPPERS HEADING WEST.
YOU'VE GOT INCOMING IN UNDER EIGHT MILES.
GOT IT. WE'RE READY FOR THEM.
POLICE

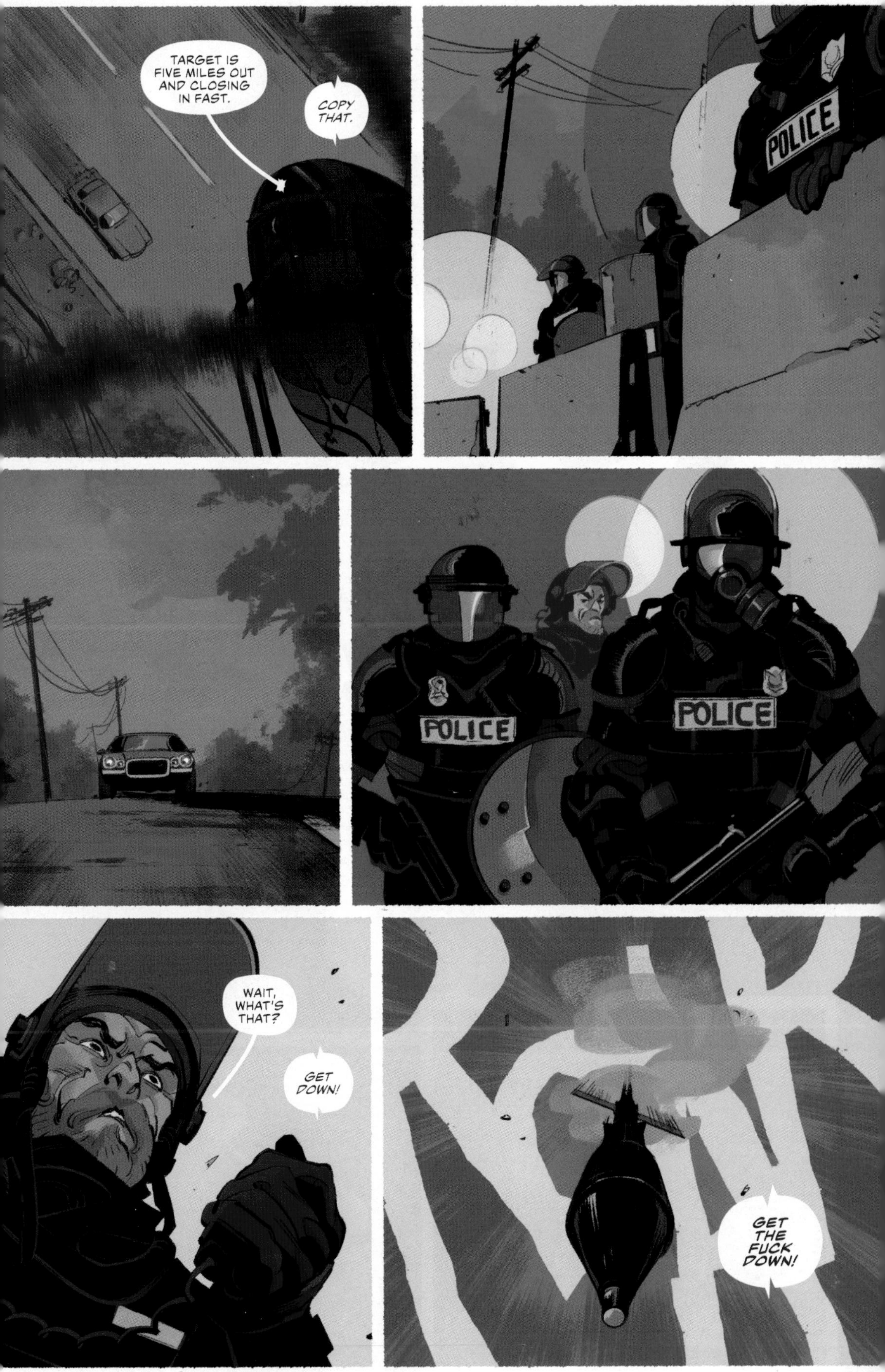
TARGET IS FIVE MILES OUT AND CLOSING IN FAST.
COPY THAT.
POLICE
POLICE
POLICE
WAIT, WHAT'S THAT?
GET DOWN!
GET THE FUCK DOWN!

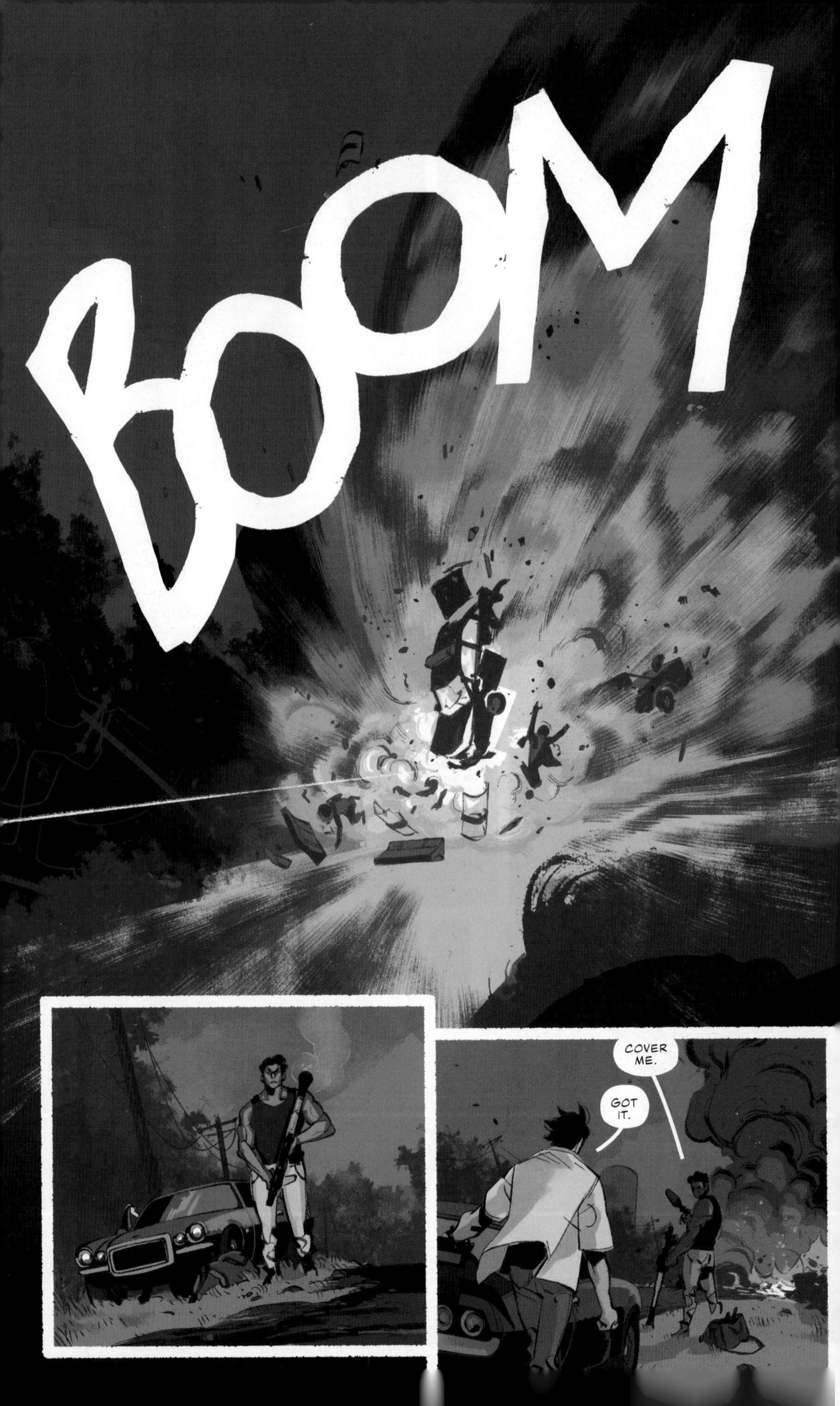
BOOM
COVER ME.
GOT IT.

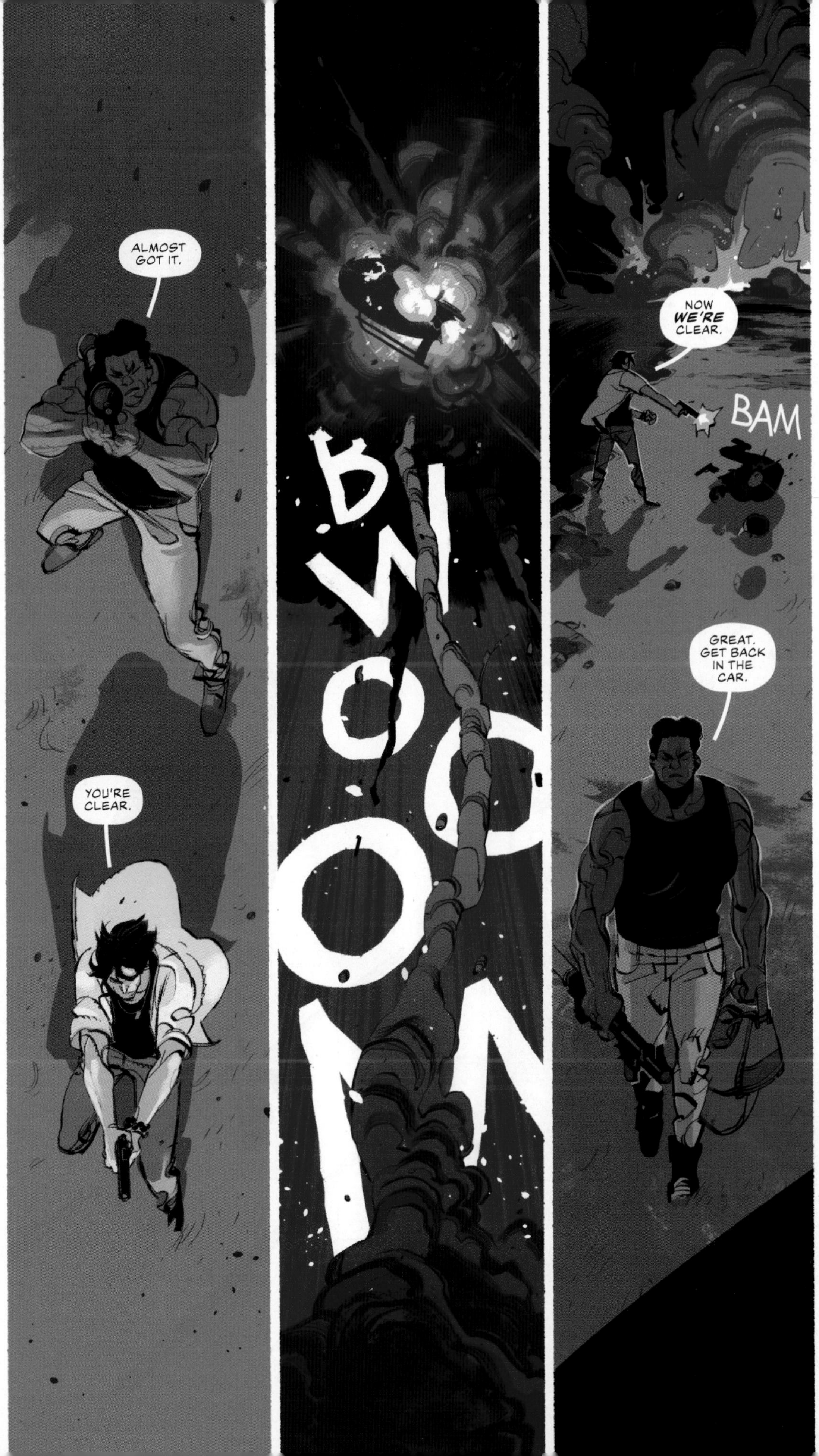
ALMOST GOT IT.
YOU'RE CLEAR.
BWOOOM
NOW *WE'RE* CLEAR.
BAM
GREAT. GET BACK IN THE CAR.

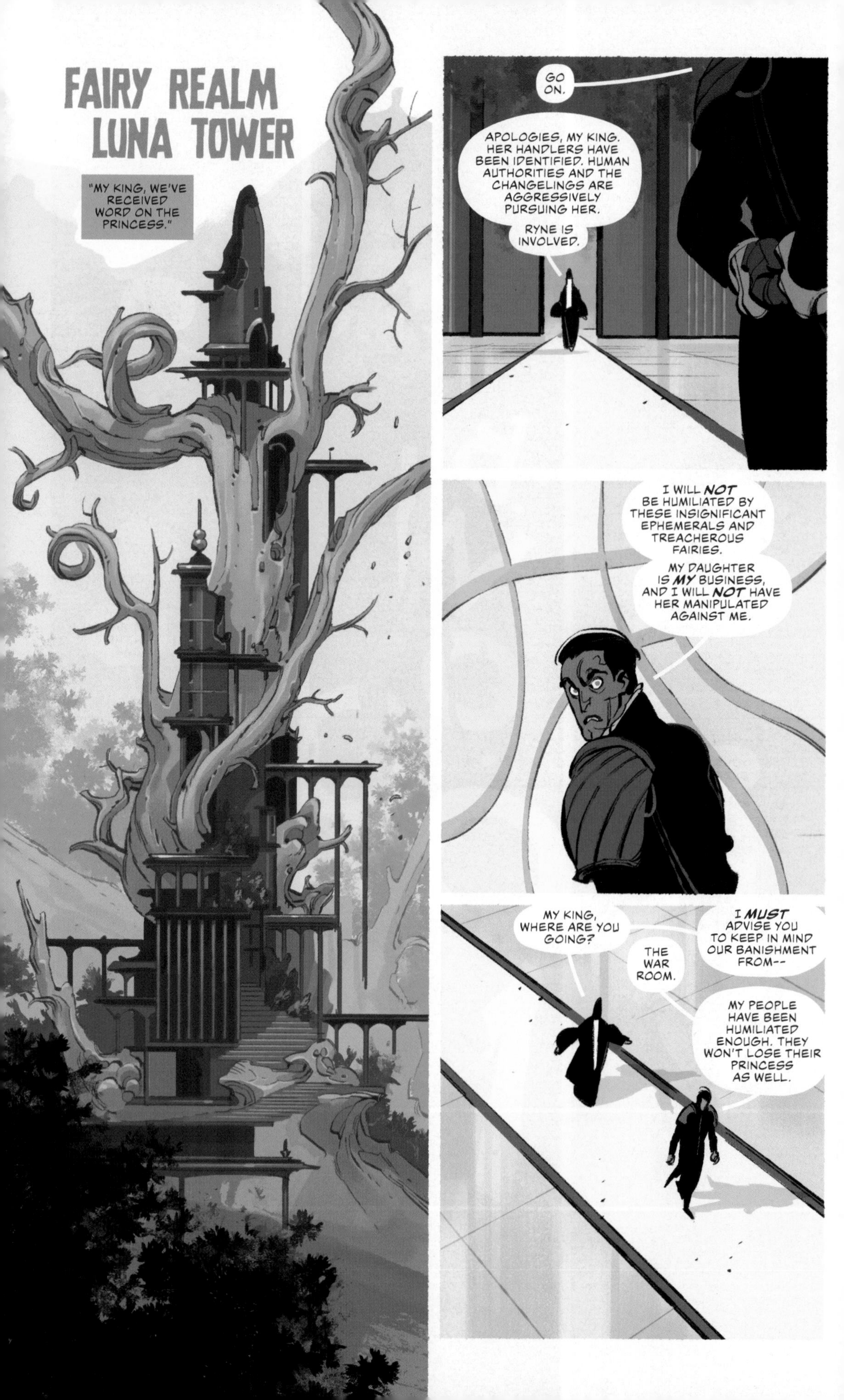
FAIRY REALM
LUNA TOWER
"MY KING, WE'VE RECEIVED WORD ON THE PRINCESS."
GO ON.
APOLOGIES, MY KING. HER HANDLERS HAVE BEEN IDENTIFIED. HUMAN AUTHORITIES AND THE CHANGELINGS ARE AGGRESSIVELY PURSUING HER.
RYNE IS INVOLVED.
I WILL NOT BE HUMILIATED BY THESE INSIGNIFICANT EPHEMERALS AND TREACHEROUS FAIRIES.
MY DAUGHTER IS MY BUSINESS, AND I WILL NOT HAVE HER MANIPULATED AGAINST ME.
MY KING, WHERE ARE YOU GOING?
THE WAR ROOM.
I MUST ADVISE YOU TO KEEP IN MIND OUR BANISHMENT FROM--
MY PEOPLE HAVE BEEN HUMILIATED ENOUGH. THEY WON'T LOSE THEIR PRINCESS AS WELL.

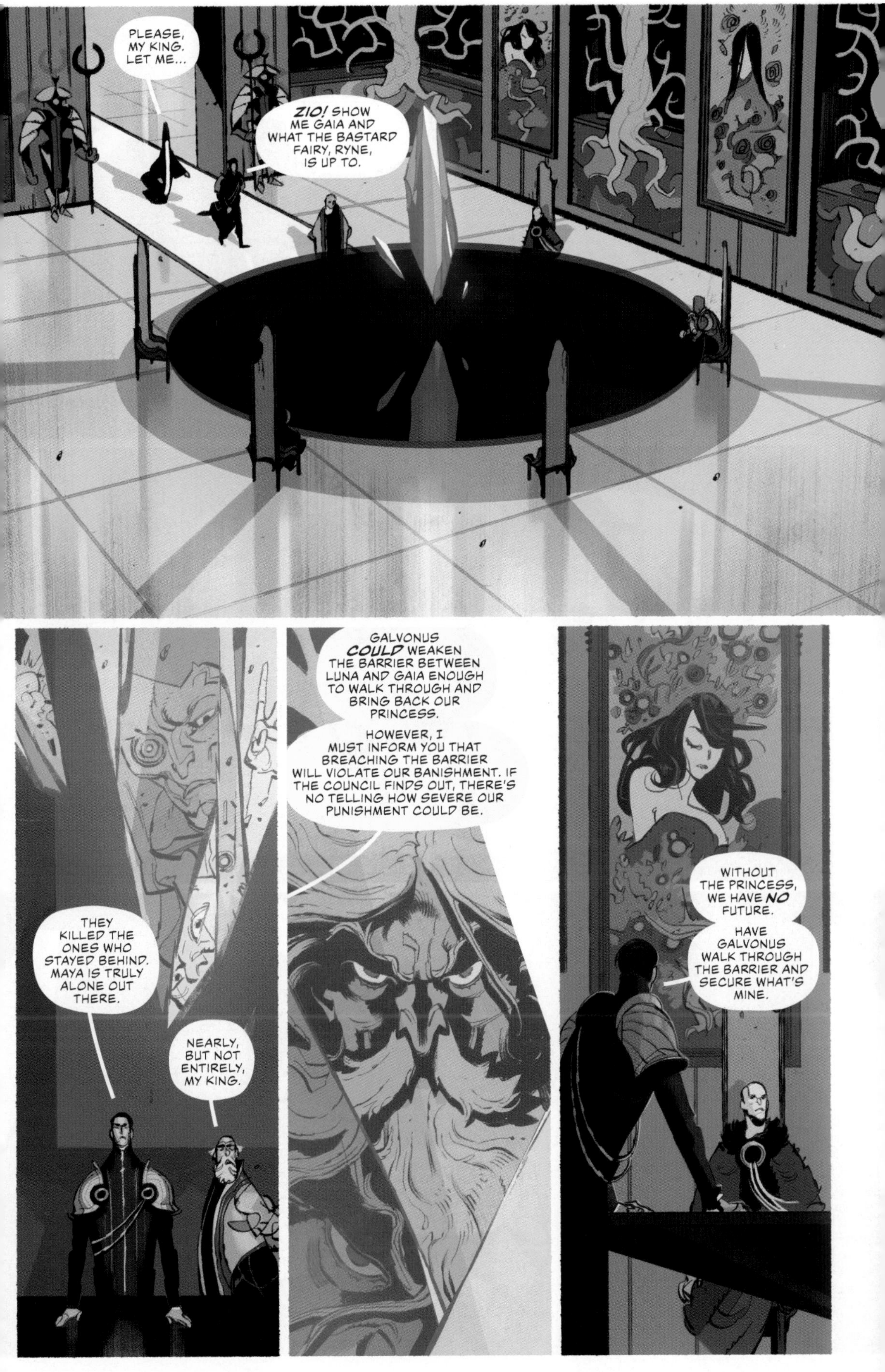
PLEASE, MY KING. LET ME...
ZIO! SHOW ME GAIA AND WHAT THE BASTARD FAIRY, RYNE, IS UP TO.
THEY KILLED THE ONES WHO STAYED BEHIND. MAYA IS TRULY ALONE OUT THERE.
NEARLY, BUT NOT ENTIRELY, MY KING.
GALVONUS COULD WEAKEN THE BARRIER BETWEEN LUNA AND GAIA ENOUGH TO WALK THROUGH AND BRING BACK OUR PRINCESS.
HOWEVER, I MUST INFORM YOU THAT BREACHING THE BARRIER WILL VIOLATE OUR BANISHMENT. IF THE COUNCIL FINDS OUT, THERE'S NO TELLING HOW SEVERE OUR PUNISHMENT COULD BE.
WITHOUT THE PRINCESS, WE HAVE NO FUTURE.
HAVE GALVONUS WALK THROUGH THE BARRIER AND SECURE WHAT'S MINE.

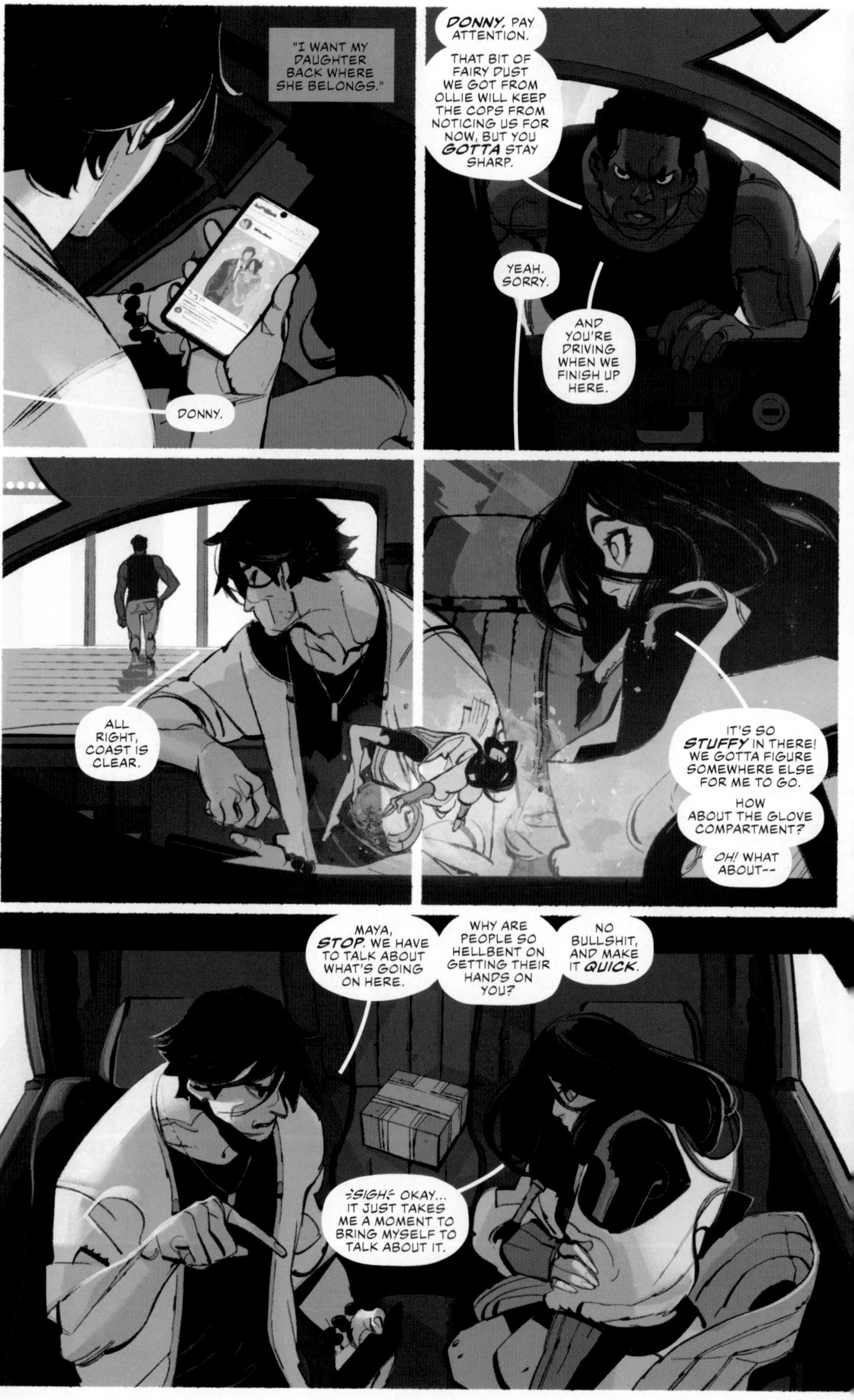
"I WANT MY DAUGHTER BACK WHERE SHE BELONGS."
DONNY.
DONNY. PAY ATTENTION.
THAT BIT OF FAIRY DUST WE GOT FROM OLLIE WILL KEEP THE COPS FROM NOTICING US FOR NOW, BUT YOU GOTTA STAY SHARP.
YEAH. SORRY.
AND YOU'RE DRIVING WHEN WE FINISH UP HERE.
ALL RIGHT, COAST IS CLEAR.
IT'S SO STUFFY IN THERE! WE GOTTA FIGURE SOMEWHERE ELSE FOR ME TO GO.
HOW ABOUT THE GLOVE COMPARTMENT?
OH! WHAT ABOUT--
MAYA, STOP. WE HAVE TO TALK ABOUT WHAT'S GOING ON HERE.
WHY ARE PEOPLE SO HELLBENT ON GETTING THEIR HANDS ON YOU?
NO BULLSHIT, AND MAKE IT QUICK.
=SIGH= OKAY... IT JUST TAKES ME A MOMENT TO BRING MYSELF TO TALK ABOUT IT.

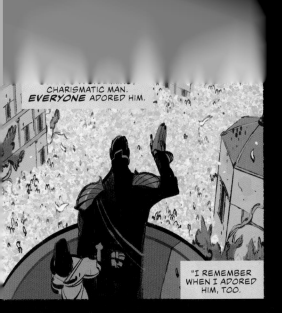

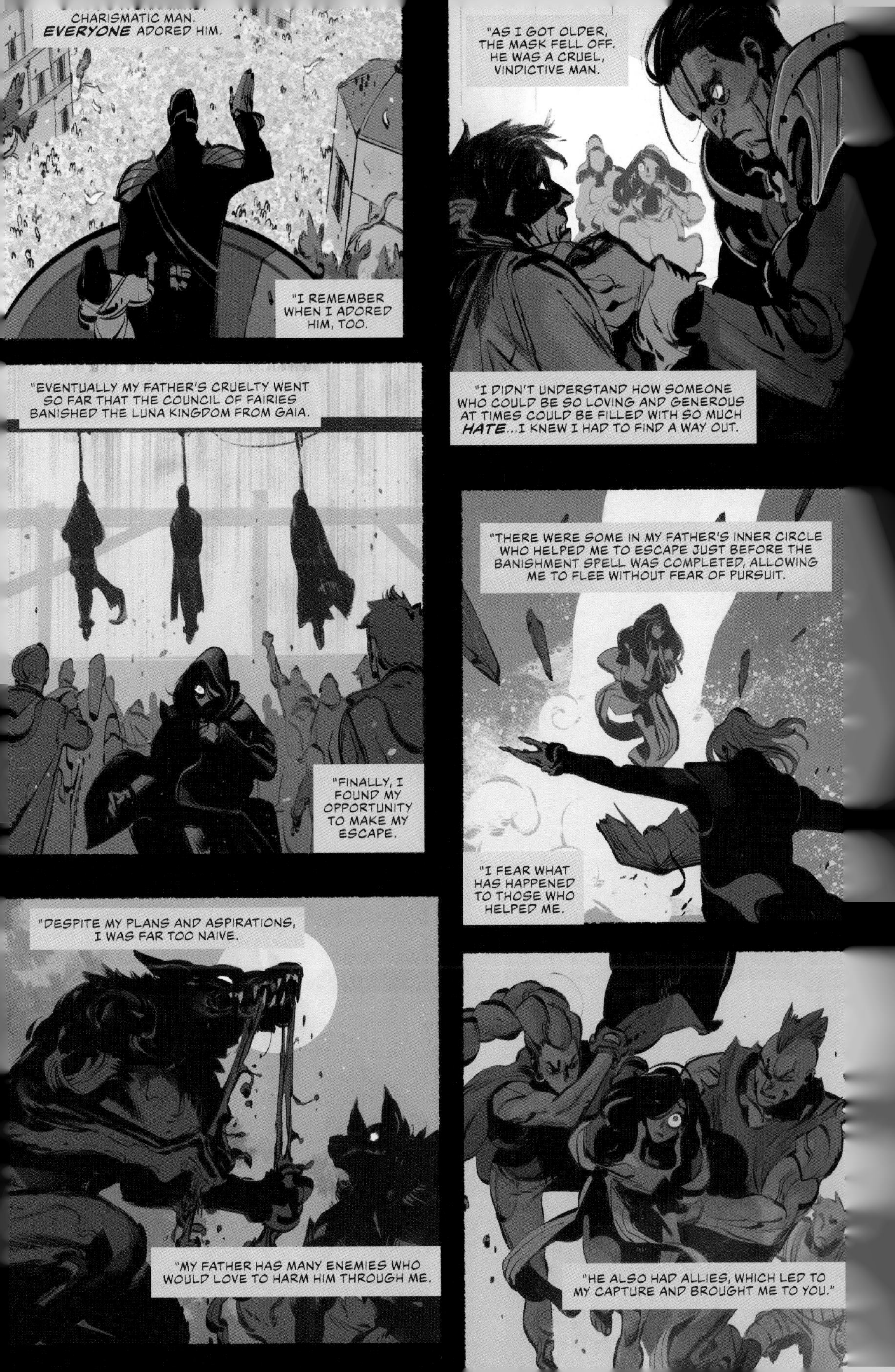
CHARISMATIC MAN. EVERYONE ADORED HIM.
"I REMEMBER WHEN I ADORED HIM, TOO.
"AS I GOT OLDER, THE MASK FELL OFF. HE WAS A CRUEL, VINDICTIVE MAN.
"I DIDN'T UNDERSTAND HOW SOMEONE WHO COULD BE SO LOVING AND GENEROUS AT TIMES COULD BE FILLED WITH SO MUCH HATE...I KNEW I HAD TO FIND A WAY OUT.
"EVENTUALLY MY FATHER'S CRUELTY WENT SO FAR THAT THE COUNCIL OF FAIRIES BANISHED THE LUNA KINGDOM FROM GAIA.
"FINALLY, I FOUND MY OPPORTUNITY TO MAKE MY ESCAPE.
"THERE WERE SOME IN MY FATHER'S INNER CIRCLE WHO HELPED ME TO ESCAPE JUST BEFORE THE BANISHMENT SPELL WAS COMPLETED, ALLOWING ME TO FLEE WITHOUT FEAR OF PURSUIT.
"I FEAR WHAT HAS HAPPENED TO THOSE WHO HELPED ME.
"DESPITE MY PLANS AND ASPIRATIONS, I WAS FAR TOO NAIVE.
"MY FATHER HAS MANY ENEMIES WHO WOULD LOVE TO HARM HIM THROUGH ME.
"HE ALSO HAD ALLIES, WHICH LED TO MY CAPTURE AND BROUGHT ME TO YOU."

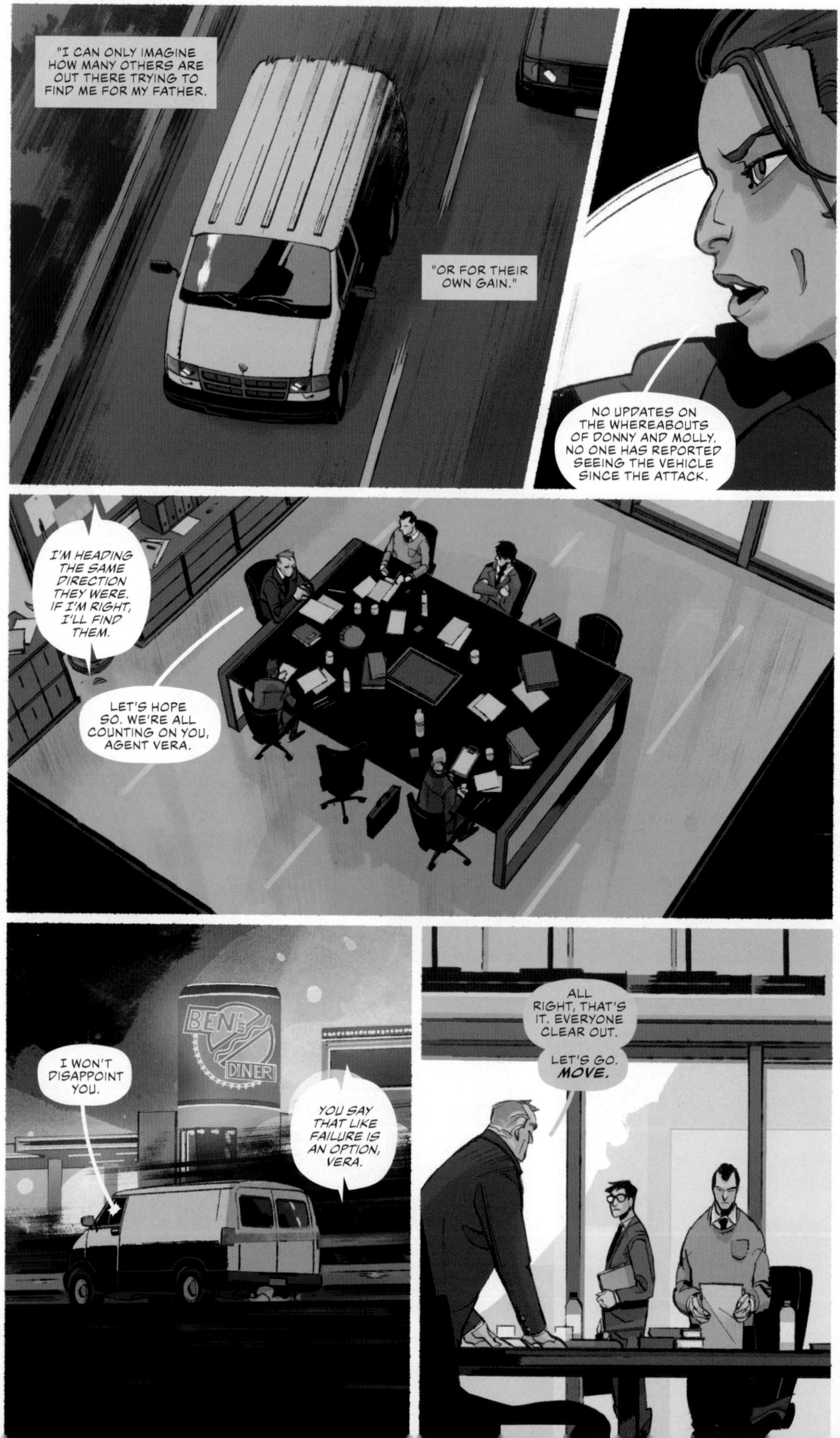
"I CAN ONLY IMAGINE HOW MANY OTHERS ARE OUT THERE TRYING TO FIND ME FOR MY FATHER.
"OR FOR THEIR OWN GAIN."
NO UPDATES ON THE WHEREABOUTS OF DONNY AND MOLLY. NO ONE HAS REPORTED SEEING THE VEHICLE SINCE THE ATTACK.
I'M HEADING THE SAME DIRECTION THEY WERE. IF I'M RIGHT, I'LL FIND THEM.
LET'S HOPE SO. WE'RE ALL COUNTING ON YOU, AGENT VERA.
BEN'S DINER
I WON'T DISAPPOINT YOU.
YOU SAY THAT LIKE FAILURE IS AN OPTION, VERA.
ALL RIGHT, THAT'S IT. EVERYONE CLEAR OUT.
LET'S GO. *MOVE.*

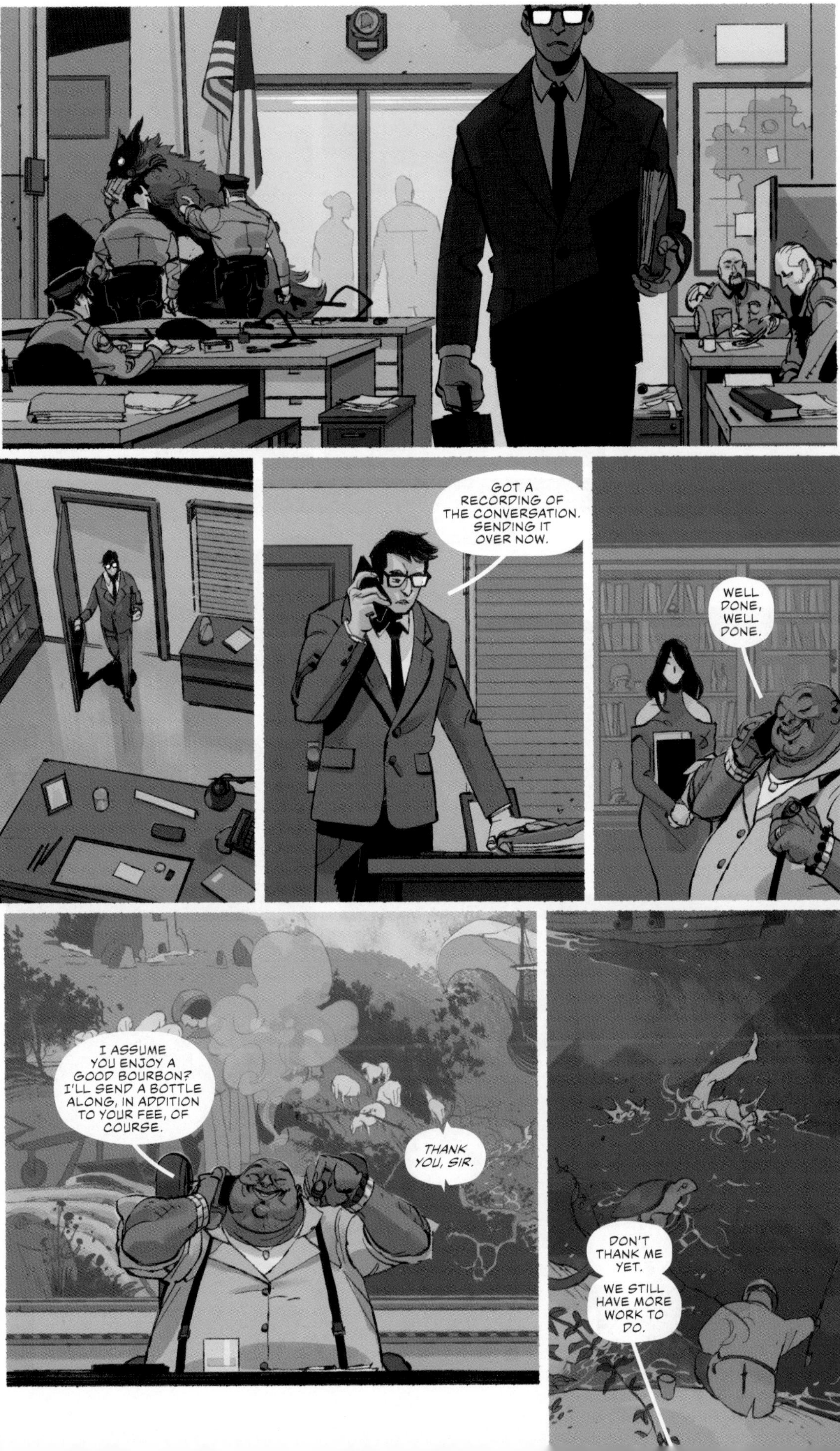
GOT A RECORDING OF THE CONVERSATION. SENDING IT OVER NOW.
WELL DONE, WELL DONE.
I ASSUME YOU ENJOY A GOOD BOURBON? I'LL SEND A BOTTLE ALONG, IN ADDITION TO YOUR FEE, OF COURSE.
THANK YOU, SIR.
DON'T THANK ME YET.
WE STILL HAVE MORE WORK TO DO.

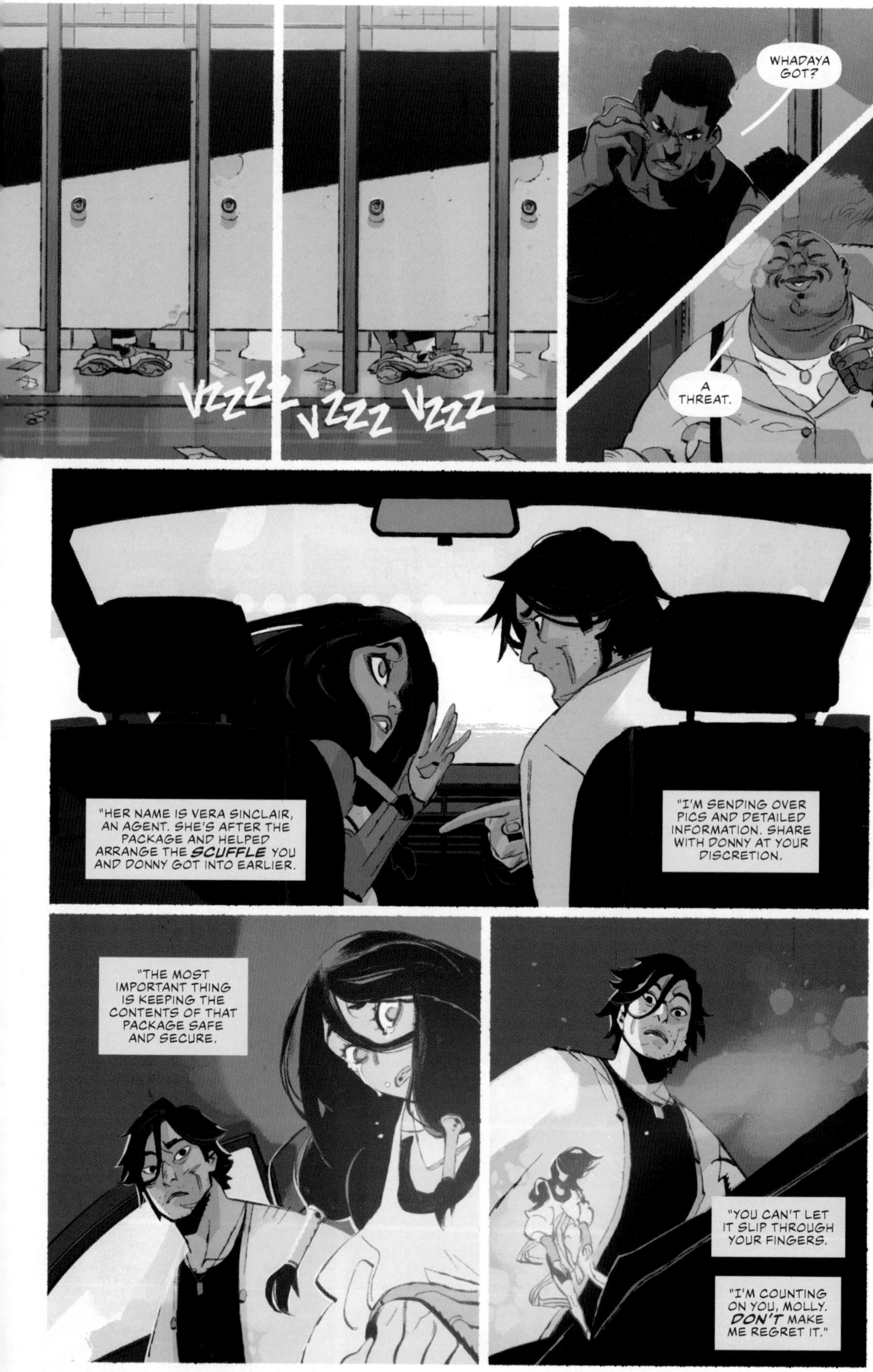
VZZZZ
VZZZ
VZZZ
WHADAYA GOT?
A THREAT.
"HER NAME IS VERA SINCLAIR, AN AGENT. SHE'S AFTER THE PACKAGE AND HELPED ARRANGE THE SCUFFLE YOU AND DONNY GOT INTO EARLIER.
"I'M SENDING OVER PICS AND DETAILED INFORMATION. SHARE WITH DONNY AT YOUR DISCRETION.
"THE MOST IMPORTANT THING IS KEEPING THE CONTENTS OF THAT PACKAGE SAFE AND SECURE.
"YOU CAN'T LET IT SLIP THROUGH YOUR FINGERS.
"I'M COUNTING ON YOU, MOLLY. DON'T MAKE ME REGRET IT."

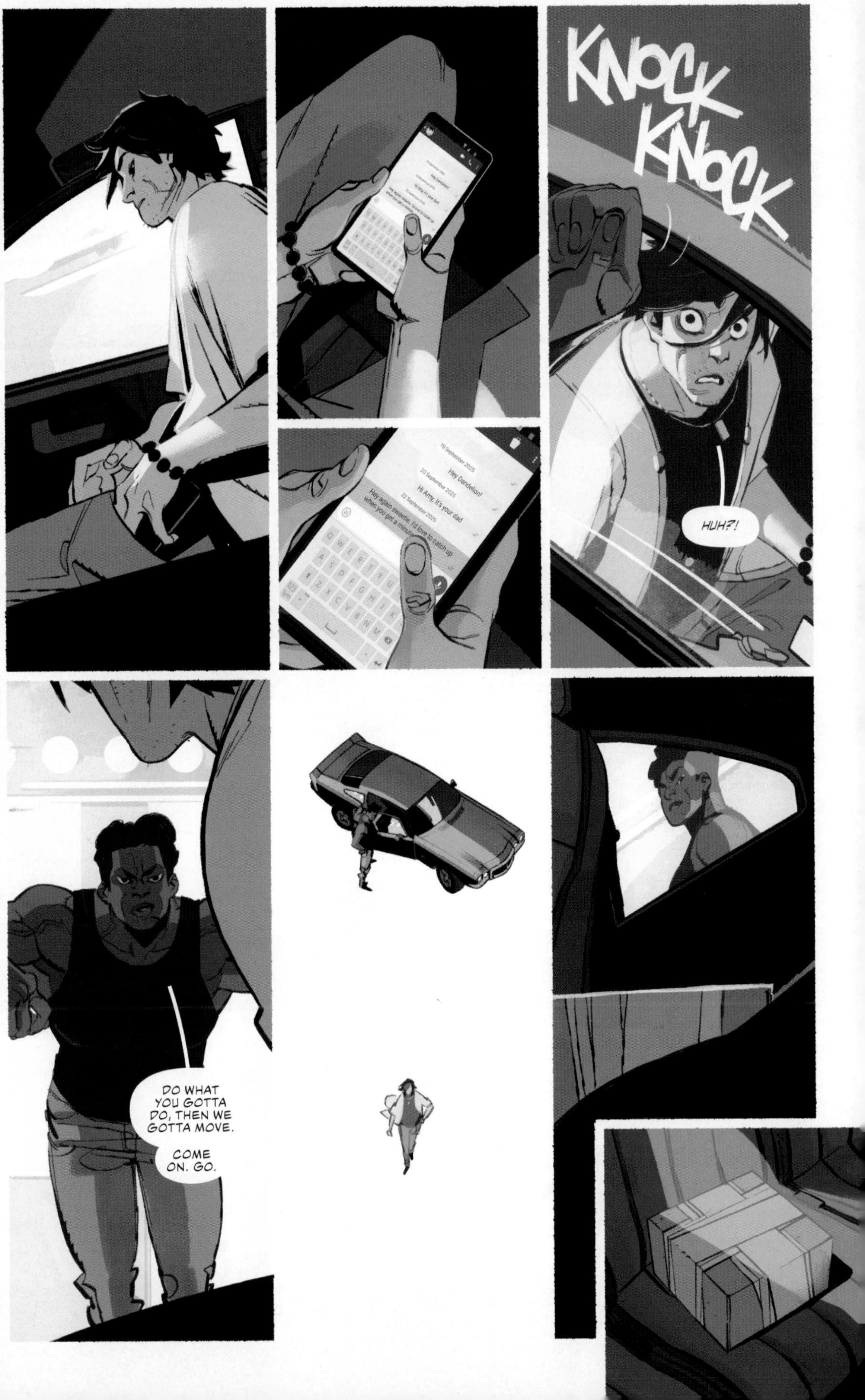
19 September 2025
Hey Dandelion!
20 September 2025
Hi Amy, It's your dad
22 September 2025
Hey again sweetie. I'd love to catch up
KNOCK KNOCK
HUH?!
DO WHAT YOU GOTTA DO, THEN WE GOTTA MOVE.
COME ON. GO.

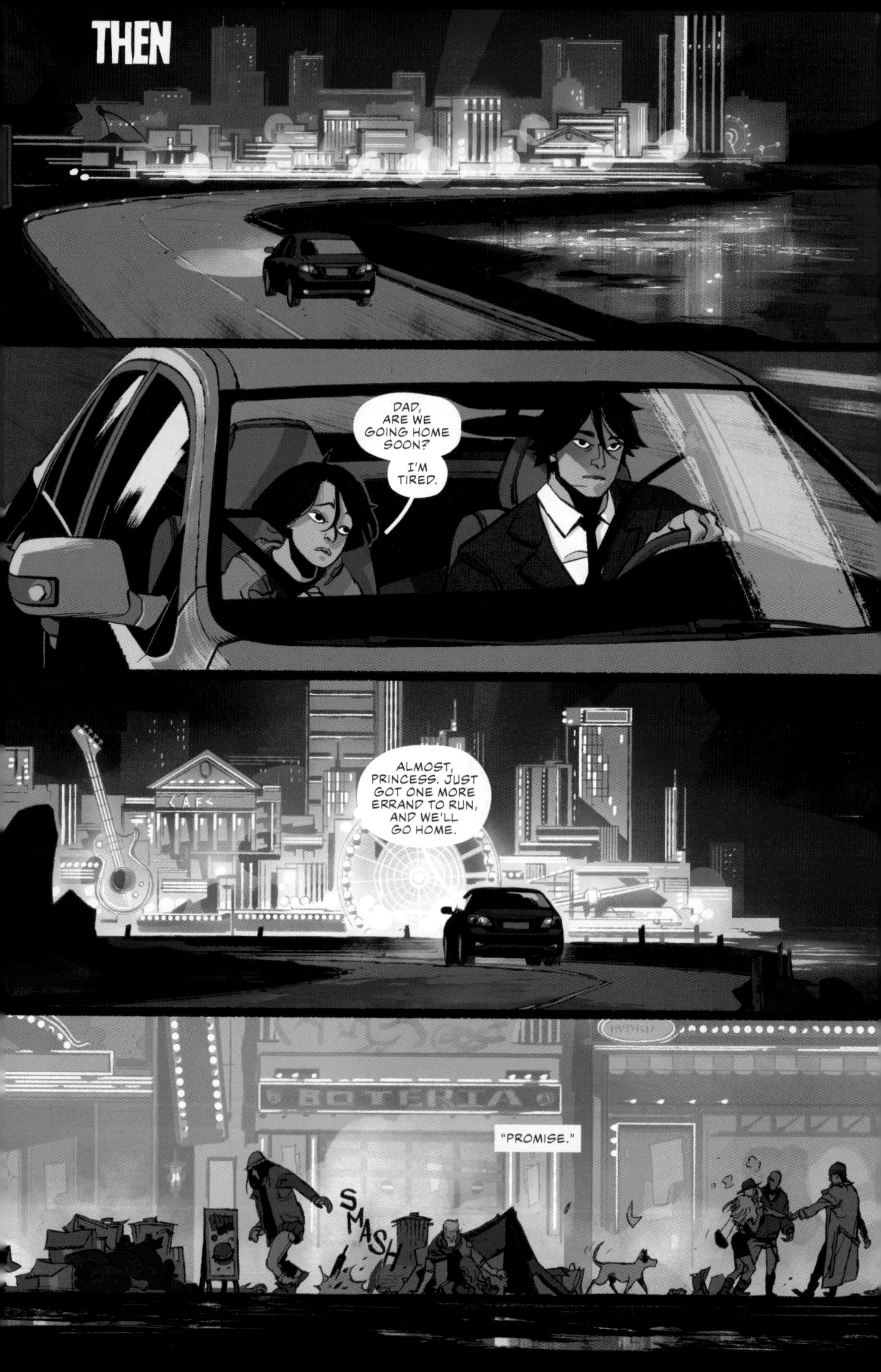
THEN
DAD, ARE WE GOING HOME SOON?
I'M TIRED.
ALMOST, PRINCESS. JUST GOT ONE MORE ERRAND TO RUN, AND WE'LL GO HOME.
BOTERIA
"PROMISE."
SMASH

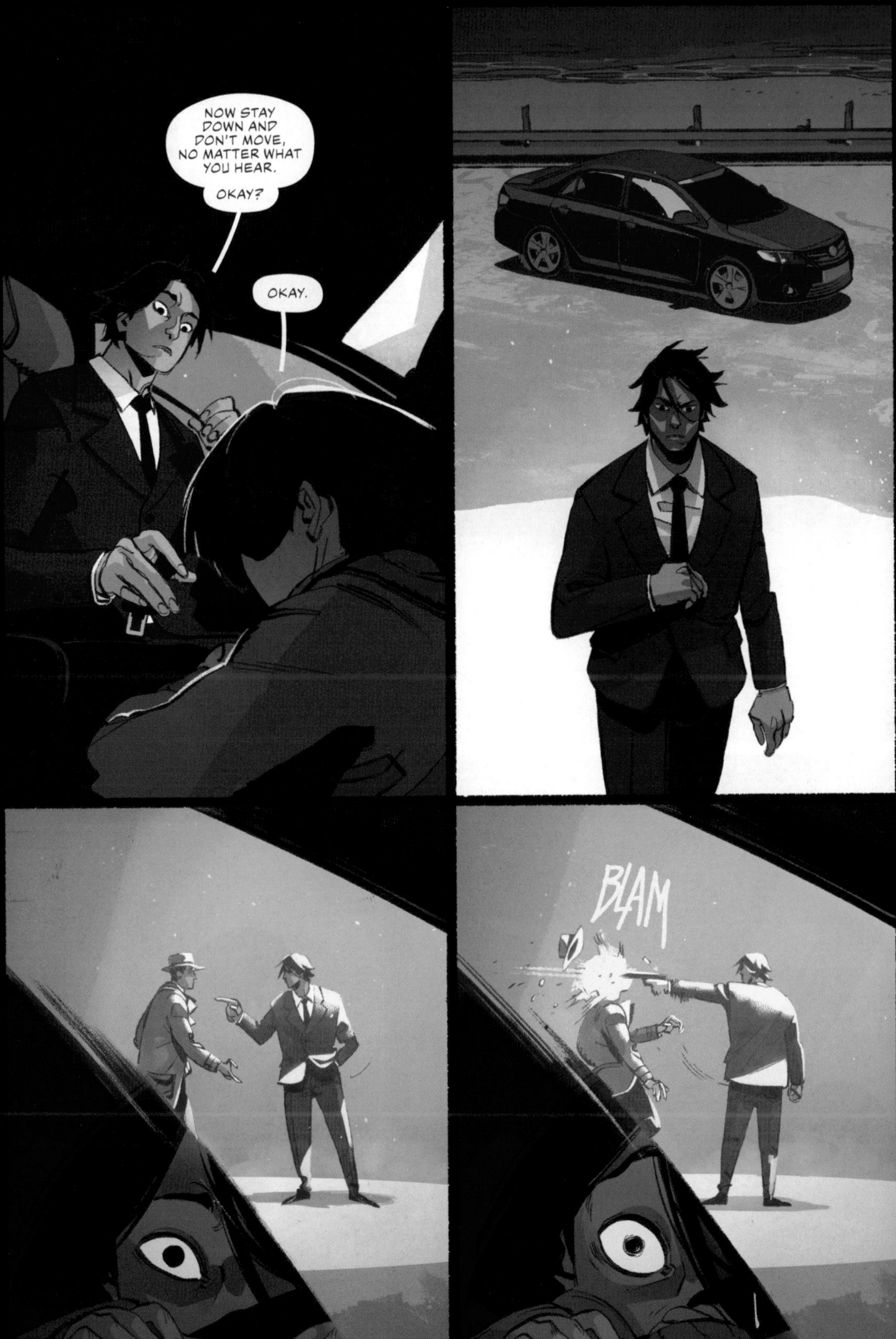
NOW STAY DOWN AND DON'T MOVE, NO MATTER WHAT YOU HEAR.
OKAY?
OKAY.
BLAM

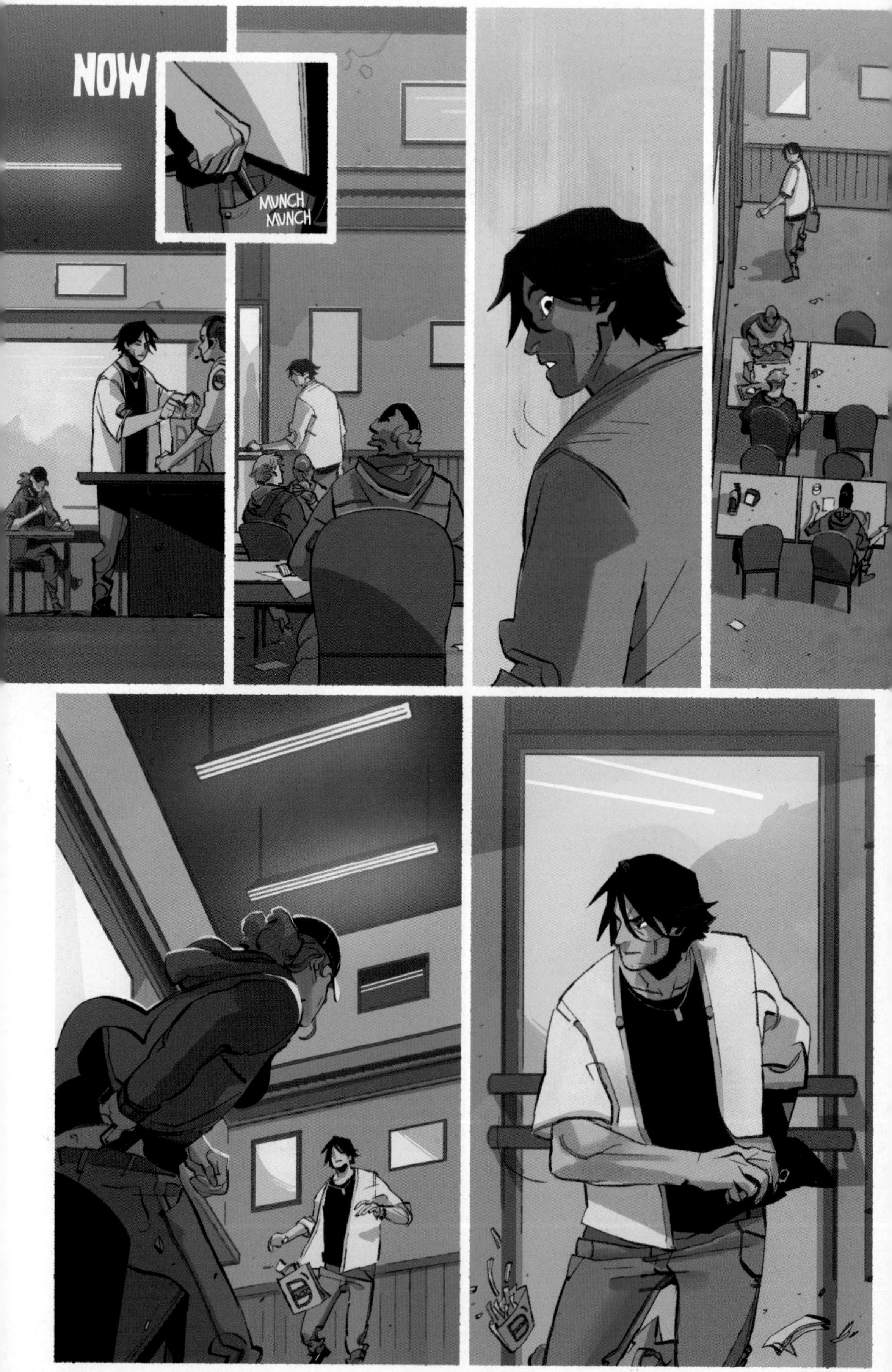
NOW
MUNCH
MUNCH

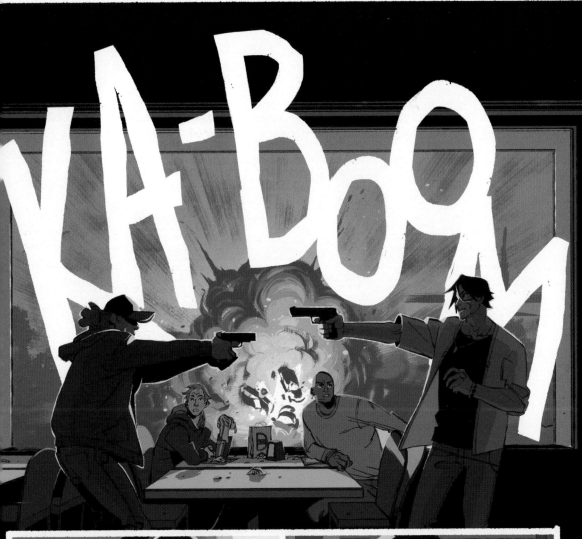

HELP!

OH, GOD! OH, GOD!

AHHHH!

THERE YOU ARE!

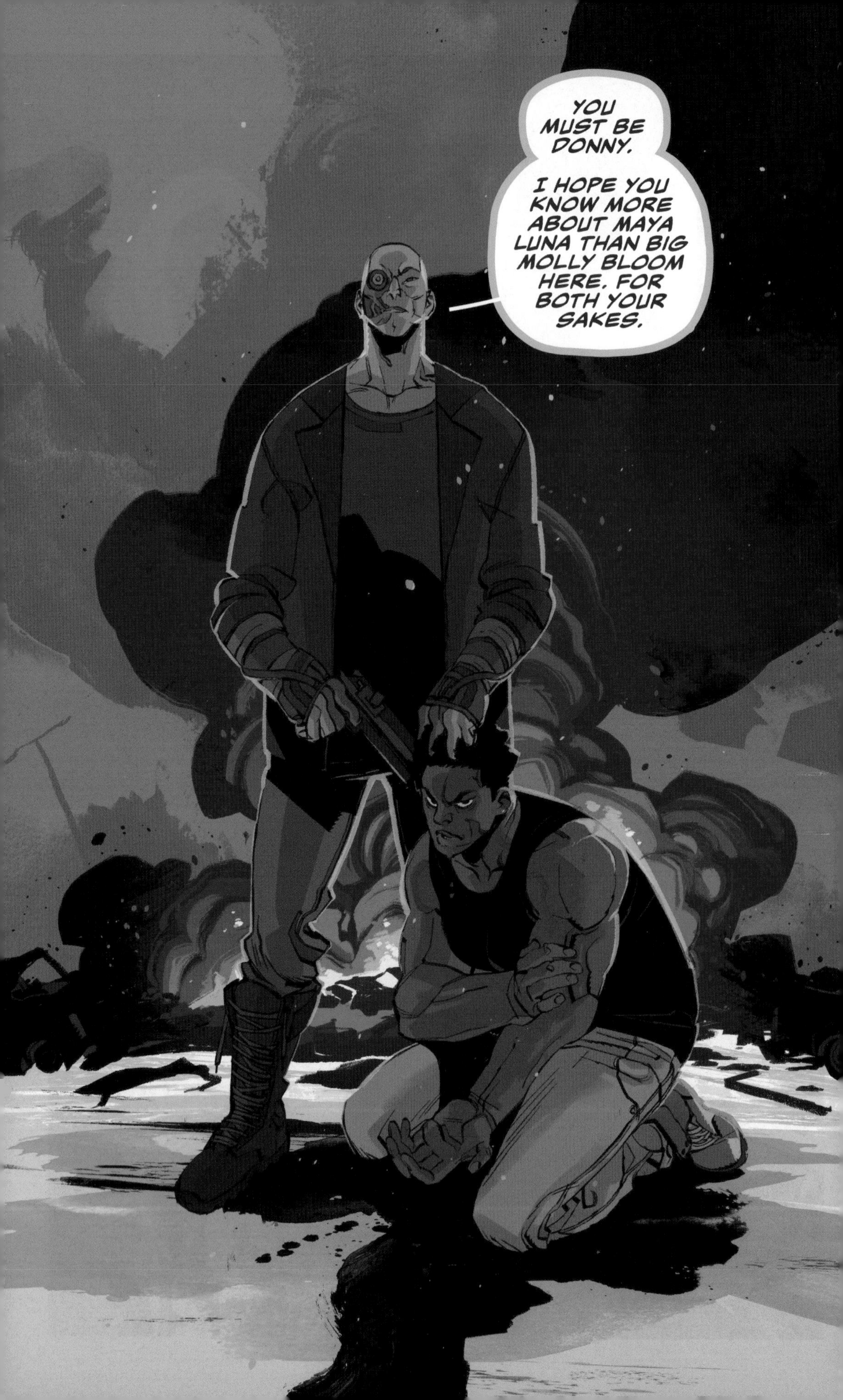
YOU MUST BE DONNY.
I HOPE YOU KNOW MORE ABOUT MAYA LUNA THAN BIG MOLLY BLOOM HERE. FOR BOTH YOUR SAKES.

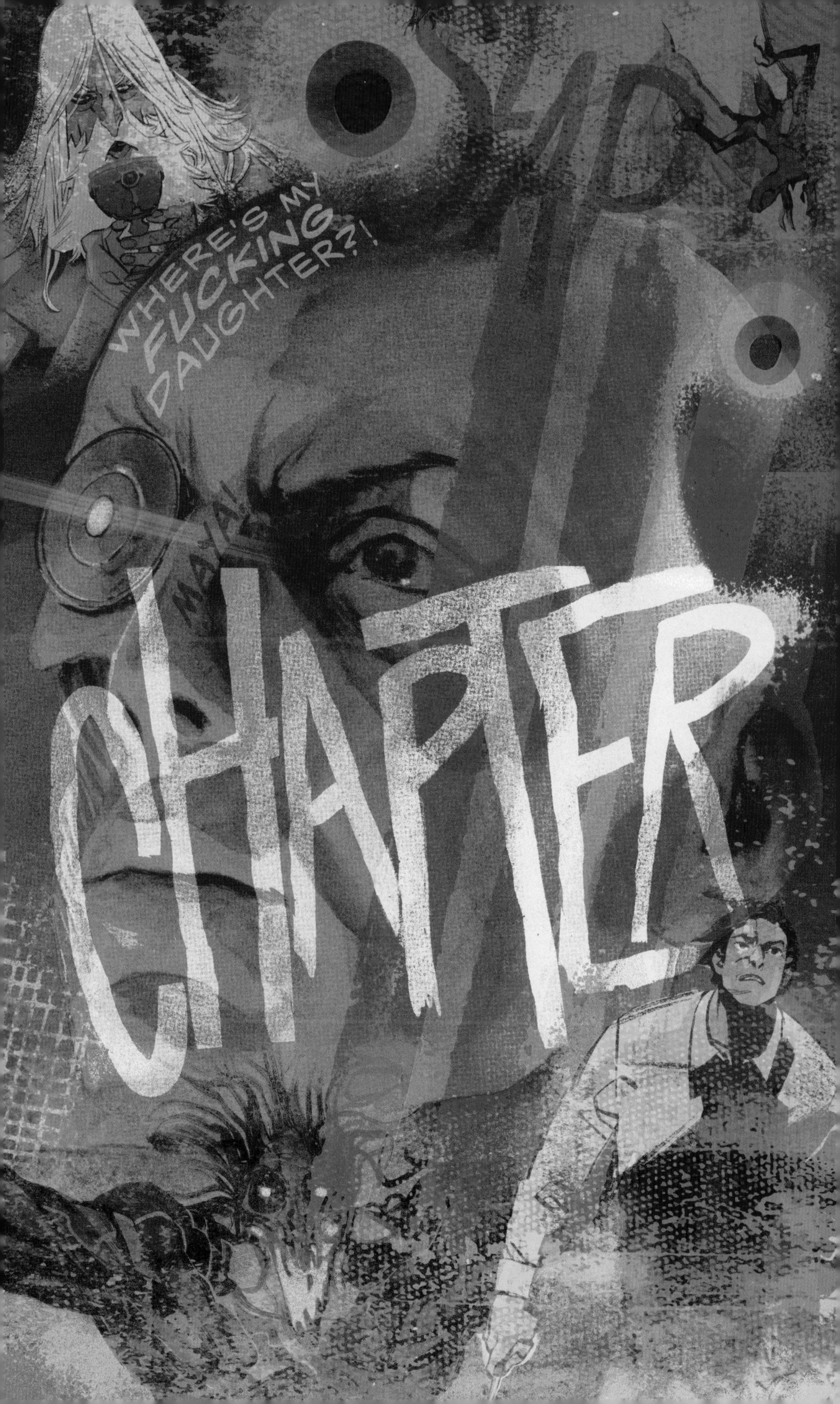
WHERE'S MY FUCKING DAUGHTER?!
CHAPTER

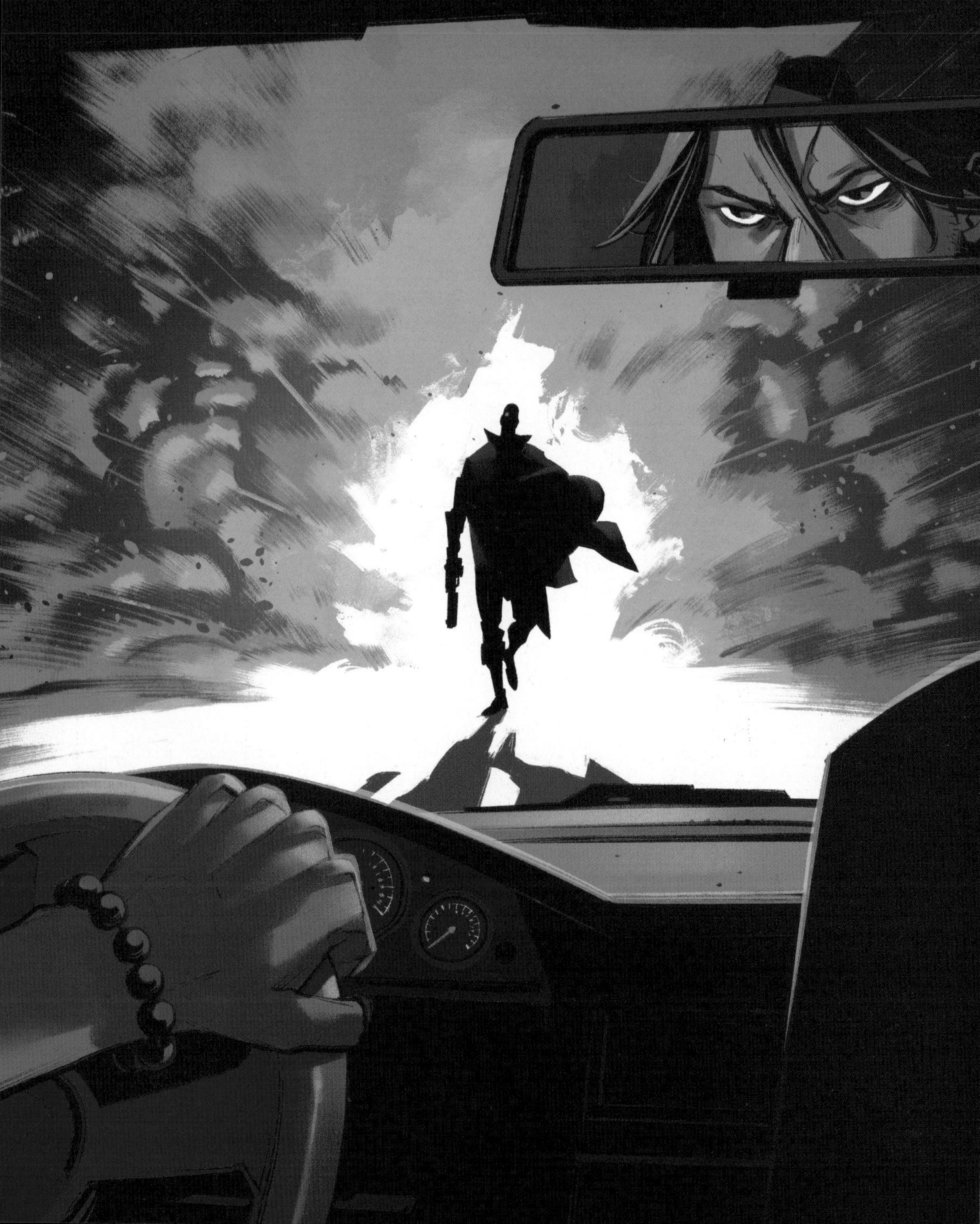

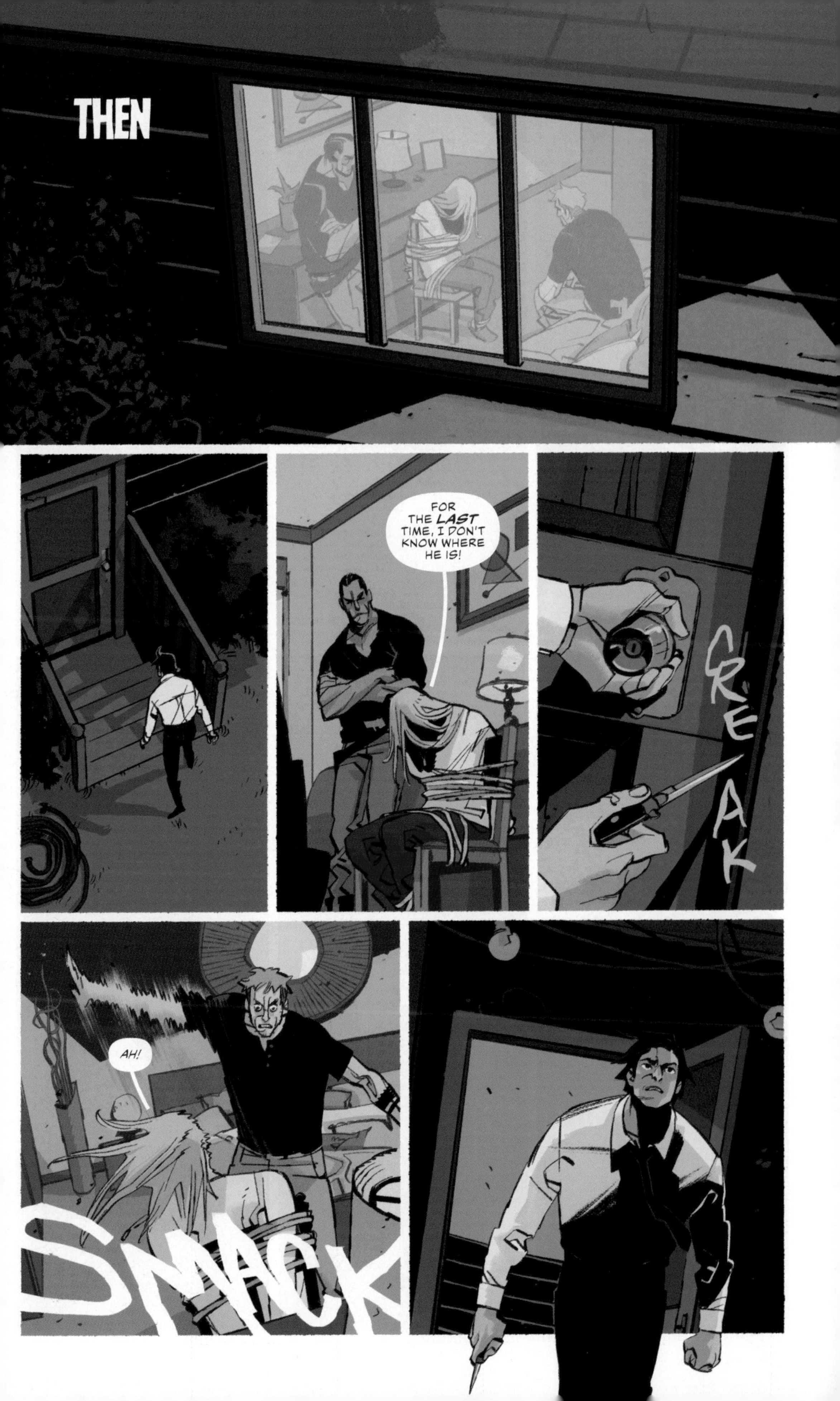
THEN
FOR THE LAST TIME, I DON'T KNOW WHERE HE IS!
CREAK
AH!
SMACK

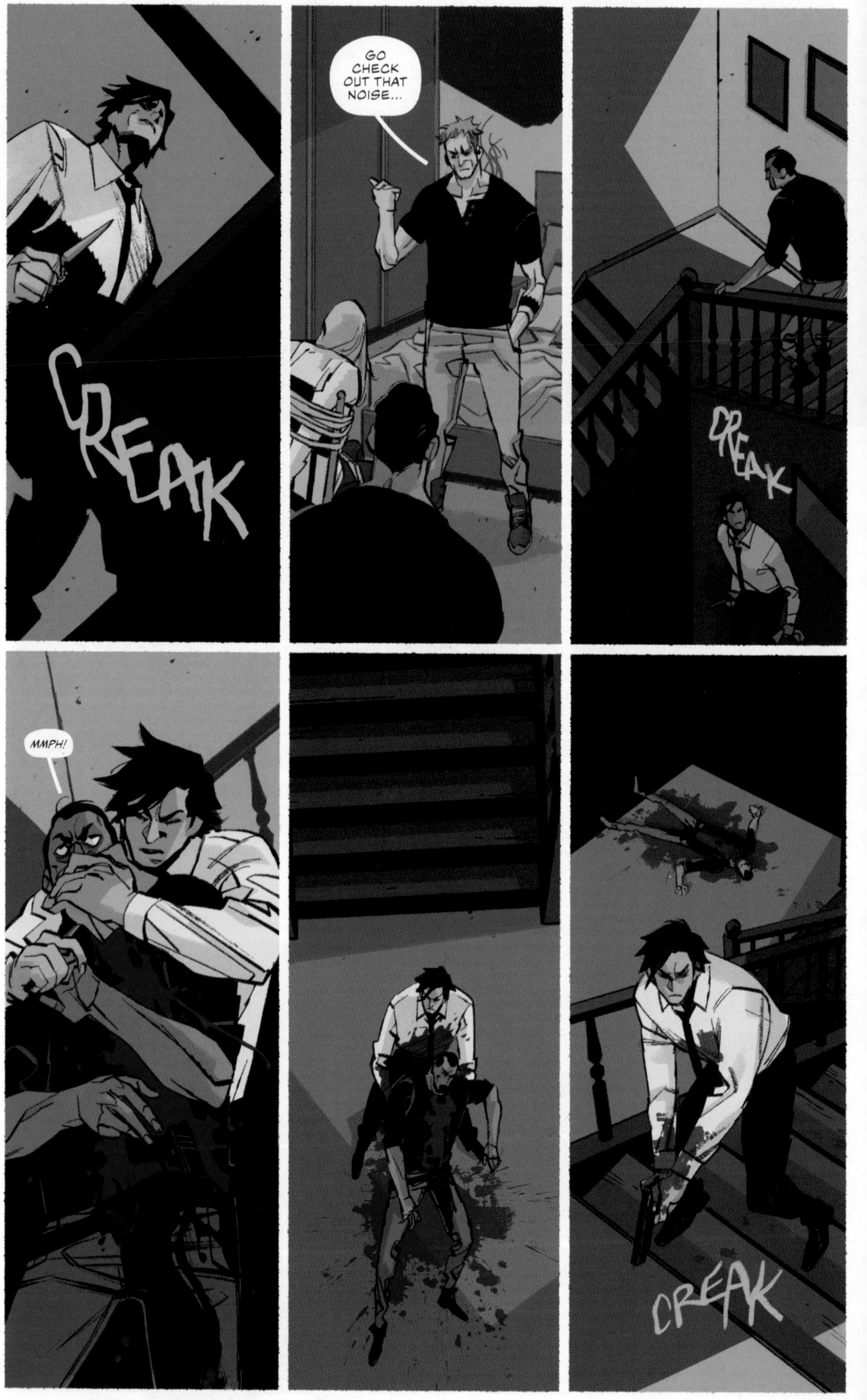
CREAK
GO CHECK OUT THAT NOISE...
CREAK
MMPH!
CREAK

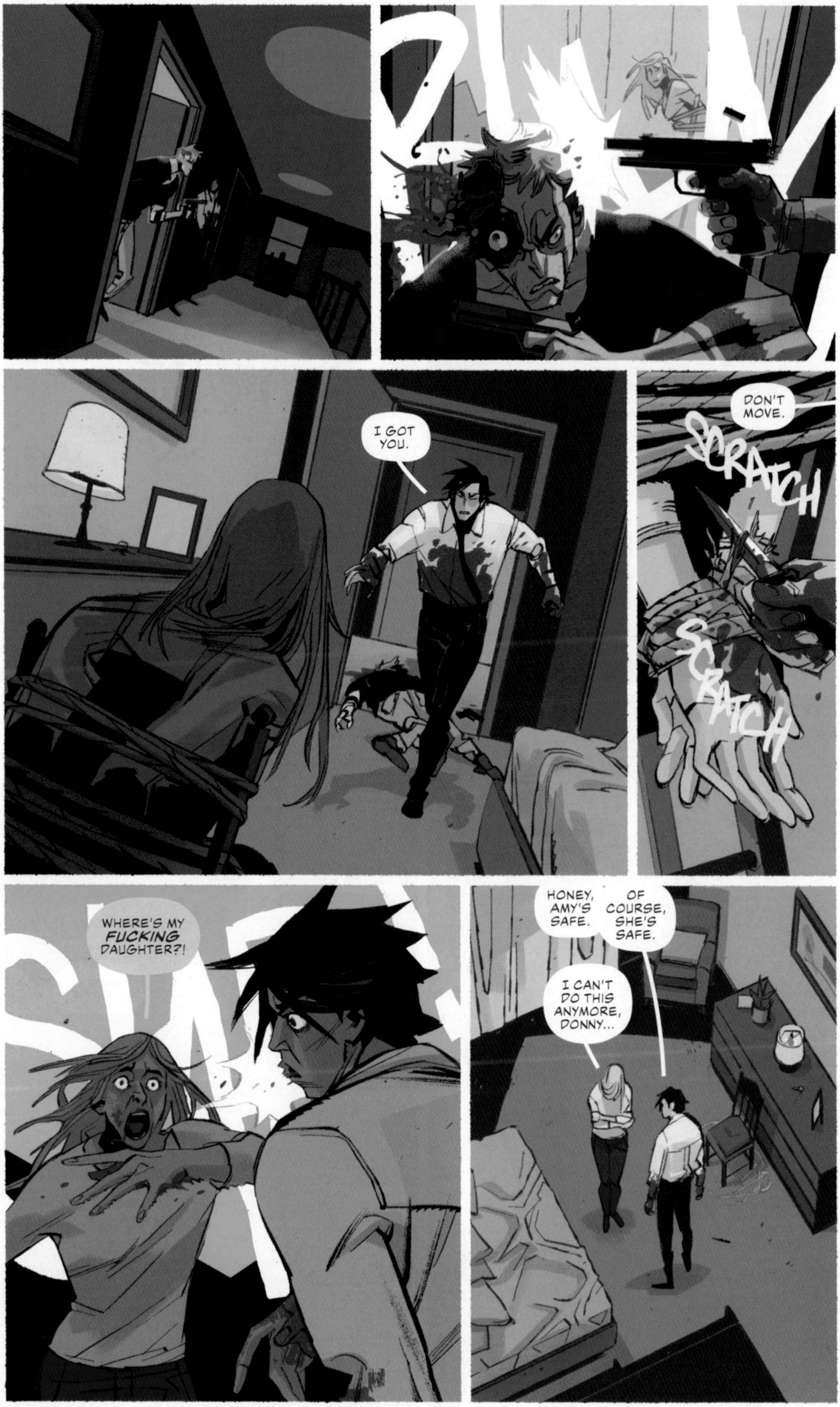
I GOT YOU.
DON'T MOVE.
SCRATCH
SCRATCH
WHERE'S MY *FUCKING* DAUGHTER?!
HONEY, AMY'S SAFE.
OF COURSE, SHE'S SAFE.
I CAN'T DO THIS ANYMORE, DONNY...

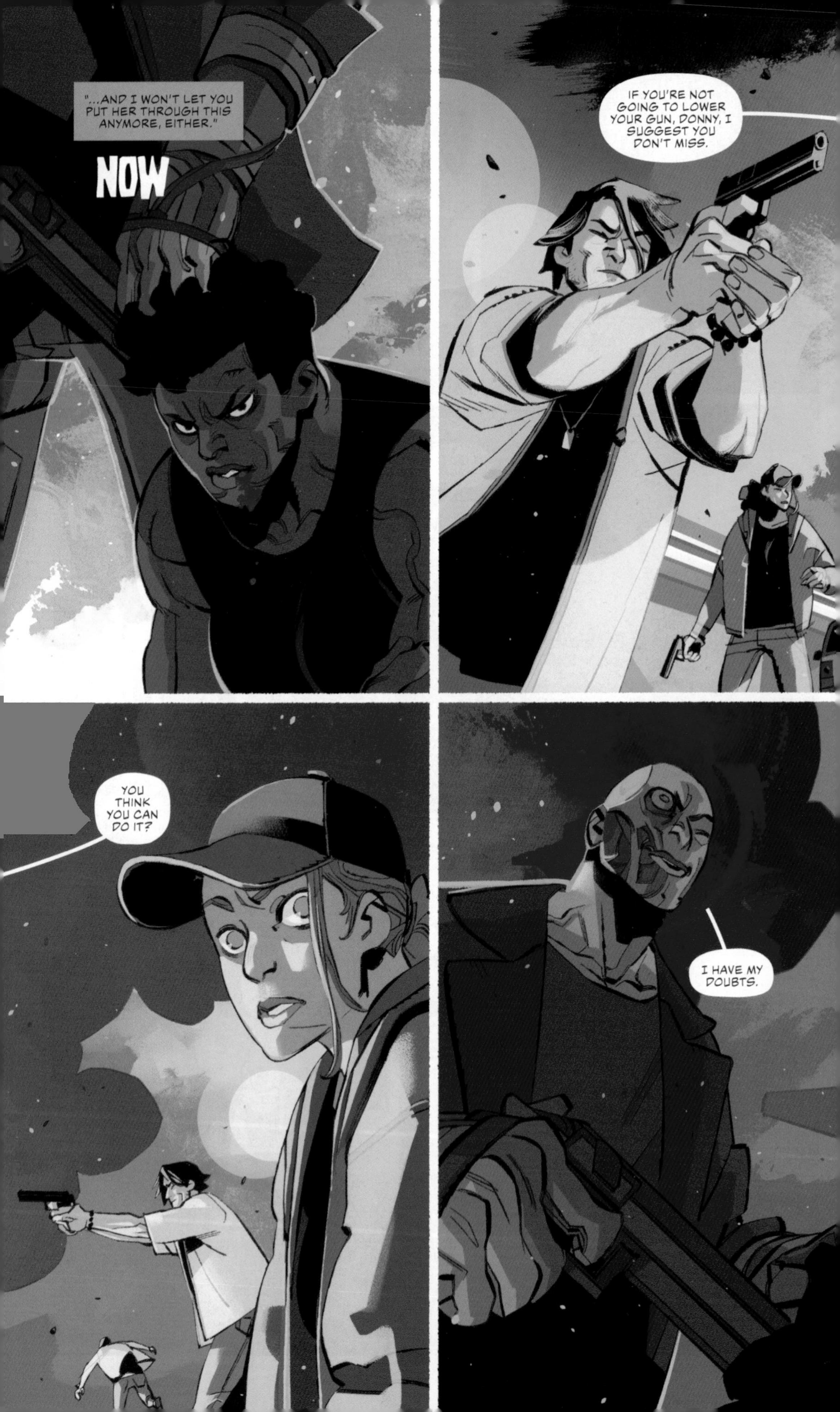
"...AND I WON'T LET YOU PUT HER THROUGH THIS ANYMORE, EITHER."
NOW
IF YOU'RE NOT GOING TO LOWER YOUR GUN, DONNY, I SUGGEST YOU DON'T MISS.
YOU THINK YOU CAN DO IT?
I HAVE MY DOUBTS.

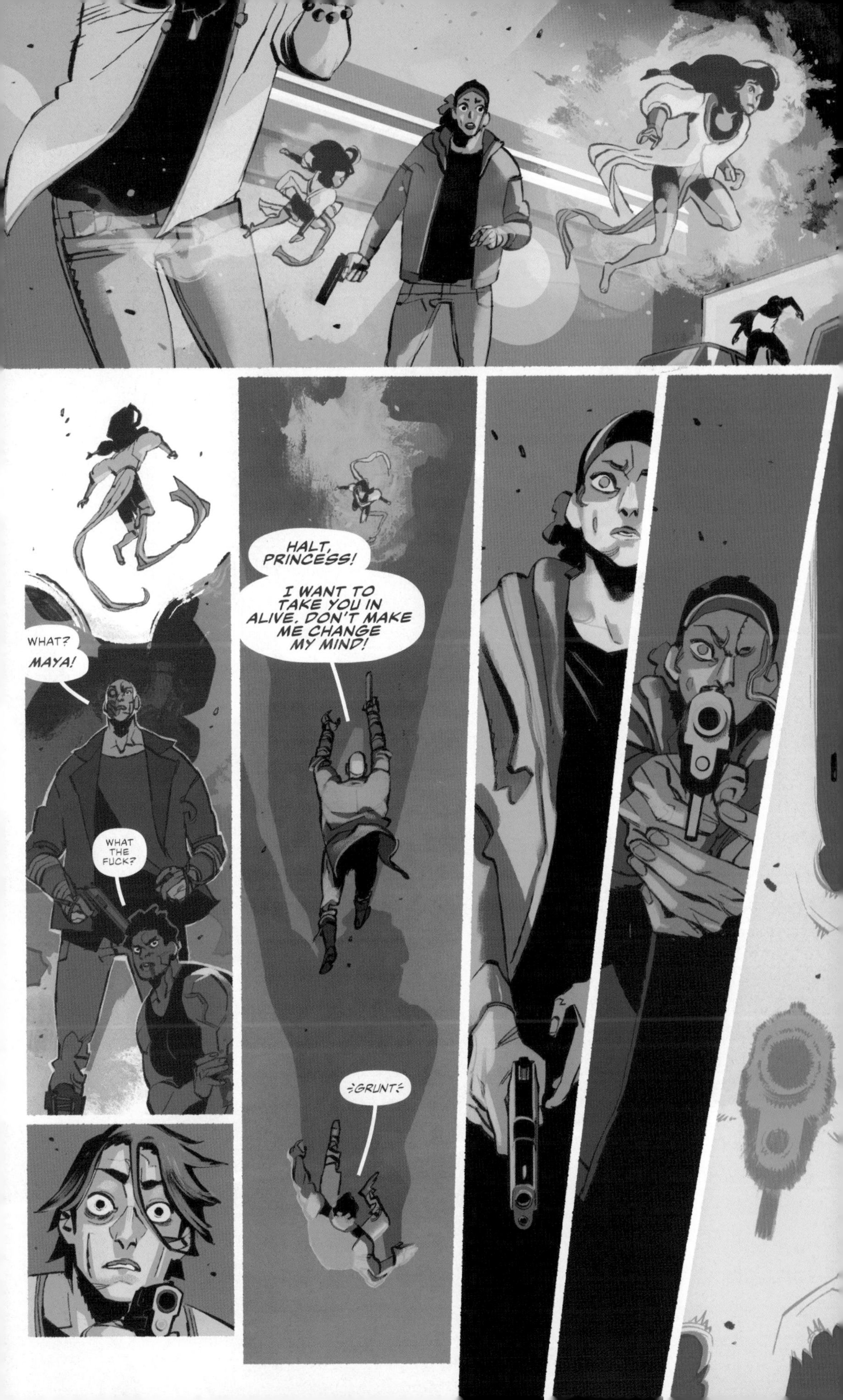
WHAT?
MAYA!
WHAT THE FUCK?
HALT, PRINCESS!
I WANT TO TAKE YOU IN ALIVE. DON'T MAKE ME CHANGE MY MIND!
GRUNT

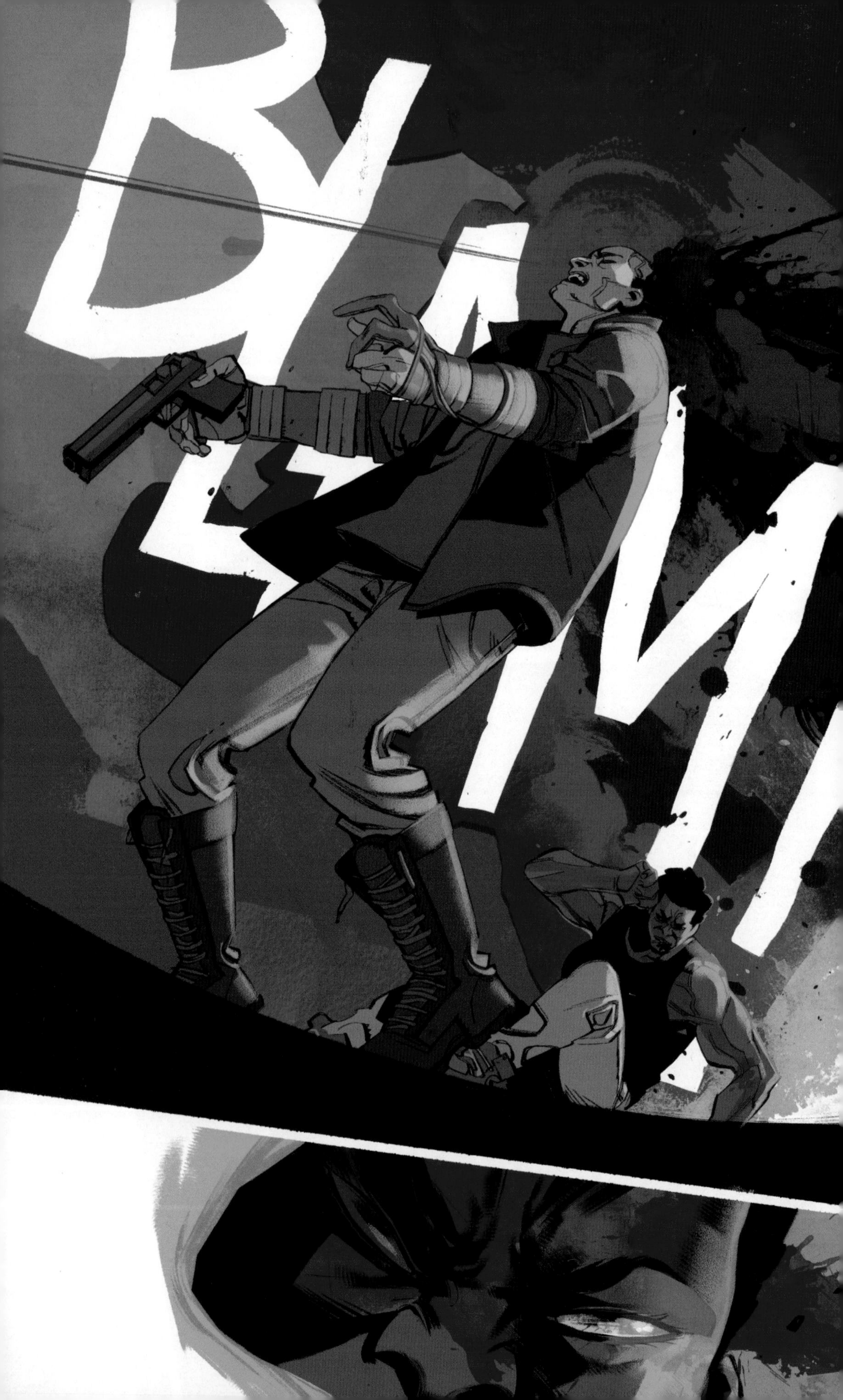

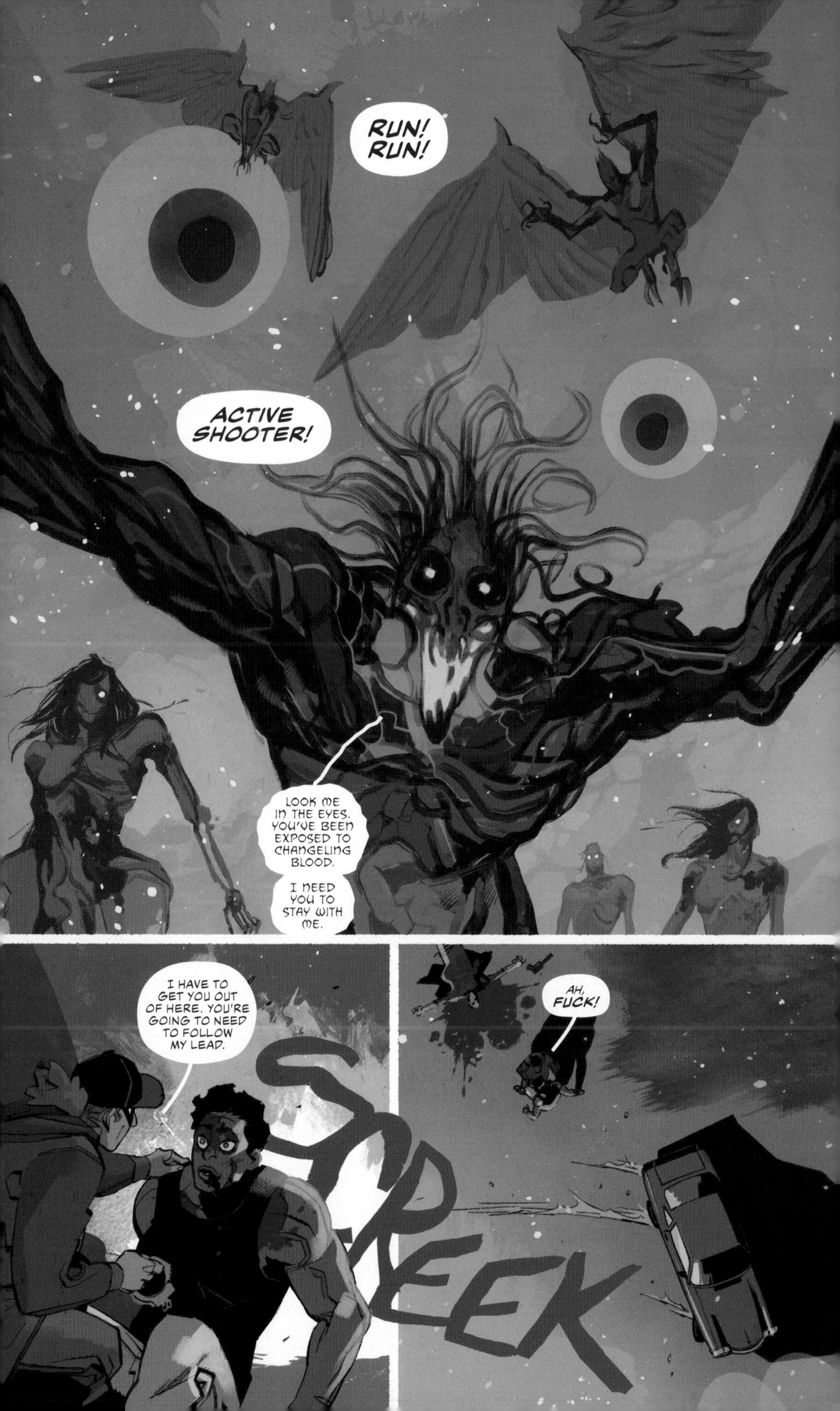
RUN! RUN!
ACTIVE SHOOTER!
LOOK ME IN THE EYES. YOU'VE BEEN EXPOSED TO CHANGELING BLOOD.
I NEED YOU TO STAY WITH ME.
I HAVE TO GET YOU OUT OF HERE. YOU'RE GOING TO NEED TO FOLLOW MY LEAD.
SCREEEK
AH, FUCK!

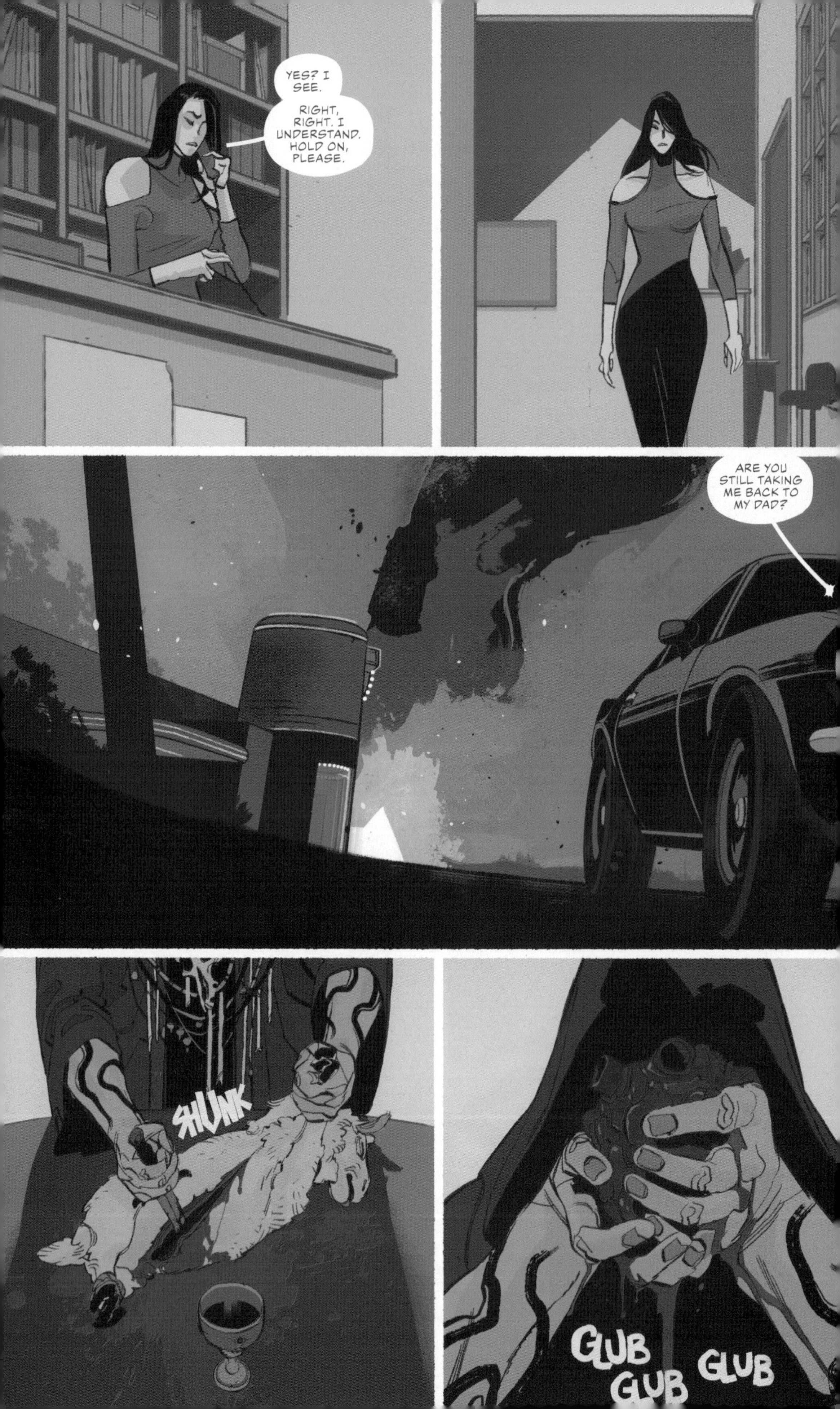
YES? I SEE.
RIGHT, RIGHT. I UNDERSTAND. HOLD ON, PLEASE.
ARE YOU STILL TAKING ME BACK TO MY DAD?
SHUNK
GLUB GLUB GLUB

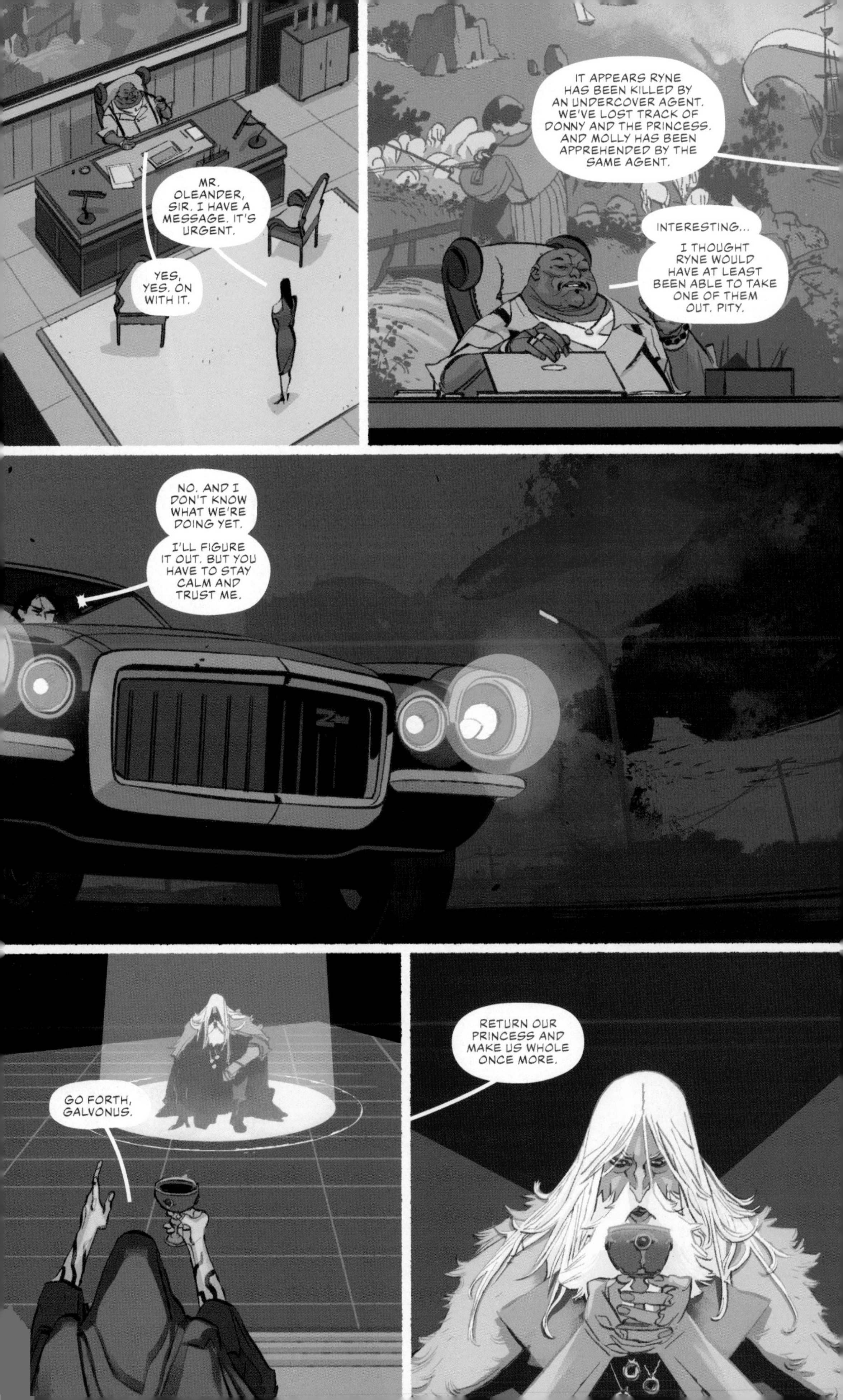
MR. OLEANDER, SIR. I HAVE A MESSAGE. IT'S URGENT.
YES, YES. ON WITH IT.
IT APPEARS RYNE HAS BEEN KILLED BY AN UNDERCOVER AGENT. WE'VE LOST TRACK OF DONNY AND THE PRINCESS. AND MOLLY HAS BEEN APPREHENDED BY THE SAME AGENT.
INTERESTING...
I THOUGHT RYNE WOULD HAVE AT LEAST BEEN ABLE TO TAKE ONE OF THEM OUT. PITY.
NO. AND I DON'T KNOW WHAT WE'RE DOING YET.
I'LL FIGURE IT OUT. BUT YOU HAVE TO STAY CALM AND TRUST ME.
GO FORTH, GALVONUS.
RETURN OUR PRINCESS AND MAKE US WHOLE ONCE MORE.

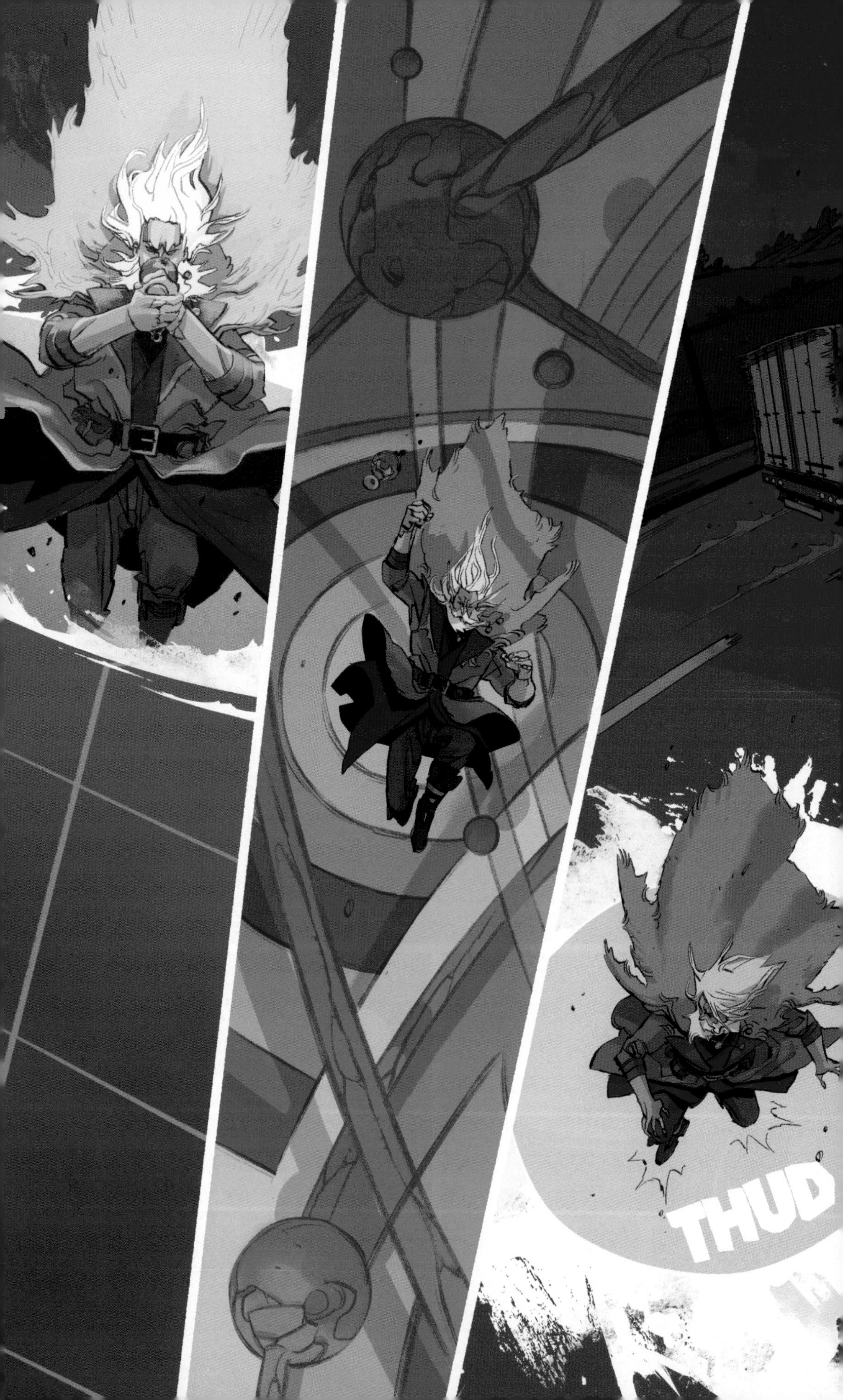
THUD

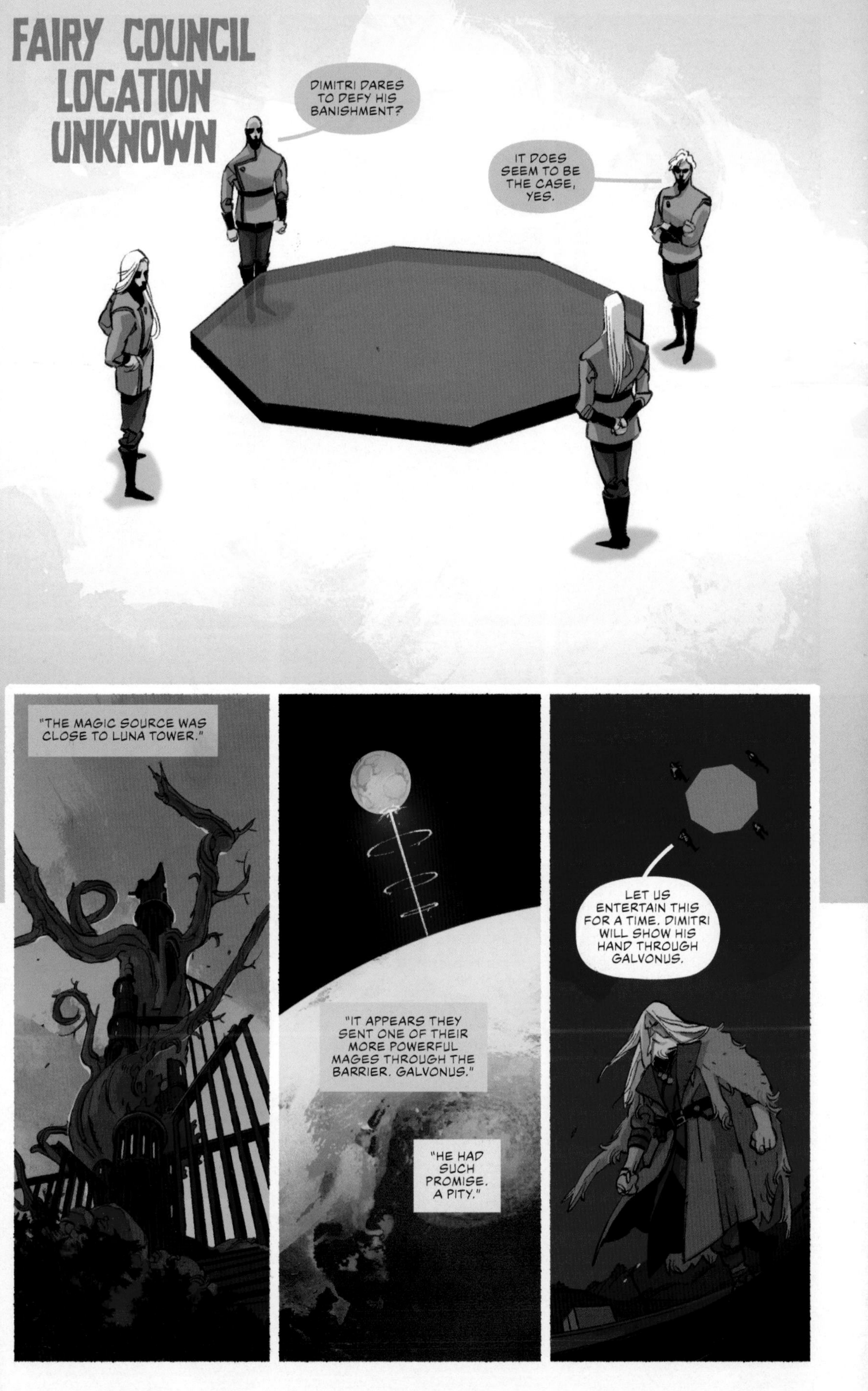
FAIRY COUNCIL LOCATION UNKNOWN
DIMITRI DARES TO DEFY HIS BANISHMENT?
IT DOES SEEM TO BE THE CASE, YES.
"THE MAGIC SOURCE WAS CLOSE TO LUNA TOWER."
"IT APPEARS THEY SENT ONE OF THEIR MORE POWERFUL MAGES THROUGH THE BARRIER. GALVONUS."
"HE HAD SUCH PROMISE. A PITY."
LET US ENTERTAIN THIS FOR A TIME. DIMITRI WILL SHOW HIS HAND THROUGH GALVONUS.

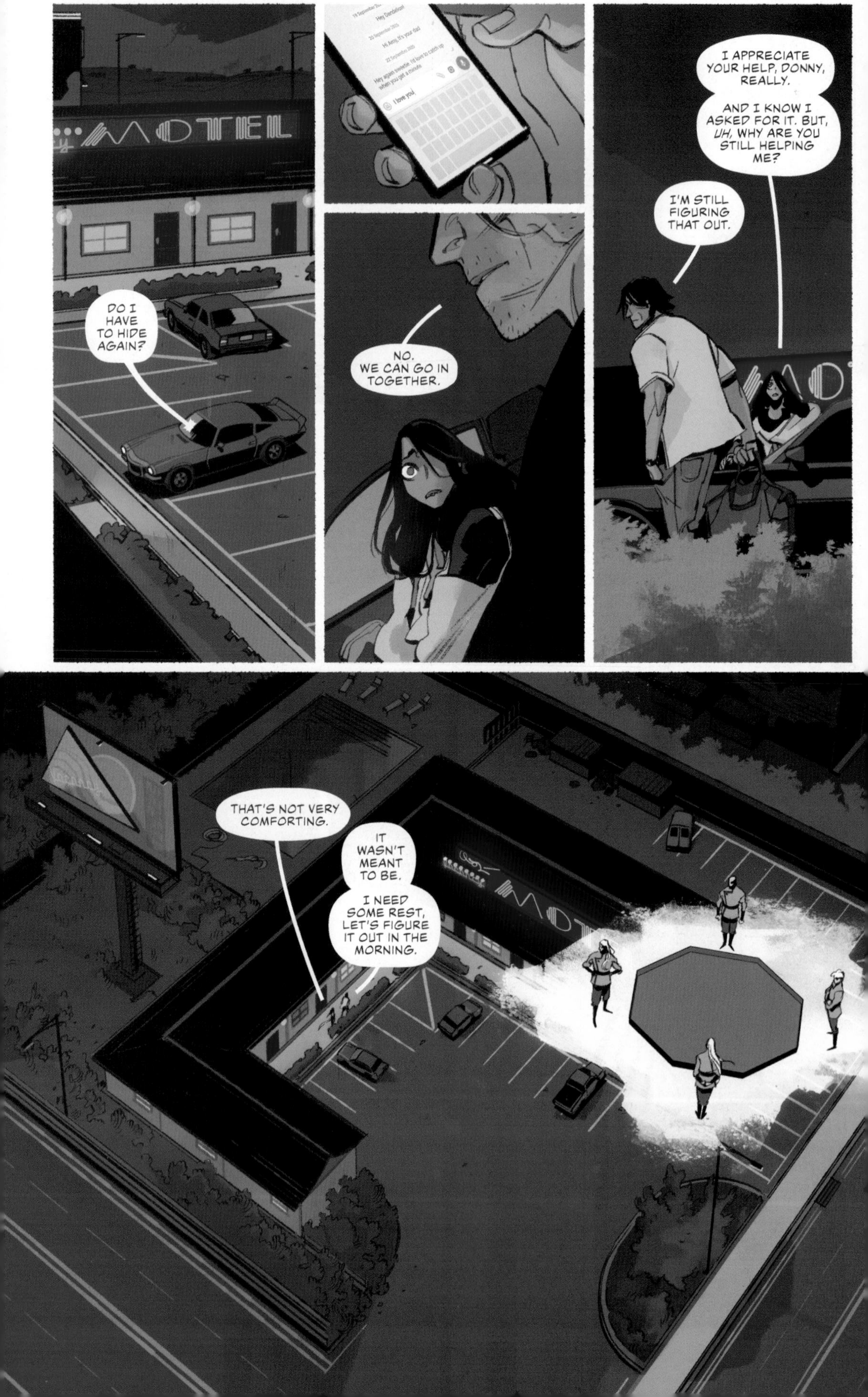
MOTEL
DO I HAVE TO HIDE AGAIN?
Hey Dandelion!
Hi Amy, it's your dad
Hey again sweetie, I'd love to catch up when you get a minute
I love you
NO. WE CAN GO IN TOGETHER.
I APPRECIATE YOUR HELP, DONNY, REALLY.
AND I KNOW I ASKED FOR IT. BUT, *UH*, WHY ARE YOU STILL HELPING ME?
I'M STILL FIGURING THAT OUT.
THAT'S NOT VERY COMFORTING.
IT WASN'T MEANT TO BE.
I NEED SOME REST, LET'S FIGURE IT OUT IN THE MORNING.

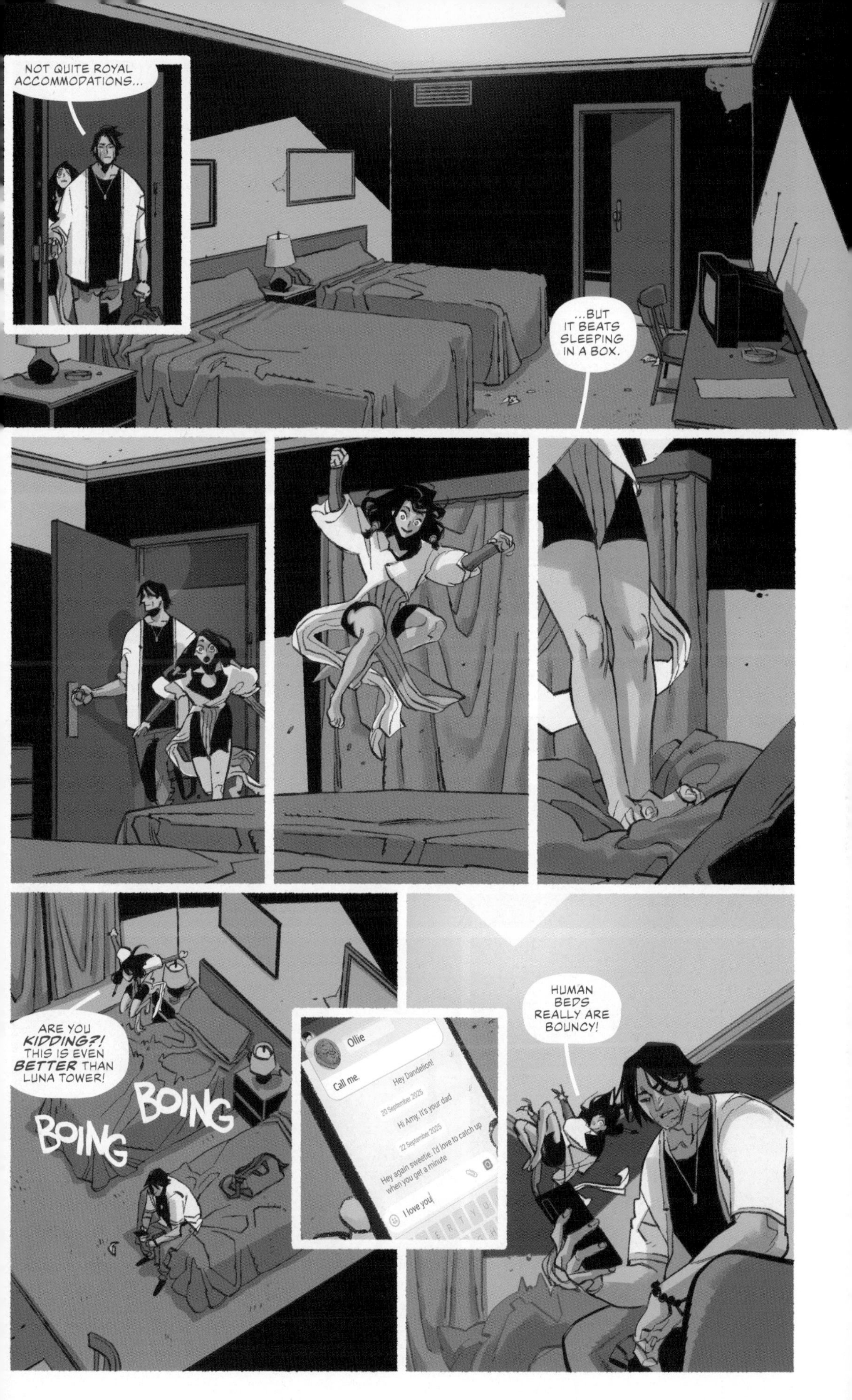
NOT QUITE ROYAL ACCOMMODATIONS...
...BUT IT BEATS SLEEPING IN A BOX.
ARE YOU *KIDDING?!* THIS IS EVEN *BETTER* THAN LUNA TOWER!
BOING
BOING
Ollie
Call me.
Hey Dandelion!
20 September 2025
Hi Amy, it's your dad
22 September 2025
Hey again sweetie. I'd love to catch up when you get a minute
I love you
HUMAN BEDS REALLY ARE BOUNCY!

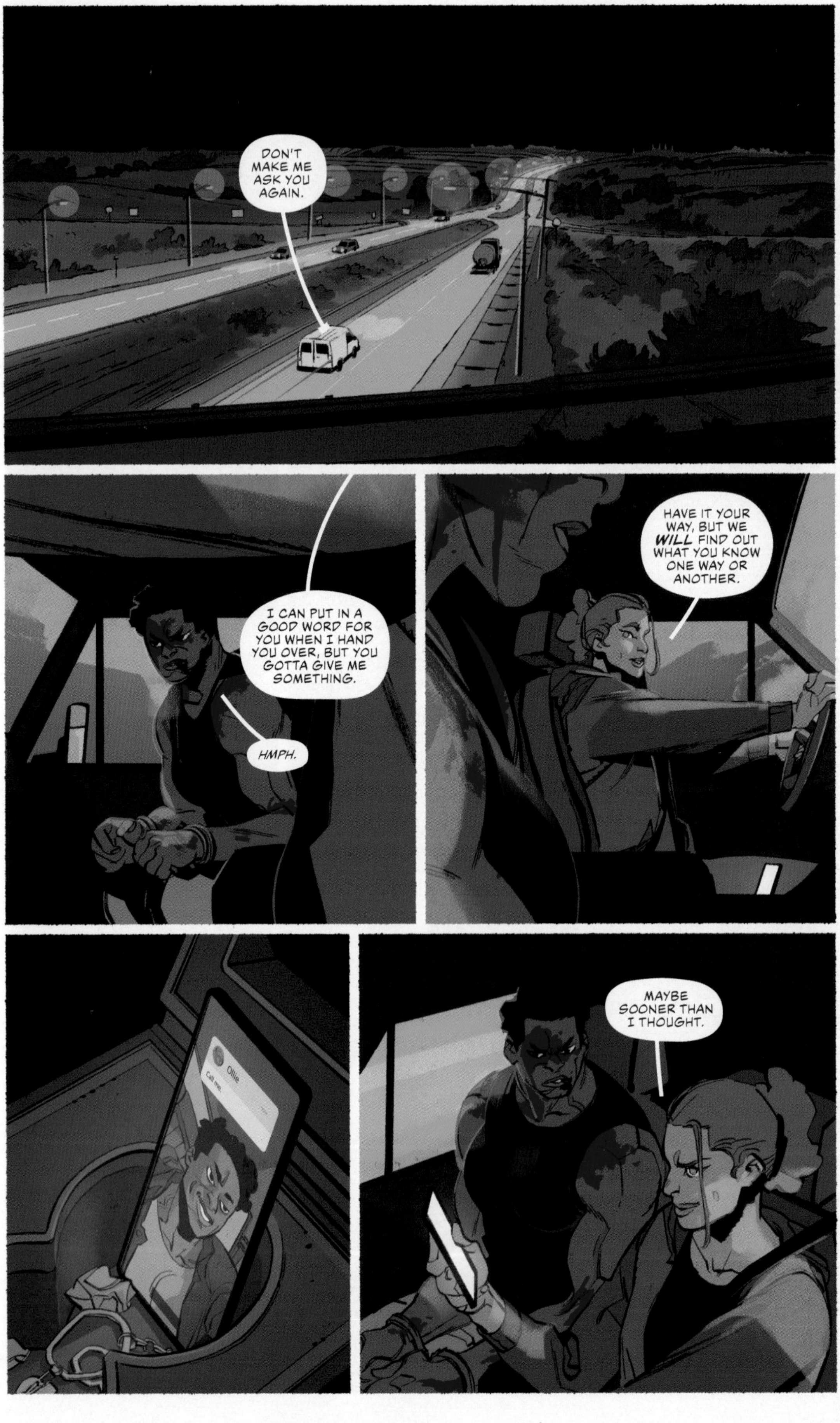
DON'T MAKE ME ASK YOU AGAIN.
I CAN PUT IN A GOOD WORD FOR YOU WHEN I HAND YOU OVER, BUT YOU GOTTA GIVE ME SOMETHING.
HMPH.
HAVE IT YOUR WAY, BUT WE **WILL** FIND OUT WHAT YOU KNOW ONE WAY OR ANOTHER.
Ollie
Call me.
MAYBE SOONER THAN I THOUGHT.

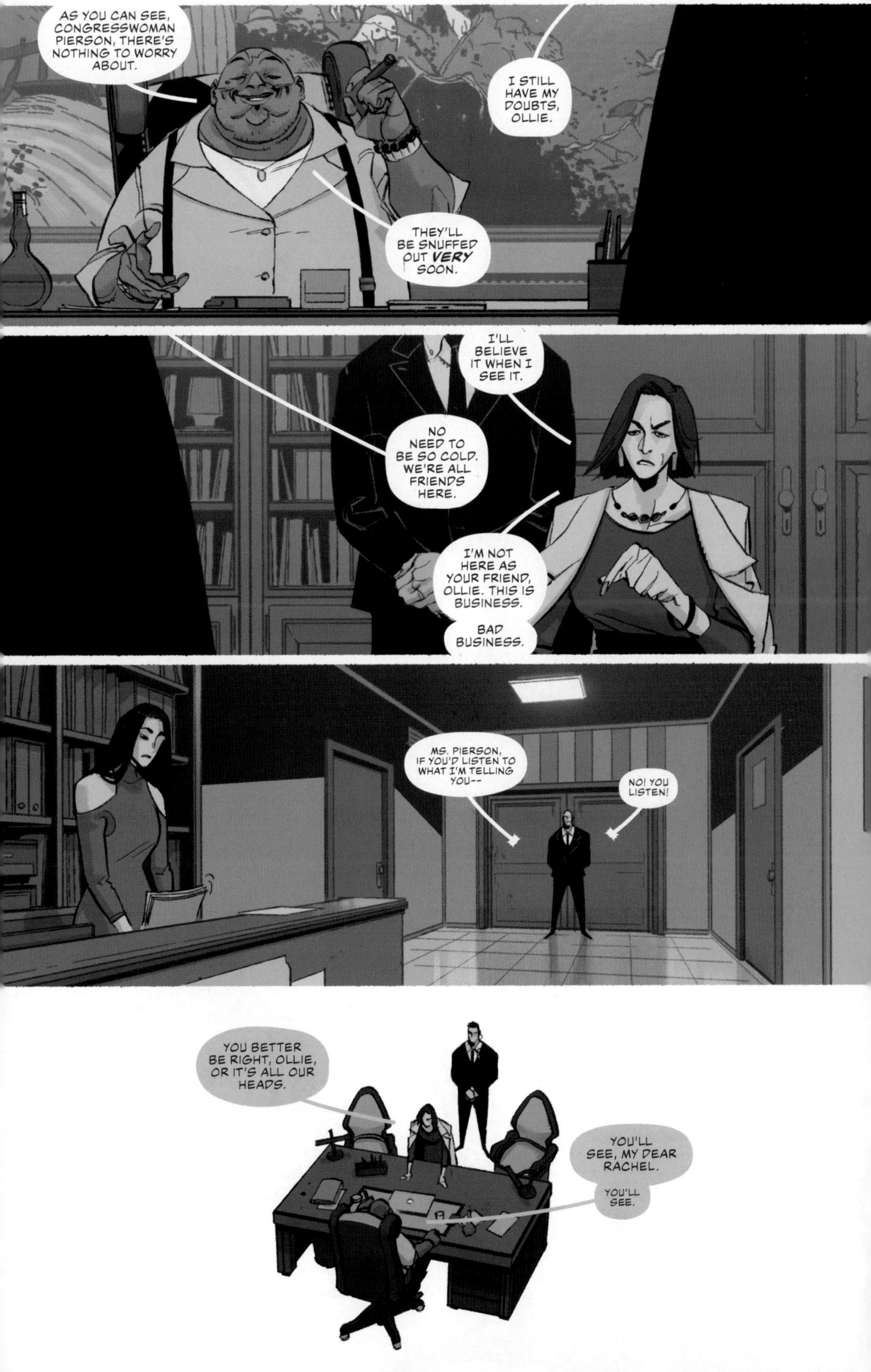

AS YOU CAN SEE, CONGRESSWOMAN PIERSON, THERE'S NOTHING TO WORRY ABOUT.
I STILL HAVE MY DOUBTS, OLLIE.
THEY'LL BE SNUFFED OUT **VERY** SOON.
I'LL BELIEVE IT WHEN I SEE IT.
NO NEED TO BE SO COLD. WE'RE ALL FRIENDS HERE.
I'M NOT HERE AS YOUR FRIEND, OLLIE. THIS IS BUSINESS.
BAD BUSINESS.
MS. PIERSON, IF YOU'D LISTEN TO WHAT I'M TELLING YOU--
NO! YOU LISTEN!
YOU BETTER BE RIGHT, OLLIE, OR IT'S ALL OUR HEADS.
YOU'LL SEE, MY DEAR RACHEL.
YOU'LL SEE.

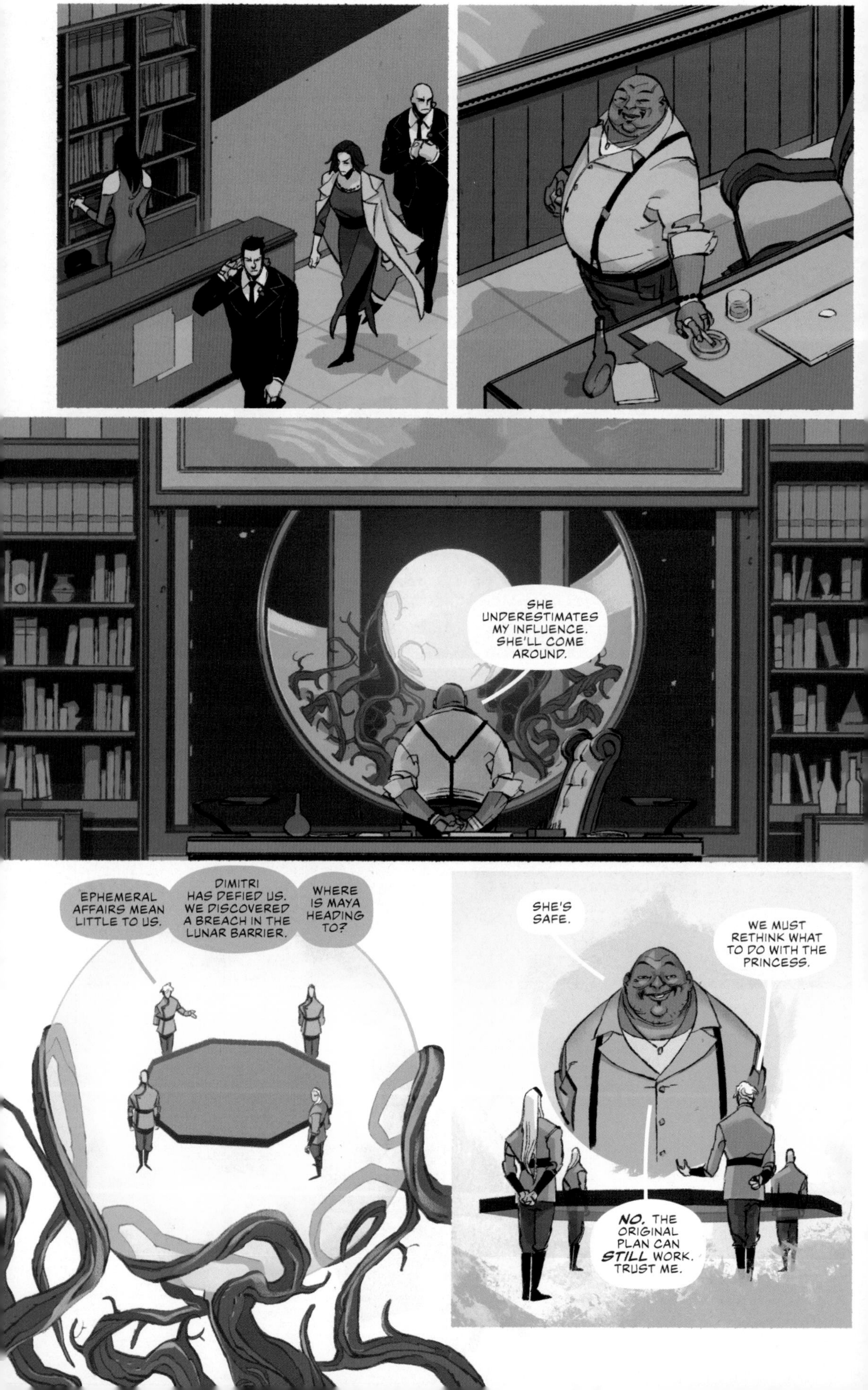
SHE UNDERESTIMATES MY INFLUENCE. SHE'LL COME AROUND.
EPHEMERAL AFFAIRS MEAN LITTLE TO US.
DIMITRI HAS DEFIED US. WE DISCOVERED A BREACH IN THE LUNAR BARRIER.
WHERE IS MAYA HEADING TO?
SHE'S SAFE.
WE MUST RETHINK WHAT TO DO WITH THE PRINCESS.
NO. THE ORIGINAL PLAN CAN STILL WORK. TRUST ME.

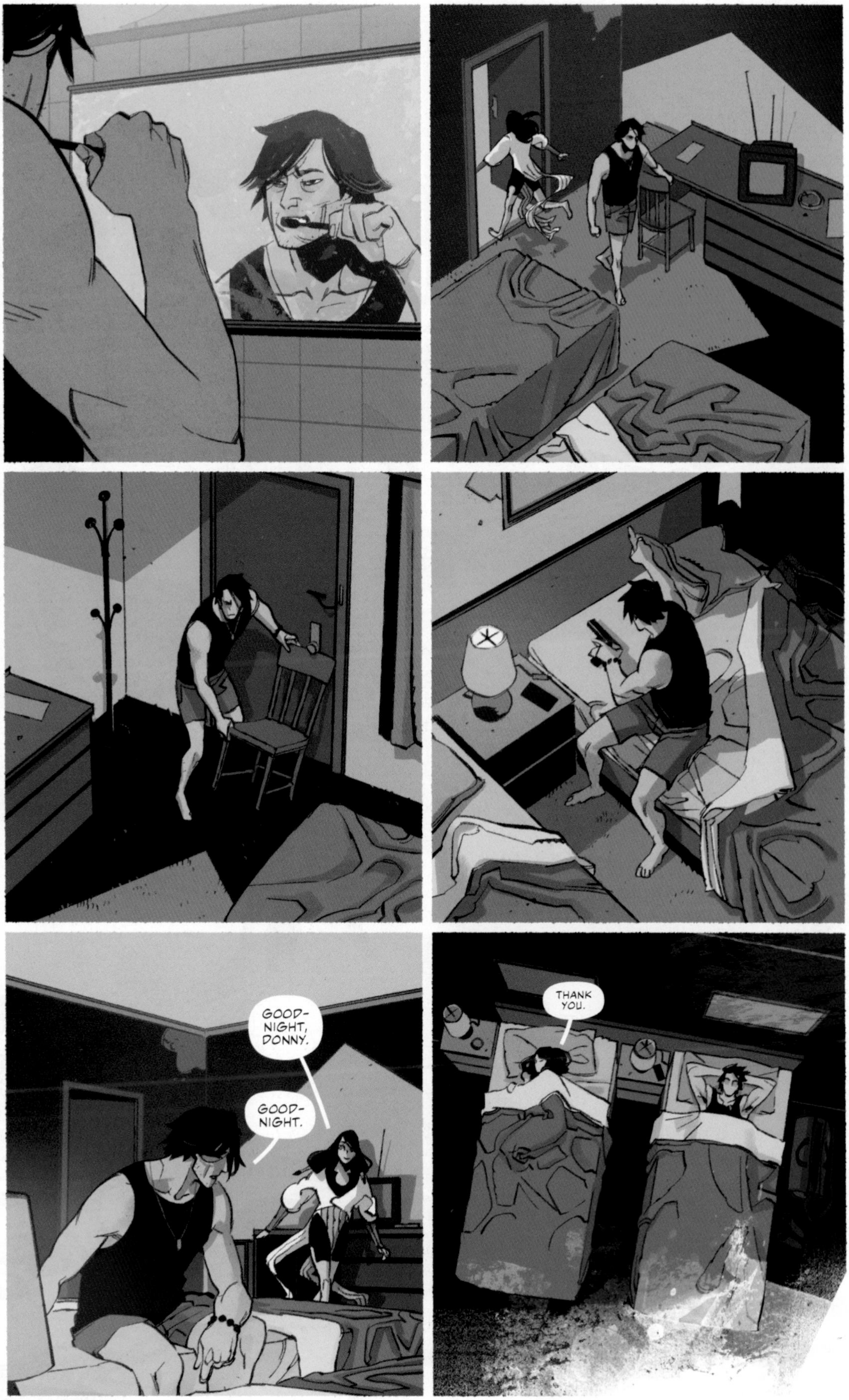
GOOD-NIGHT, DONNY.
GOOD-NIGHT.
THANK YOU.

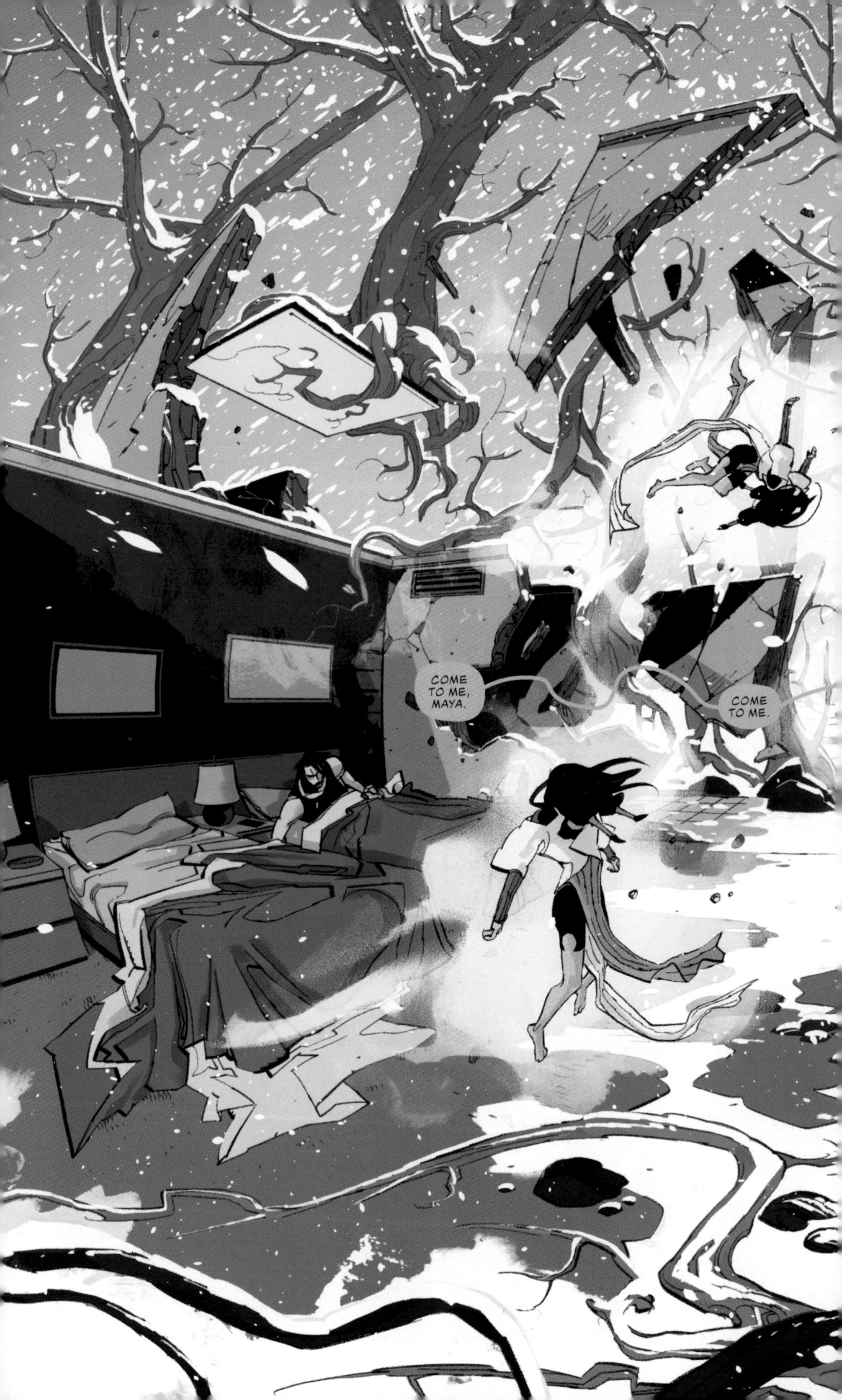
COME TO ME, MAYA.
COME TO ME.

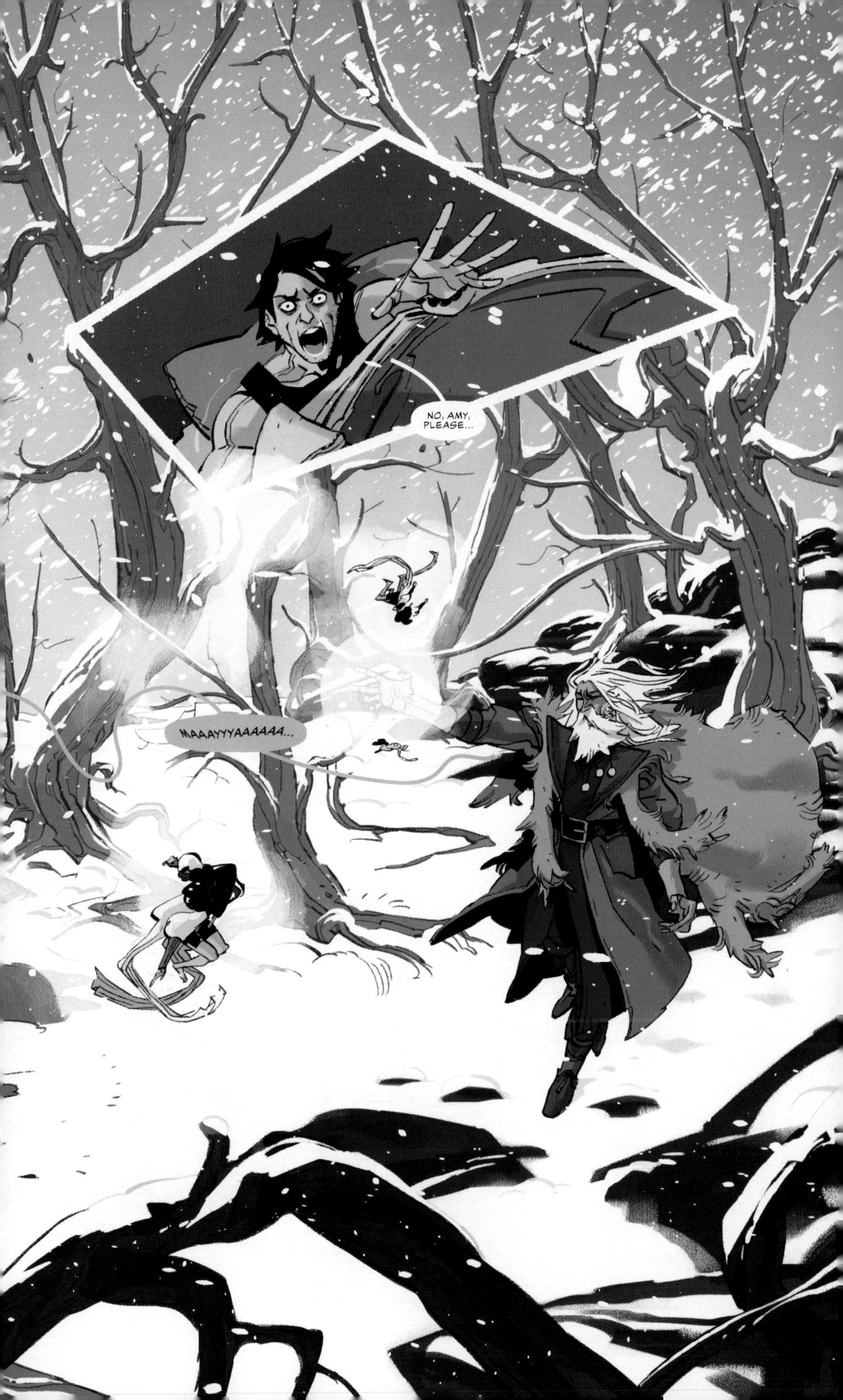
NO, AMY, PLEASE...
MAAAYYYAAAAAA...

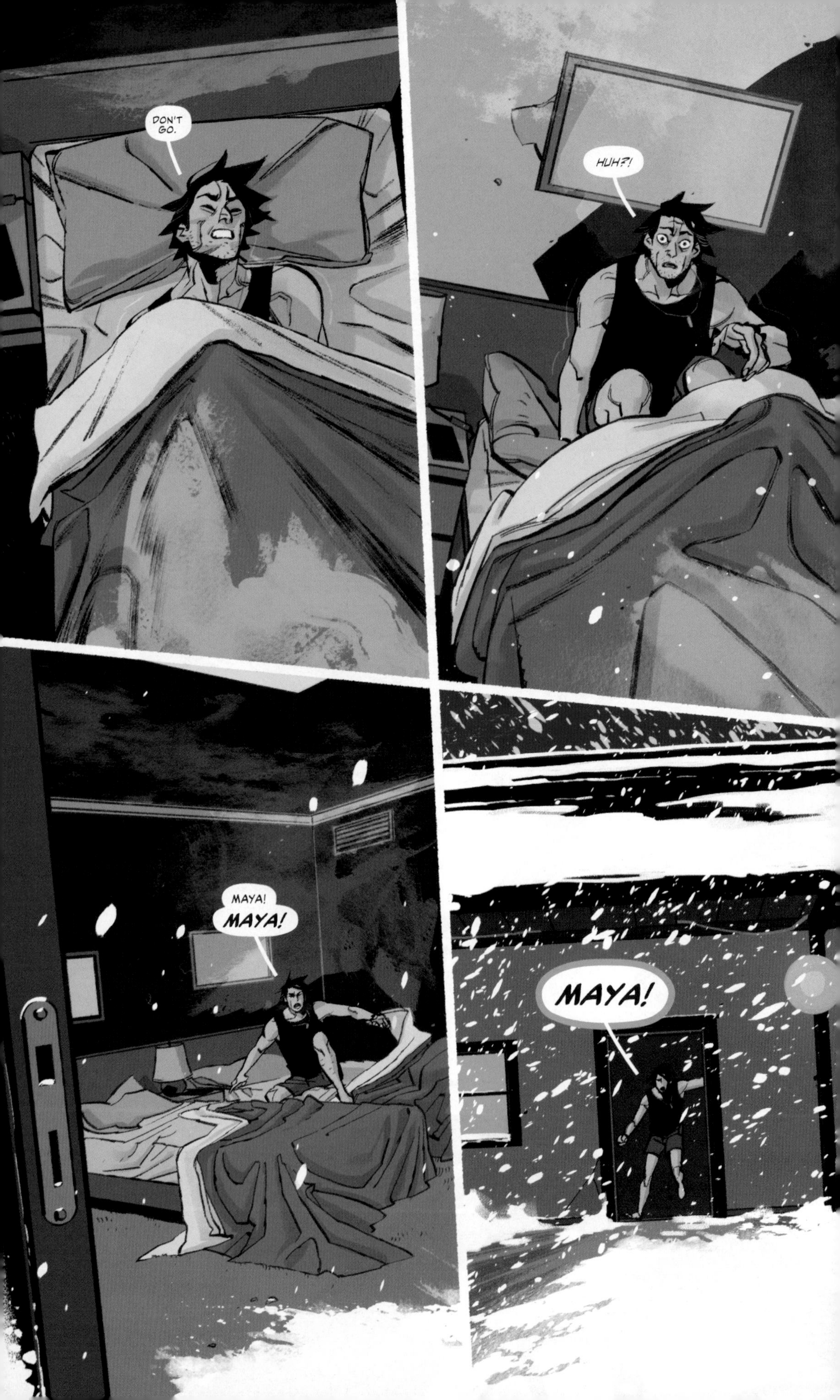
DON'T GO.
HUH?!
MAYA!
MAYA!
MAYA!

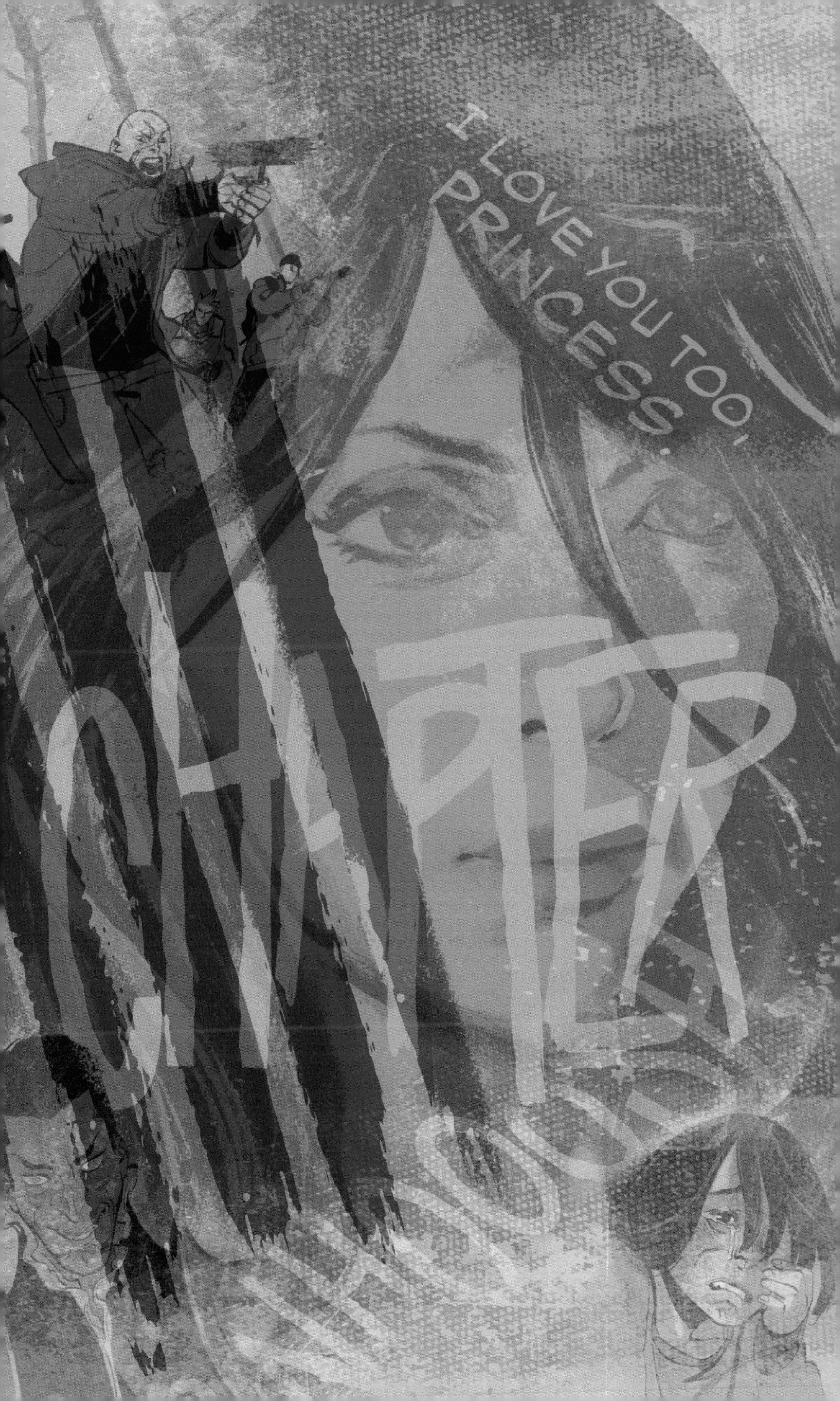
I LOVE YOU TOO, PRINCESS.
CHAPTER

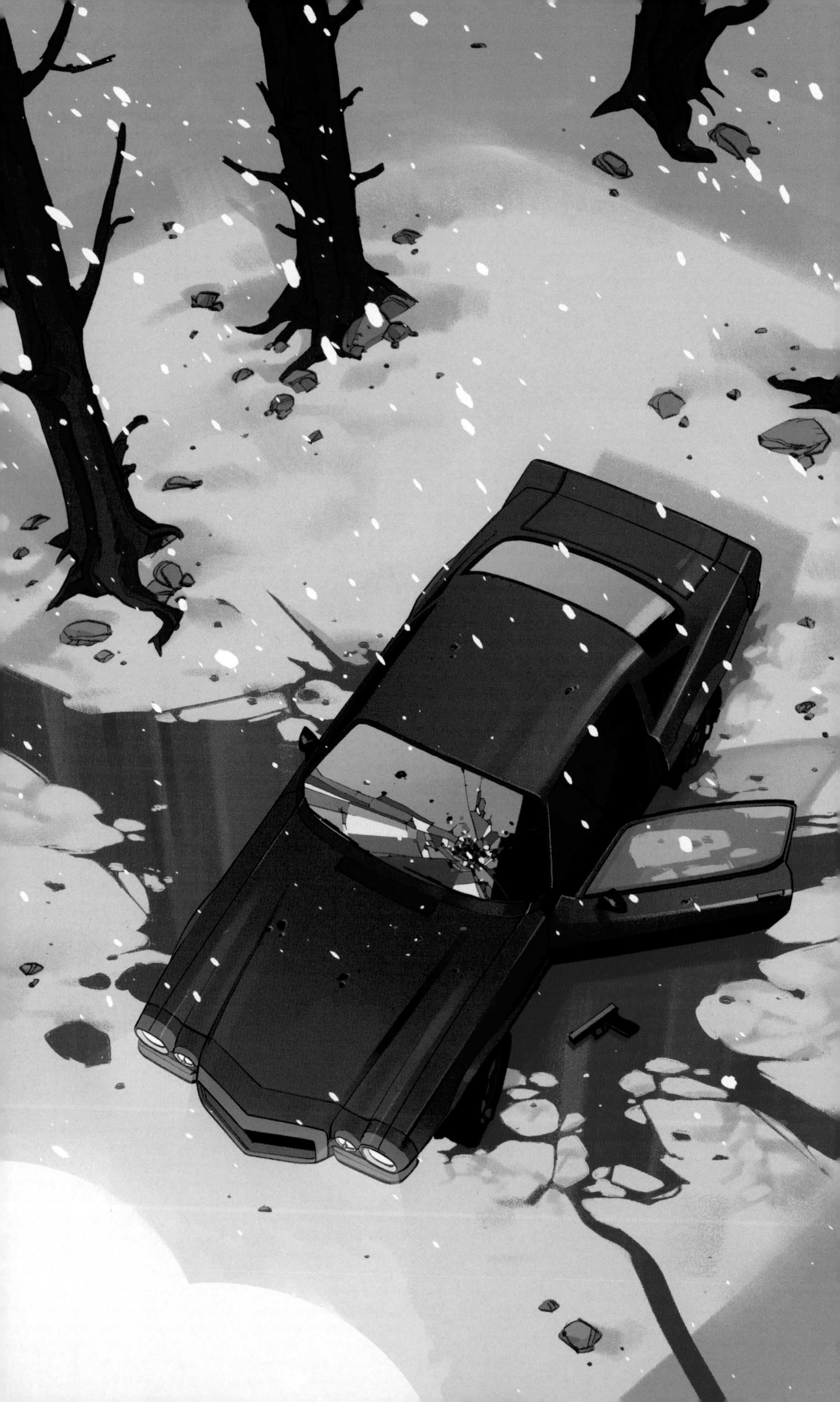

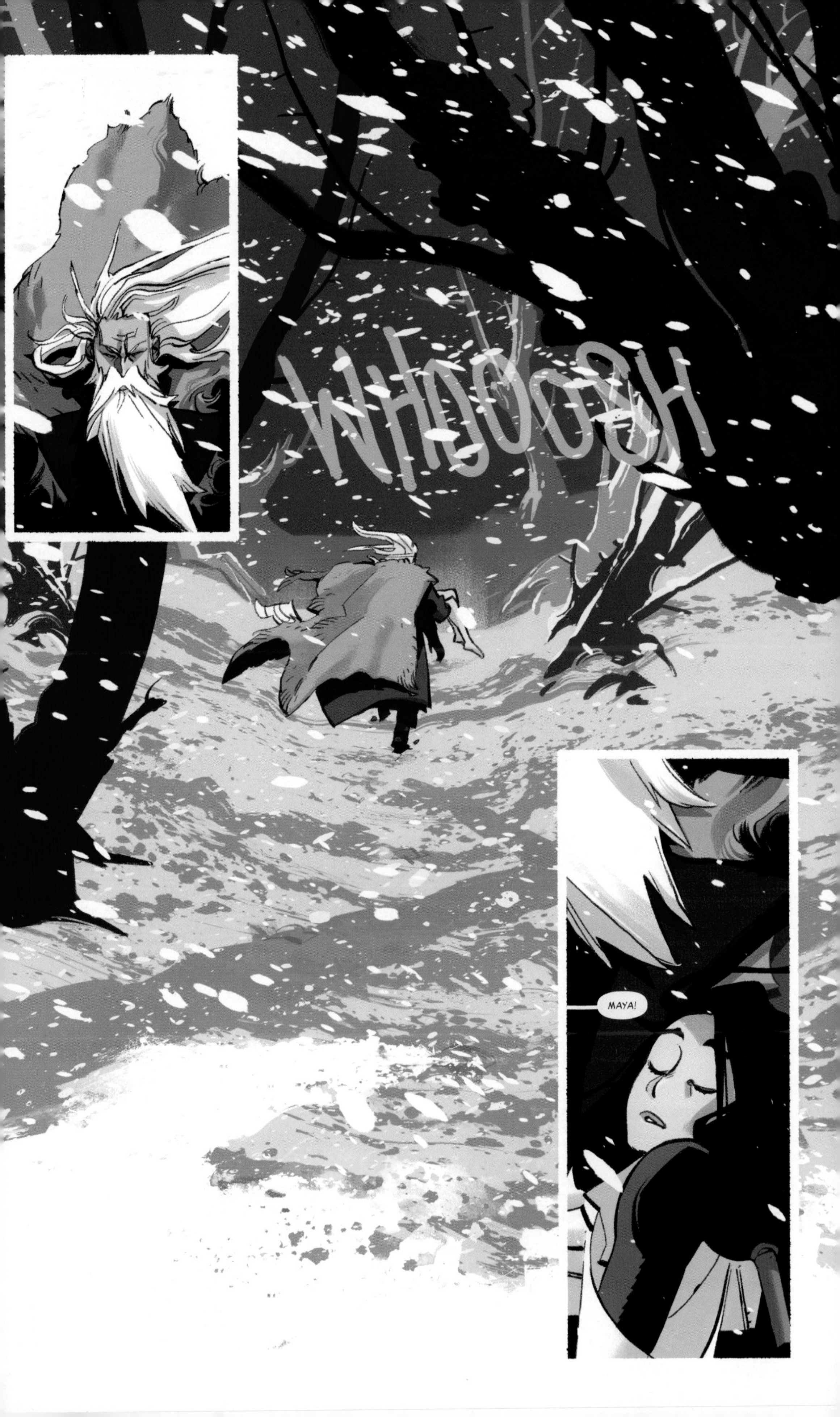
WHOOOSH
MAYA!

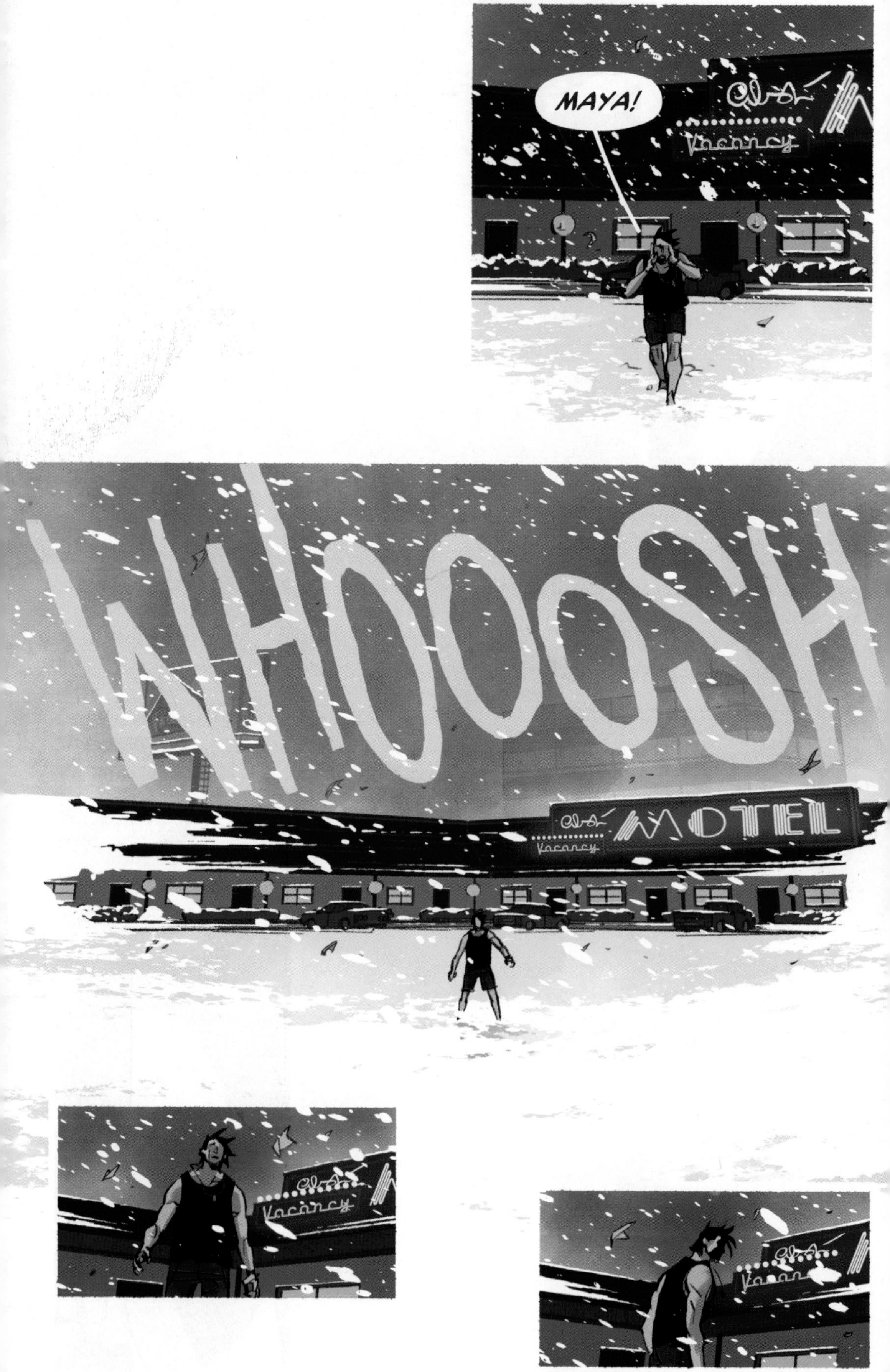
MAYA!
WHOOOSH
MOTEL
Vacancy

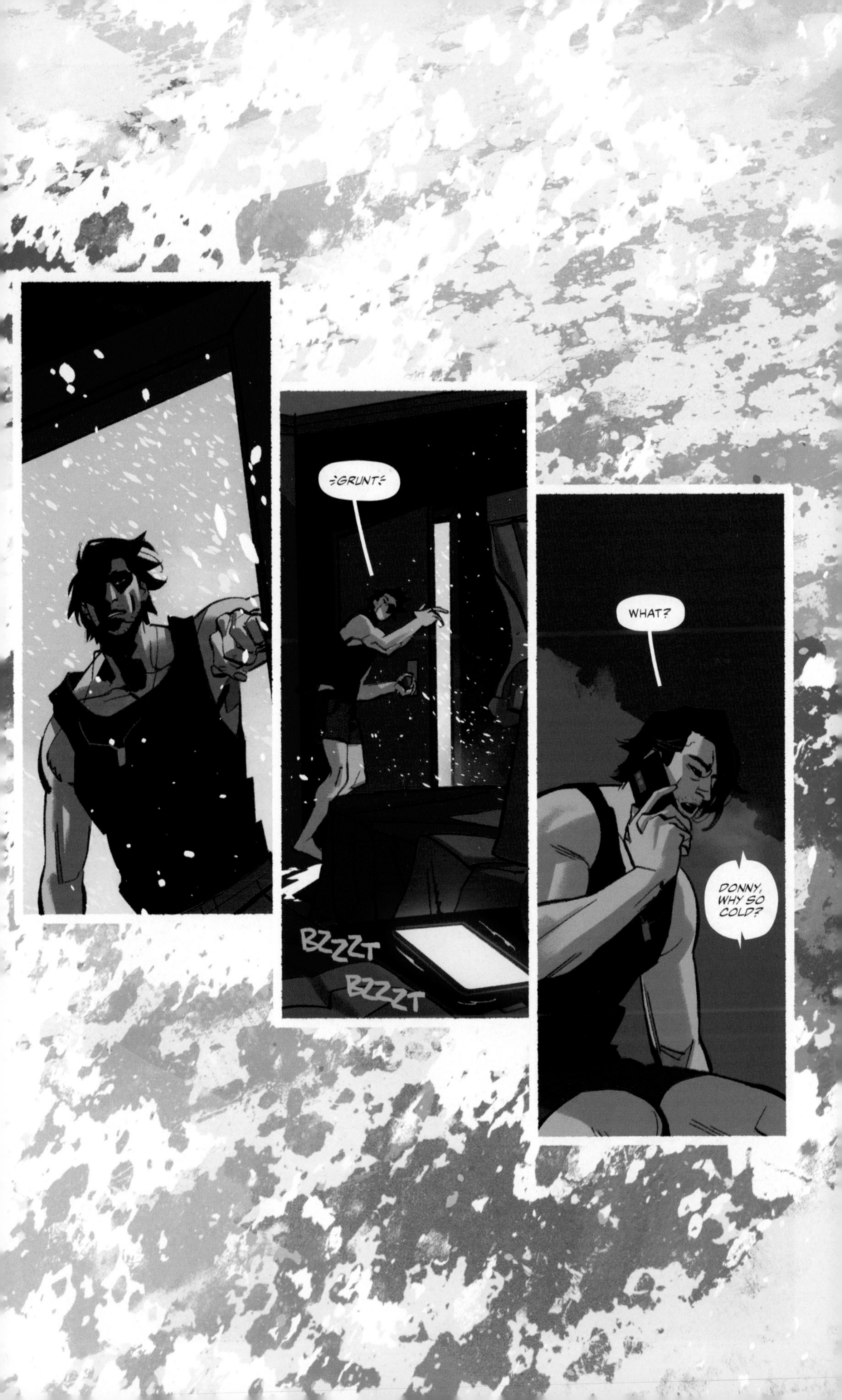

GRUNT
BZZZT
BZZZT
WHAT?
DONNY, WHY SO COLD?

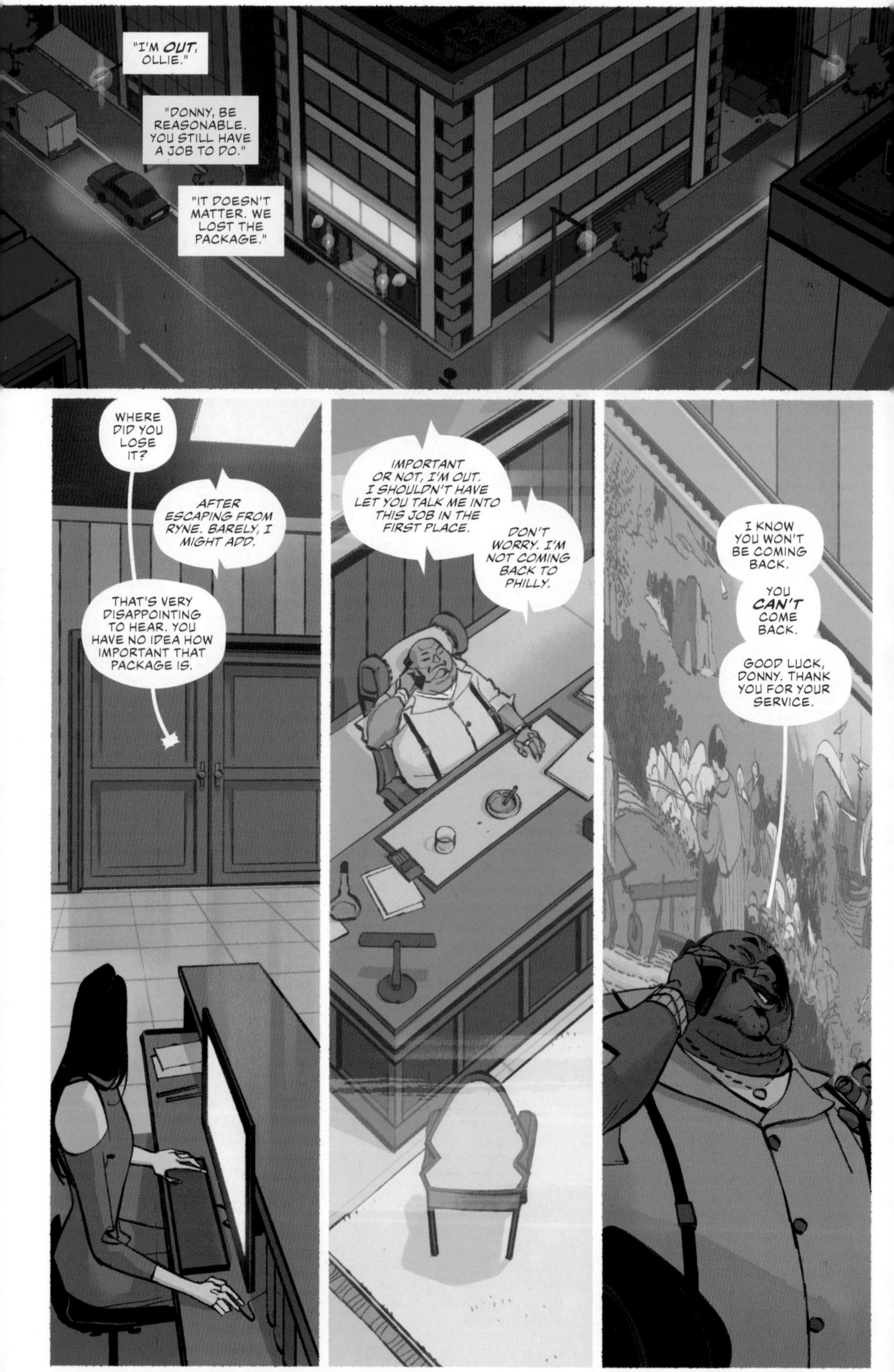
"I'M OUT, OLLIE."
"DONNY, BE REASONABLE. YOU STILL HAVE A JOB TO DO."
"IT DOESN'T MATTER. WE LOST THE PACKAGE."
WHERE DID YOU LOSE IT?
AFTER ESCAPING FROM RYNE. BARELY, I MIGHT ADD.
THAT'S VERY DISAPPOINTING TO HEAR. YOU HAVE NO IDEA HOW IMPORTANT THAT PACKAGE IS.
IMPORTANT OR NOT, I'M OUT. I SHOULDN'T HAVE LET YOU TALK ME INTO THIS JOB IN THE FIRST PLACE.
DON'T WORRY. I'M NOT COMING BACK TO PHILLY.
I KNOW YOU WON'T BE COMING BACK.
YOU CAN'T COME BACK.
GOOD LUCK, DONNY. THANK YOU FOR YOUR SERVICE.

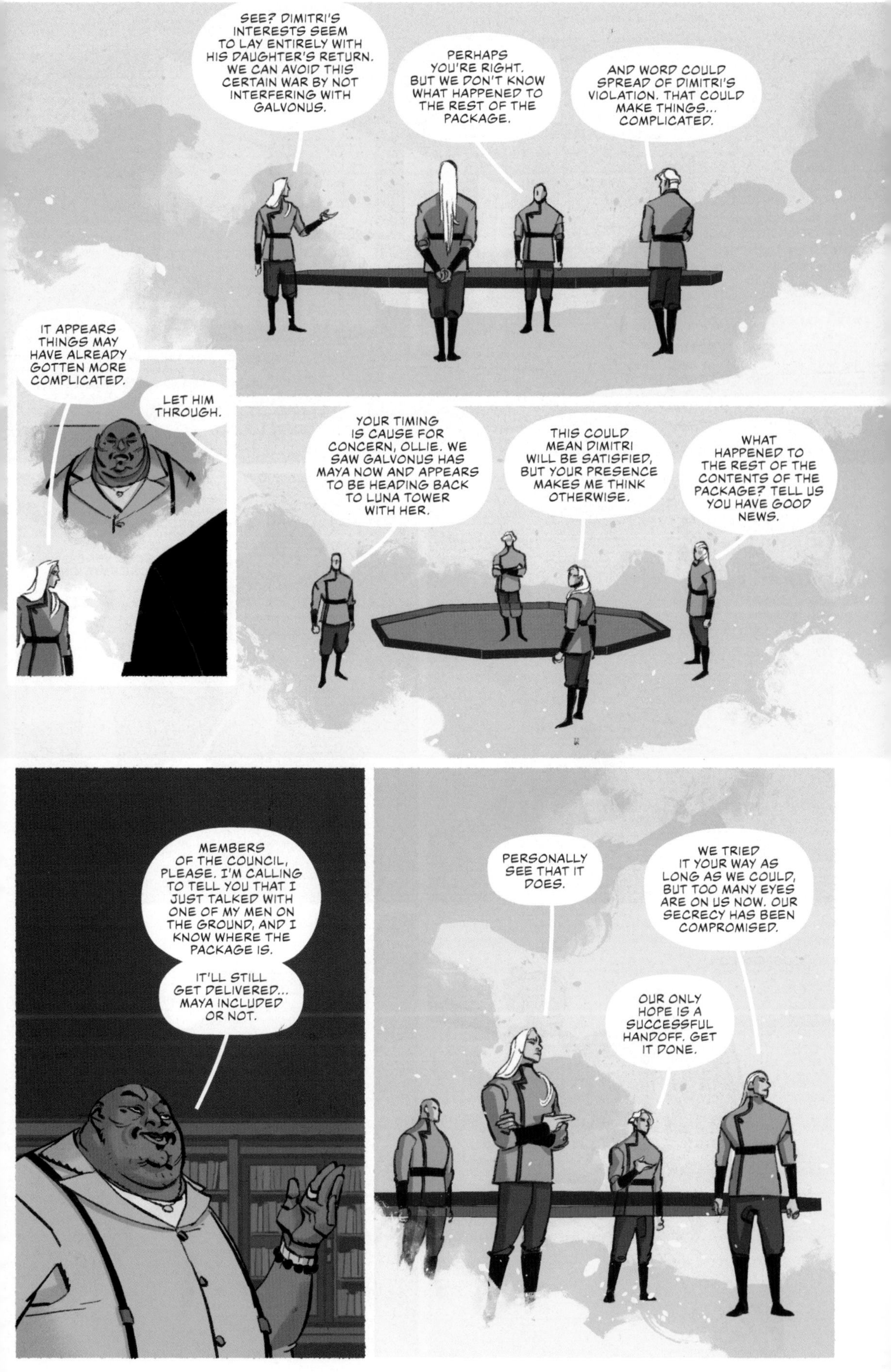
SEE? DIMITRI'S INTERESTS SEEM TO LAY ENTIRELY WITH HIS DAUGHTER'S RETURN. WE CAN AVOID THIS CERTAIN WAR BY NOT INTERFERING WITH GALVONUS.
PERHAPS YOU'RE RIGHT. BUT WE DON'T KNOW WHAT HAPPENED TO THE REST OF THE PACKAGE.
AND WORD COULD SPREAD OF DIMITRI'S VIOLATION. THAT COULD MAKE THINGS... COMPLICATED.
IT APPEARS THINGS MAY HAVE ALREADY GOTTEN MORE COMPLICATED.
LET HIM THROUGH.
YOUR TIMING IS CAUSE FOR CONCERN, OLLIE. WE SAW GALVONUS HAS MAYA NOW AND APPEARS TO BE HEADING BACK TO LUNA TOWER WITH HER.
THIS COULD MEAN DIMITRI WILL BE SATISFIED, BUT YOUR PRESENCE MAKES ME THINK OTHERWISE.
WHAT HAPPENED TO THE REST OF THE CONTENTS OF THE PACKAGE? TELL US YOU HAVE GOOD NEWS.
MEMBERS OF THE COUNCIL, PLEASE. I'M CALLING TO TELL YOU THAT I JUST TALKED WITH ONE OF MY MEN ON THE GROUND, AND I KNOW WHERE THE PACKAGE IS.
IT'LL STILL GET DELIVERED... MAYA INCLUDED OR NOT.
PERSONALLY SEE THAT IT DOES.
WE TRIED IT YOUR WAY AS LONG AS WE COULD, BUT TOO MANY EYES ARE ON US NOW. OUR SECRECY HAS BEEN COMPROMISED.
OUR ONLY HOPE IS A SUCCESSFUL HANDOFF. GET IT DONE.

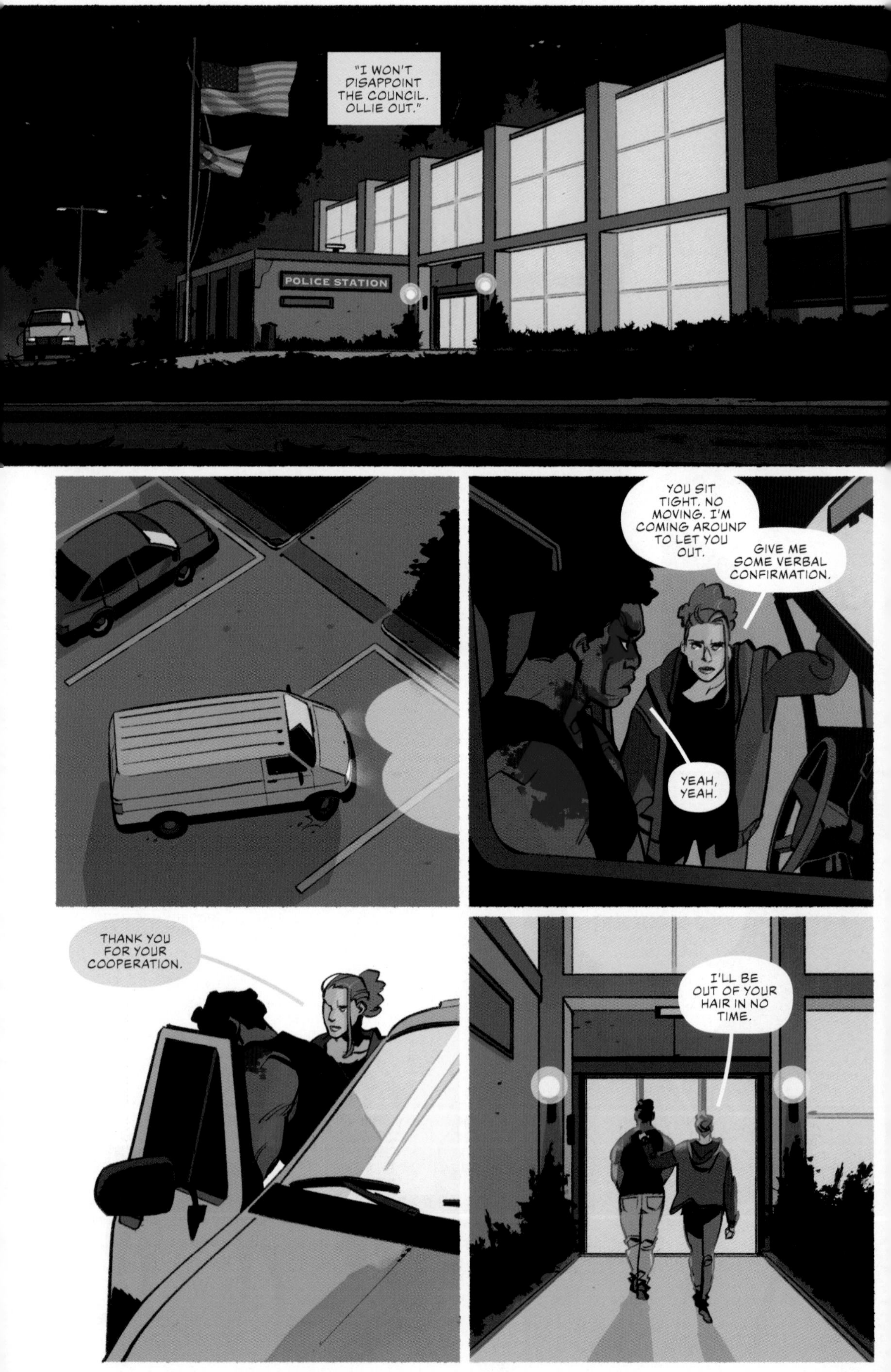
"I WON'T DISAPPOINT THE COUNCIL. OLLIE OUT."
POLICE STATION
YOU SIT TIGHT. NO MOVING. I'M COMING AROUND TO LET YOU OUT.
GIVE ME SOME VERBAL CONFIRMATION.
YEAH, YEAH.
THANK YOU FOR YOUR COOPERATION.
I'LL BE OUT OF YOUR HAIR IN NO TIME.

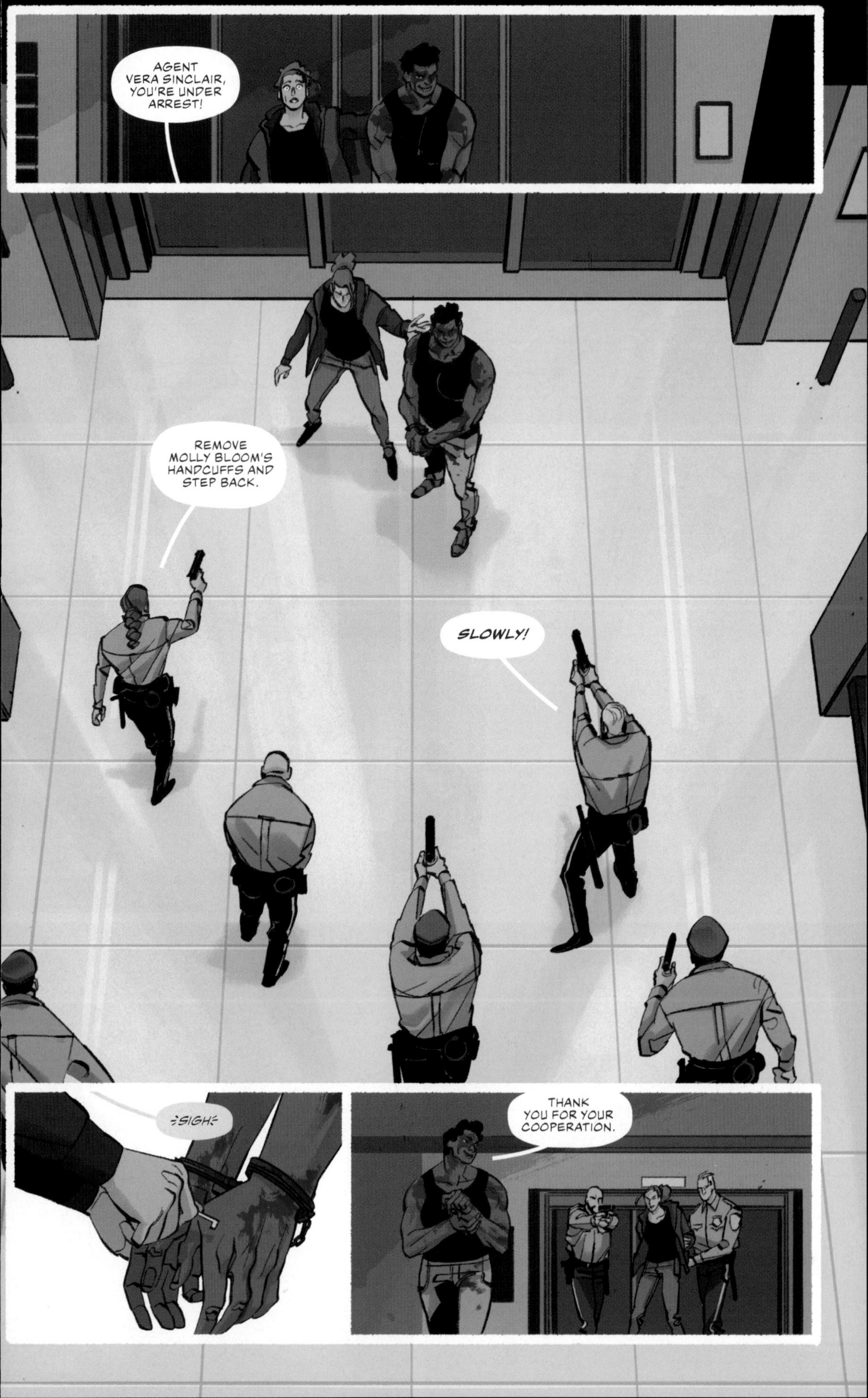
AGENT VERA SINCLAIR, YOU'RE UNDER ARREST!
REMOVE MOLLY BLOOM'S HANDCUFFS AND STEP BACK.
SLOWLY!
-SIGH-
THANK YOU FOR YOUR COOPERATION.

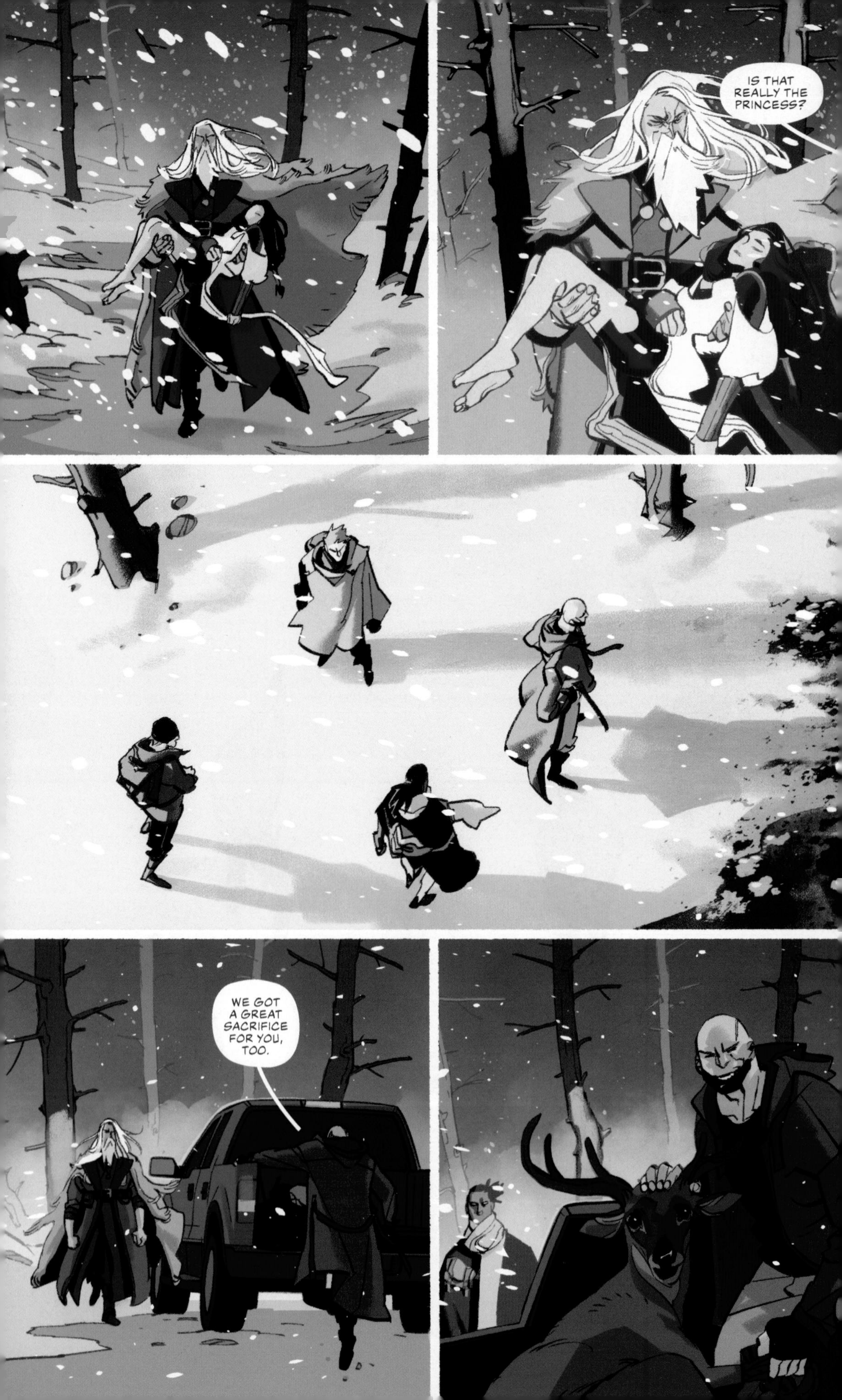
IS THAT REALLY THE PRINCESS?
WE GOT A GREAT SACRIFICE FOR YOU, TOO.

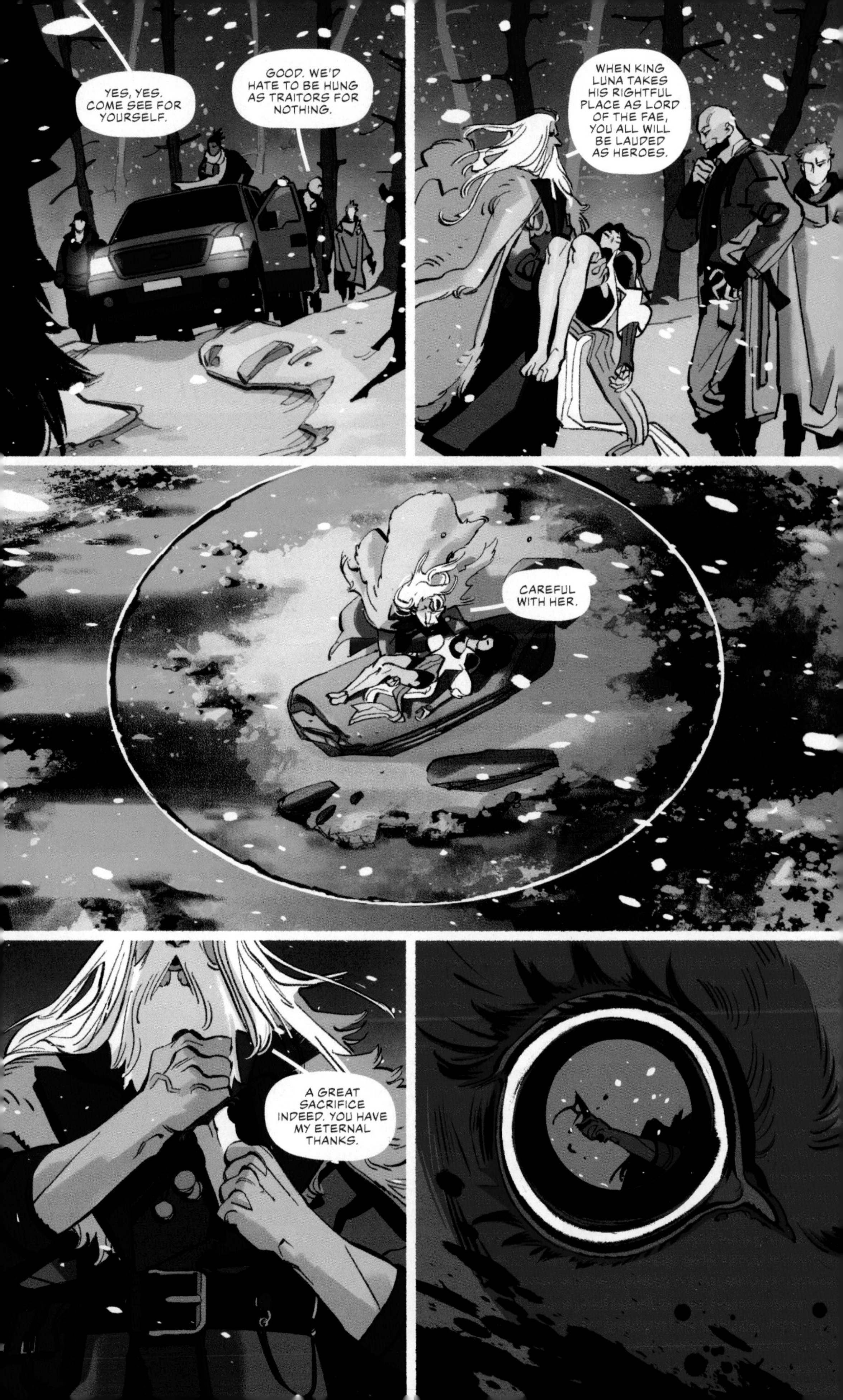
YES, YES. COME SEE FOR YOURSELF.
GOOD. WE'D HATE TO BE HUNG AS TRAITORS FOR NOTHING.
WHEN KING LUNA TAKES HIS RIGHTFUL PLACE AS LORD OF THE FAE, YOU ALL WILL BE LAUDED AS HEROES.
CAREFUL WITH HER.
A GREAT SACRIFICE INDEED. YOU HAVE MY ETERNAL THANKS.

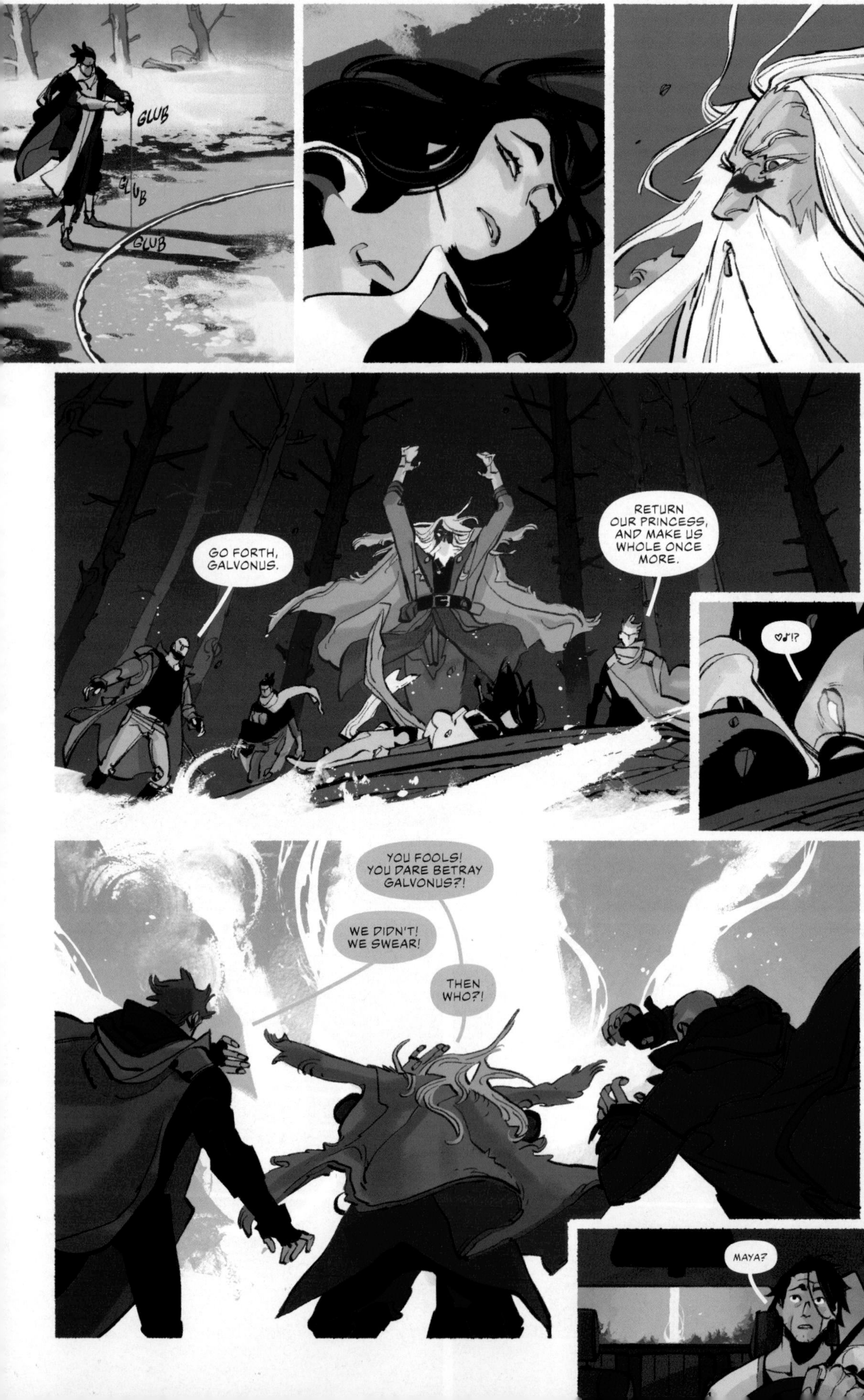
GLUB
GLUB
GLUB
GO FORTH, GALVONUS.
RETURN OUR PRINCESS, AND MAKE US WHOLE ONCE MORE.
YOU FOOLS! YOU DARE BETRAY GALVONUS?!
WE DIDN'T! WE SWEAR!
THEN WHO?!
MAYA?

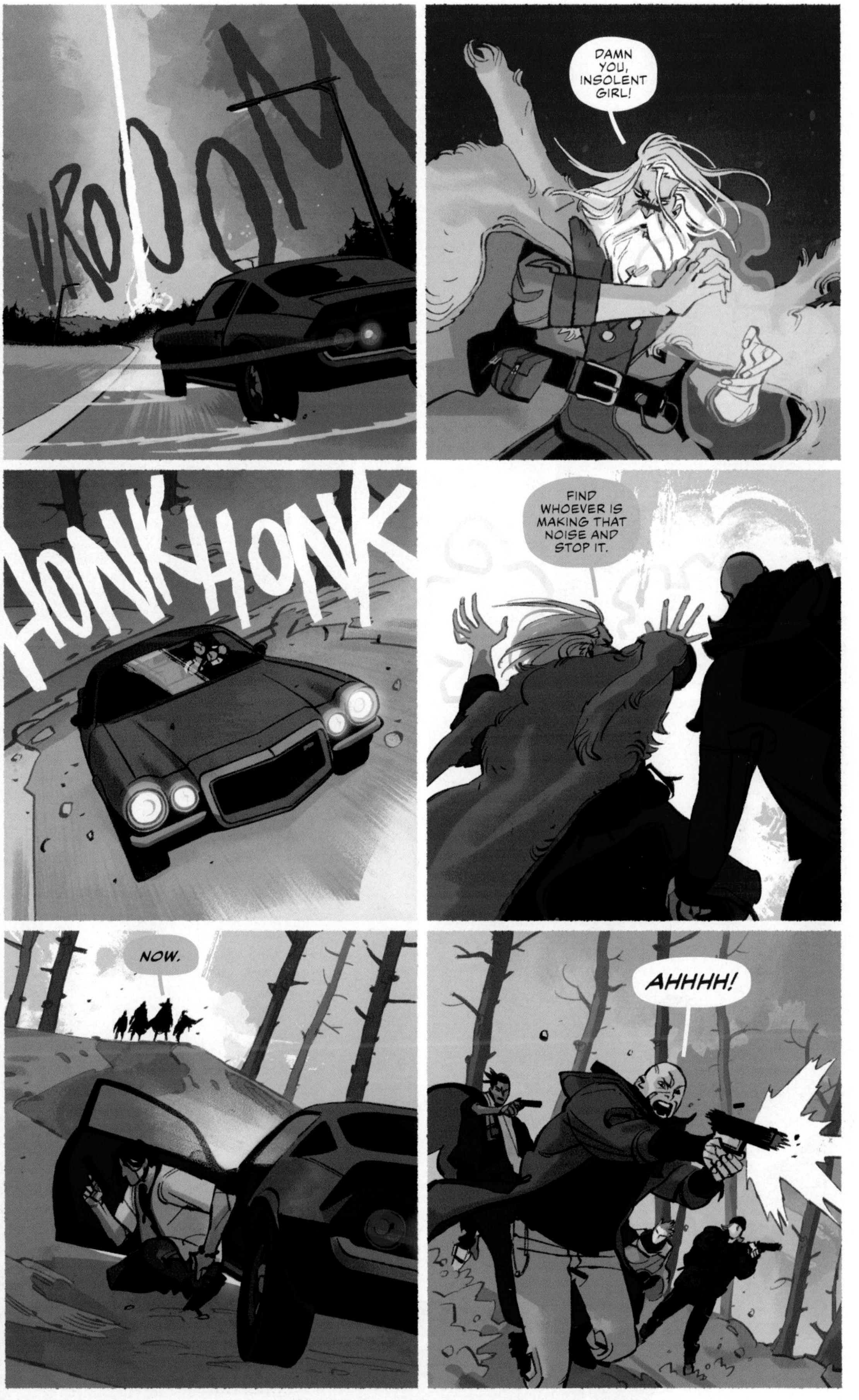
VROOOM
DAMN YOU, INSOLENT GIRL!
HONKHONK
FIND WHOEVER IS MAKING THAT NOISE AND STOP IT.
NOW.
AHHHH!

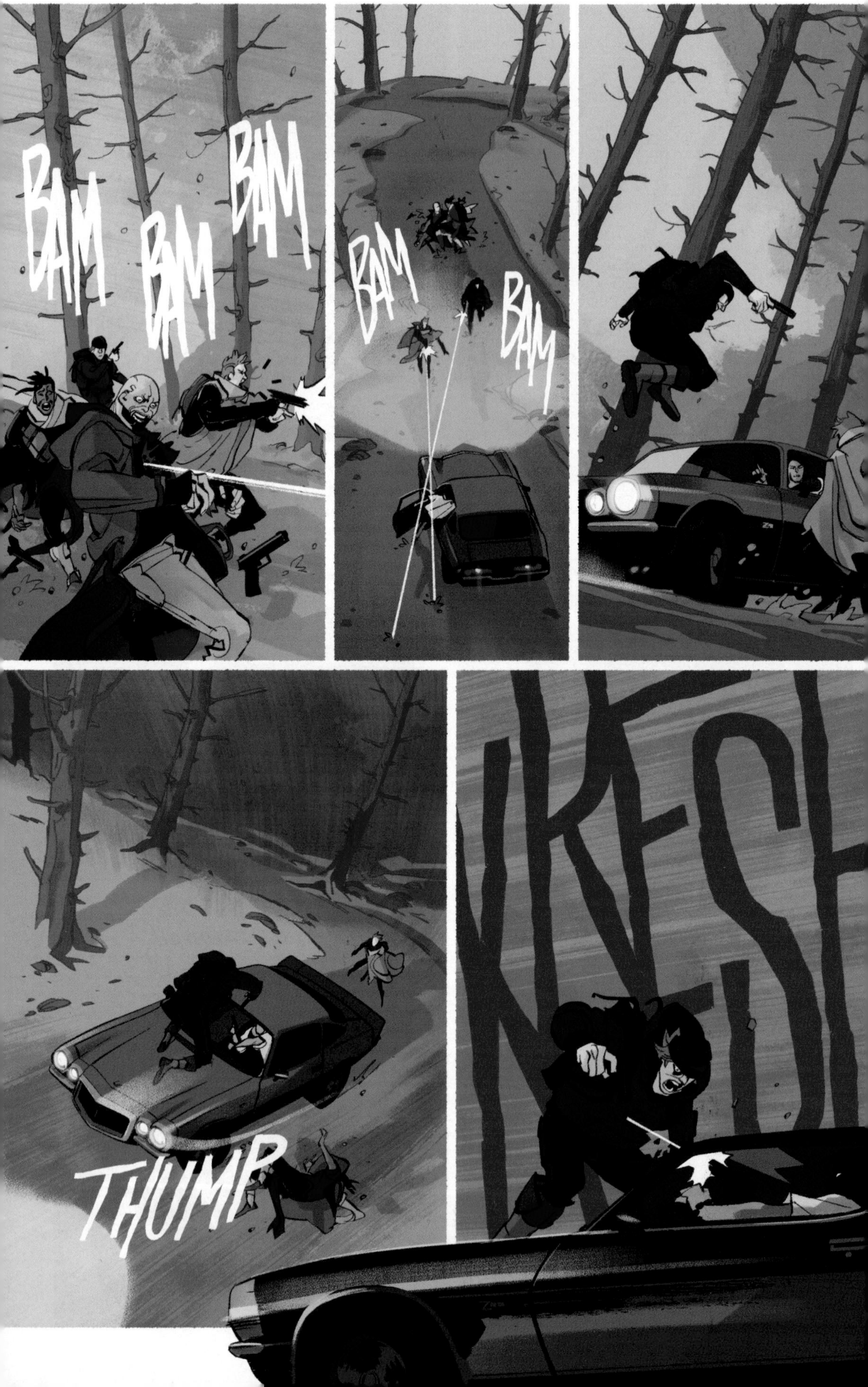
BAM
BAM
BAM
BAM
BAM
THUMP

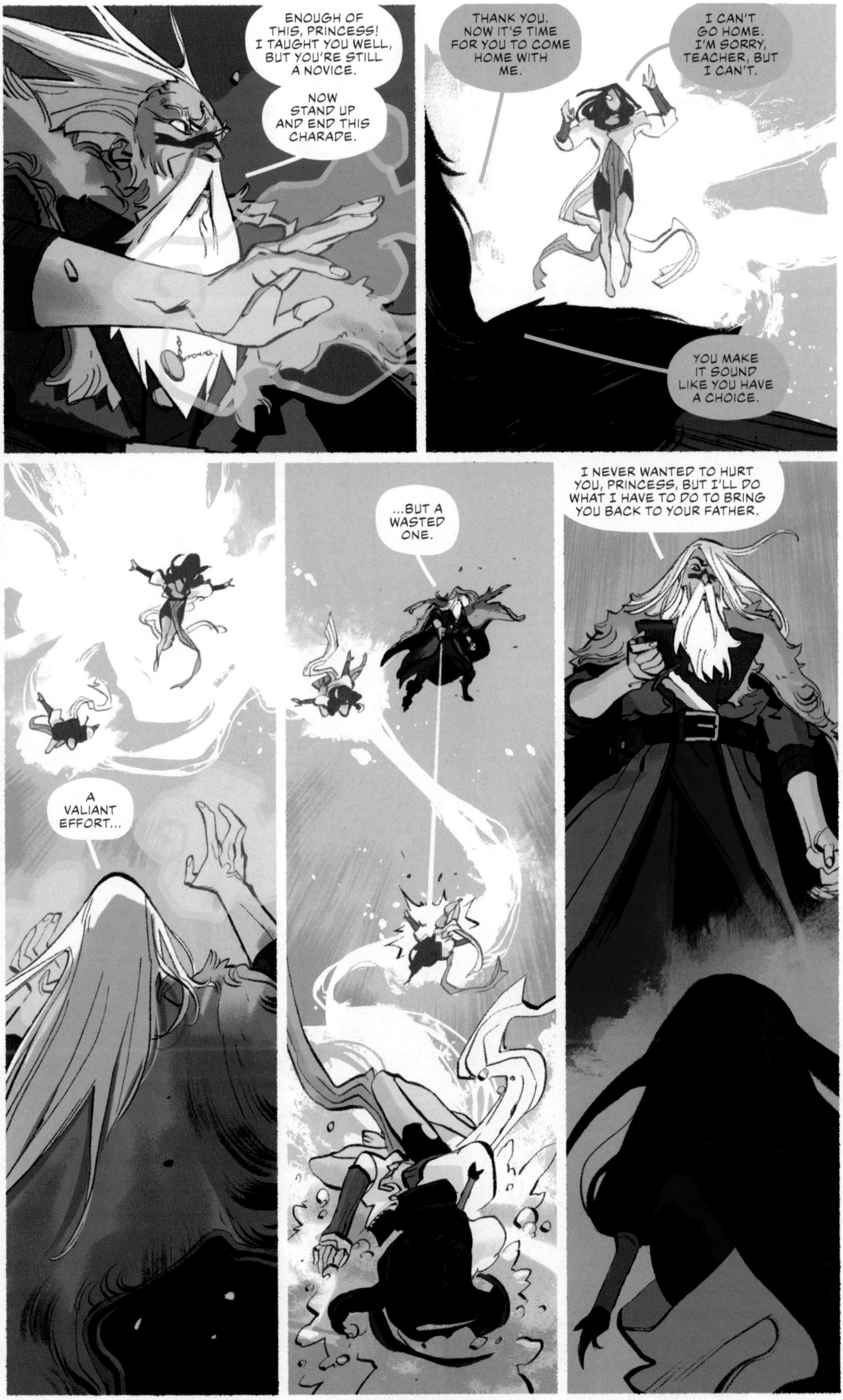
ENOUGH OF THIS, PRINCESS! I TAUGHT YOU WELL, BUT YOU'RE STILL A NOVICE.
NOW STAND UP AND END THIS CHARADE.
THANK YOU. NOW IT'S TIME FOR YOU TO COME HOME WITH ME.
I CAN'T GO HOME. I'M SORRY, TEACHER, BUT I CAN'T.
YOU MAKE IT SOUND LIKE YOU HAVE A CHOICE.
A VALIANT EFFORT...
...BUT A WASTED ONE.
I NEVER WANTED TO HURT YOU, PRINCESS, BUT I'LL DO WHAT I HAVE TO DO TO BRING YOU BACK TO YOUR FATHER.

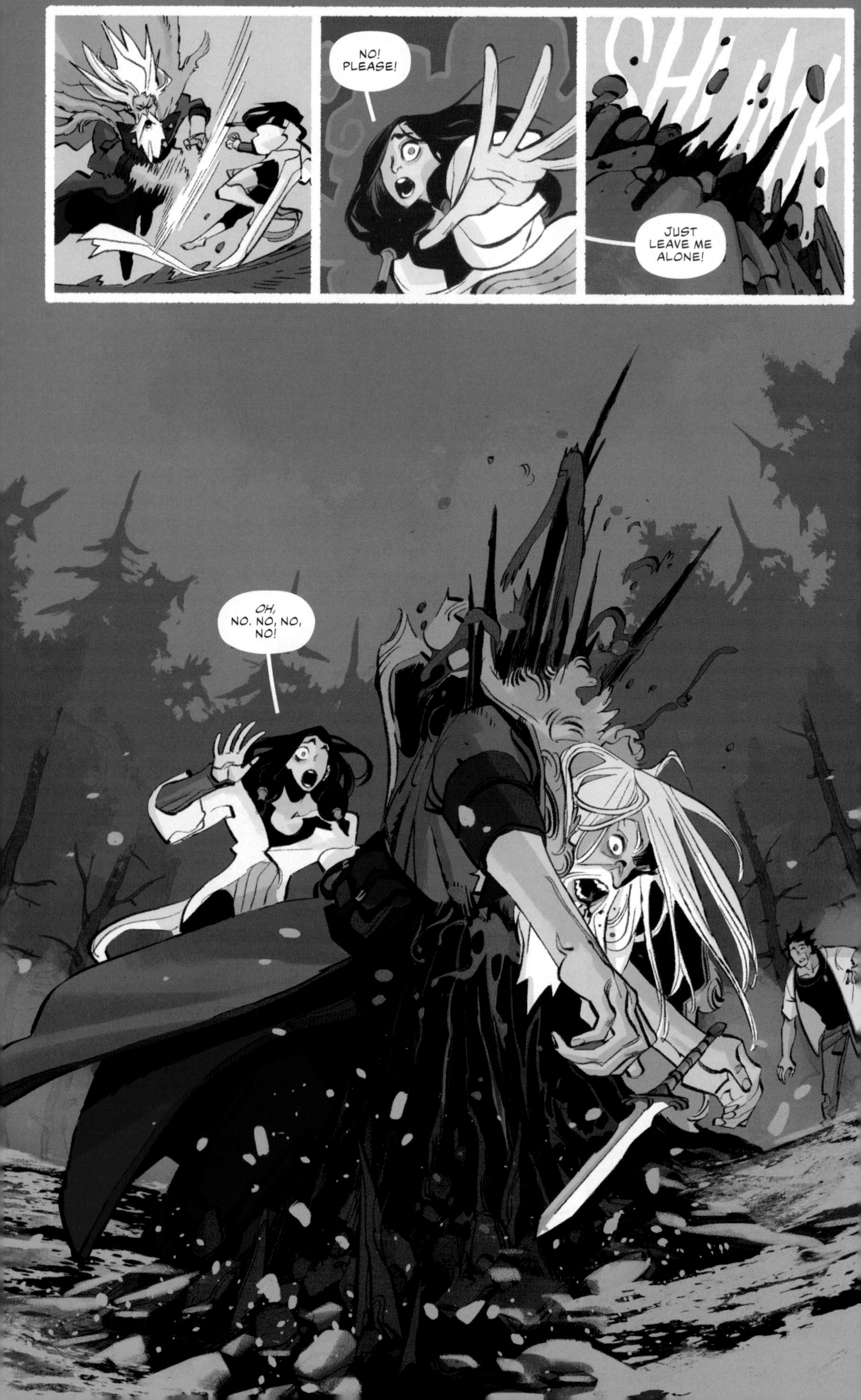
NO! PLEASE!
SHUNK
JUST LEAVE ME ALONE!
OH, NO. NO, NO, NO!

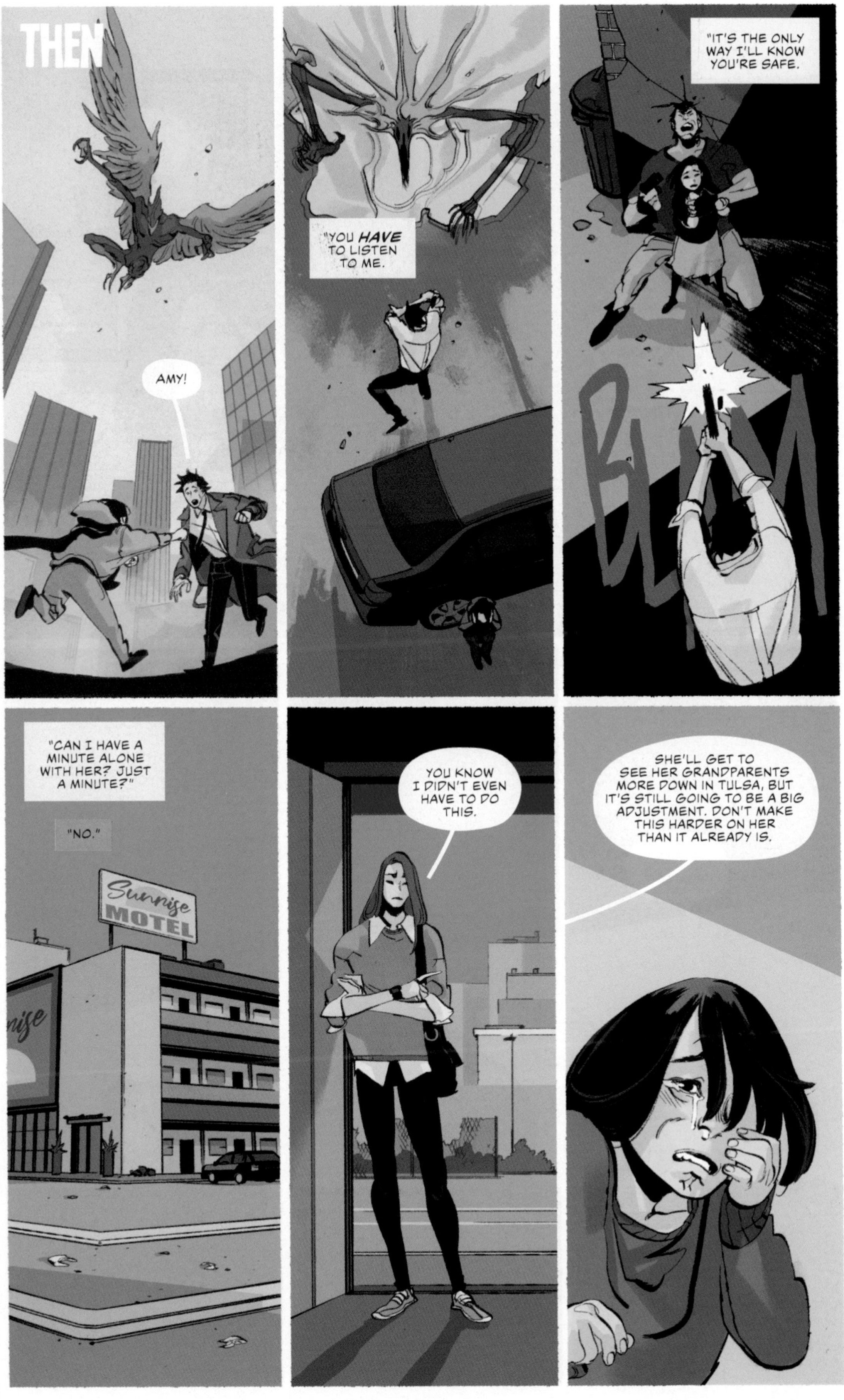
THEN
AMY!
"YOU HAVE TO LISTEN TO ME.
"IT'S THE ONLY WAY I'LL KNOW YOU'RE SAFE.
BLAM
"CAN I HAVE A MINUTE ALONE WITH HER? JUST A MINUTE?"
"NO."
Sunrise MOTEL
YOU KNOW I DIDN'T EVEN HAVE TO DO THIS.
SHE'LL GET TO SEE HER GRANDPARENTS MORE DOWN IN TULSA, BUT IT'S STILL GOING TO BE A BIG ADJUSTMENT. DON'T MAKE THIS HARDER ON HER THAN IT ALREADY IS.

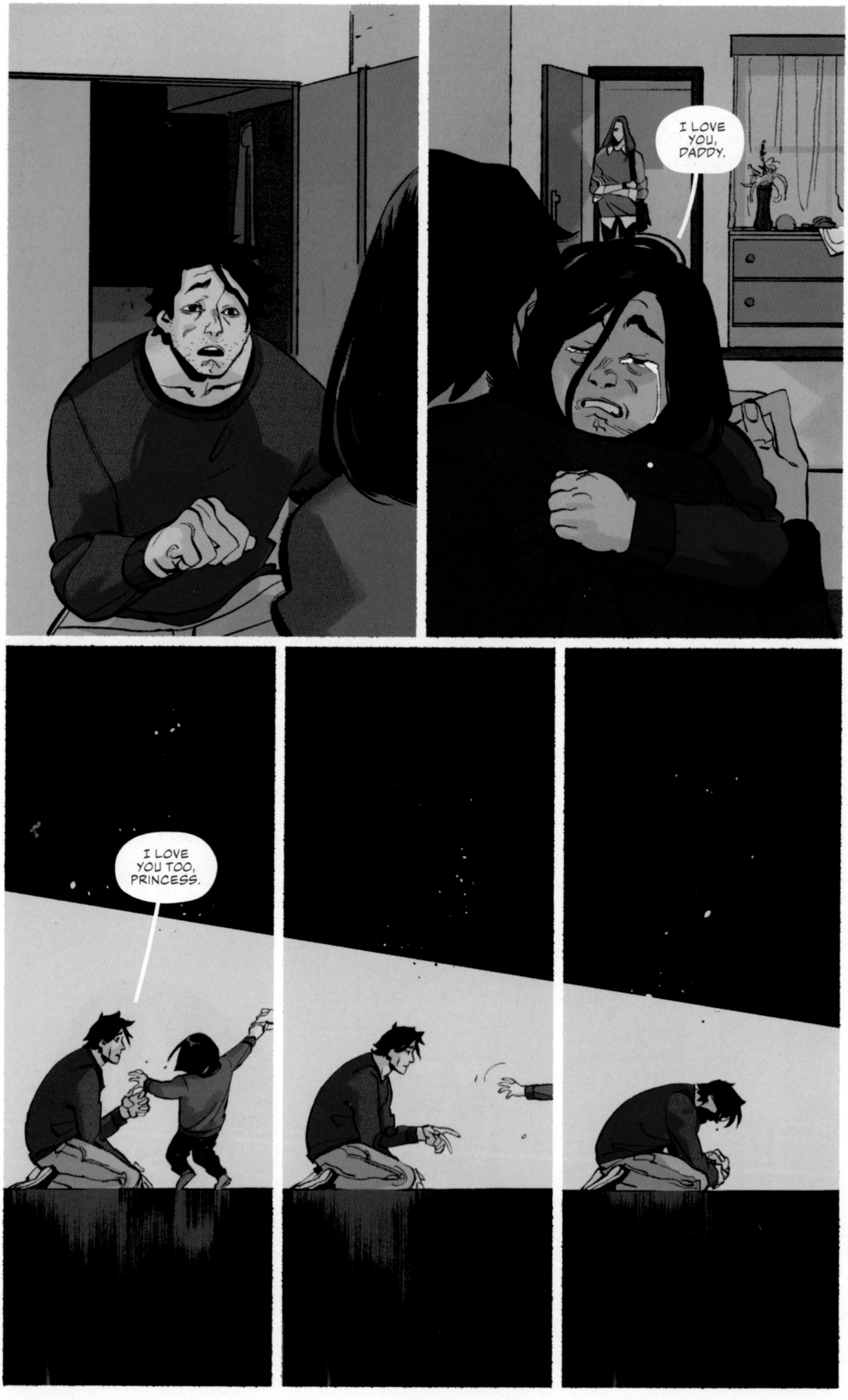
I LOVE YOU, DADDY.
I LOVE YOU TOO, PRINCESS.

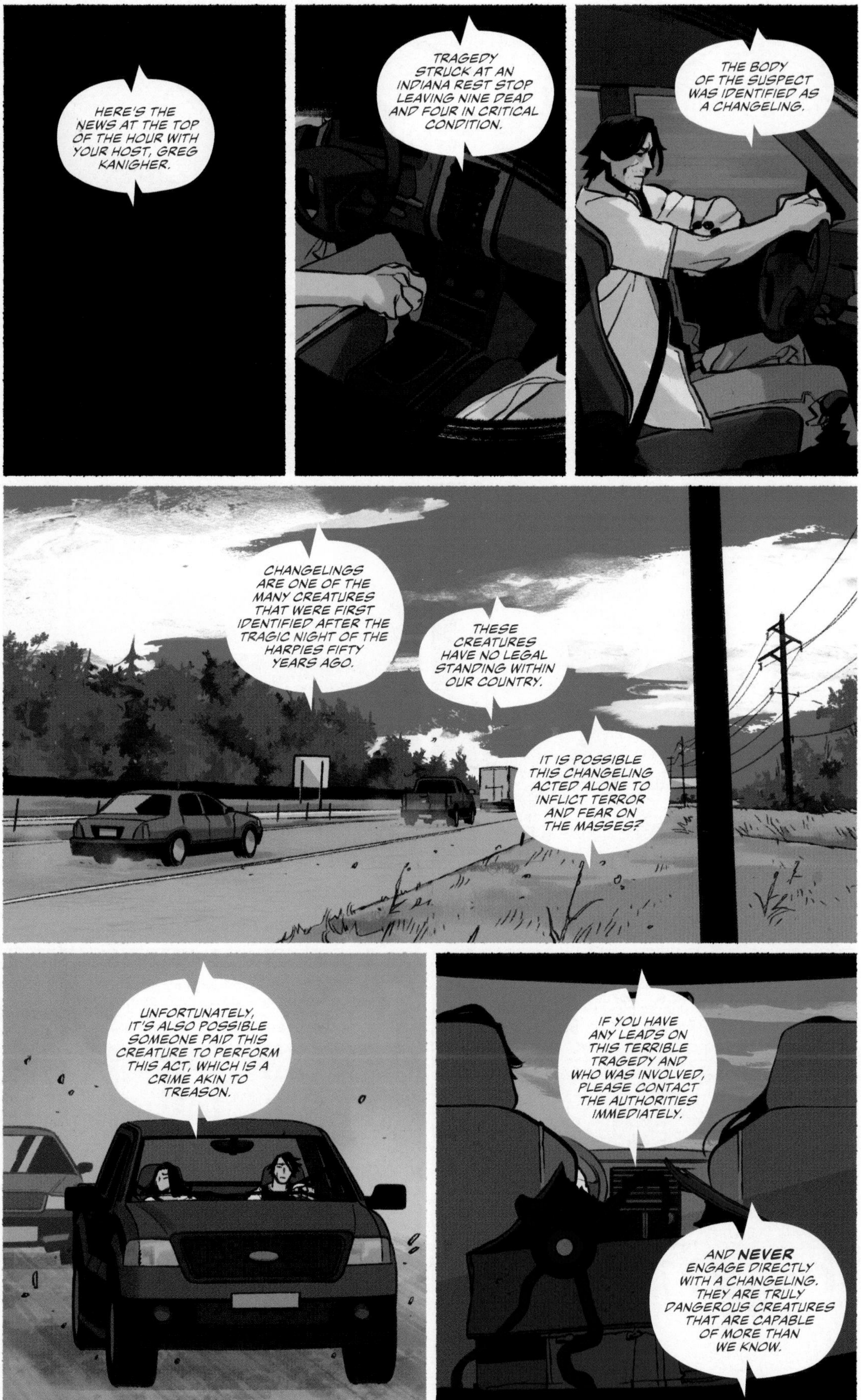
HERE'S THE NEWS AT THE TOP OF THE HOUR WITH YOUR HOST, GREG KANIGHER.
TRAGEDY STRUCK AT AN INDIANA REST STOP LEAVING NINE DEAD AND FOUR IN CRITICAL CONDITION.
THE BODY OF THE SUSPECT WAS IDENTIFIED AS A CHANGELING.
CHANGELINGS ARE ONE OF THE MANY CREATURES THAT WERE FIRST IDENTIFIED AFTER THE TRAGIC NIGHT OF THE HARPIES FIFTY YEARS AGO.
THESE CREATURES HAVE NO LEGAL STANDING WITHIN OUR COUNTRY.
IT IS POSSIBLE THIS CHANGELING ACTED ALONE TO INFLICT TERROR AND FEAR ON THE MASSES?
UNFORTUNATELY, IT'S ALSO POSSIBLE SOMEONE PAID THIS CREATURE TO PERFORM THIS ACT, WHICH IS A CRIME AKIN TO TREASON.
IF YOU HAVE ANY LEADS ON THIS TERRIBLE TRAGEDY AND WHO WAS INVOLVED, PLEASE CONTACT THE AUTHORITIES IMMEDIATELY.
AND **NEVER** ENGAGE DIRECTLY WITH A CHANGELING. THEY ARE TRULY DANGEROUS CREATURES THAT ARE CAPABLE OF MORE THAN WE KNOW.

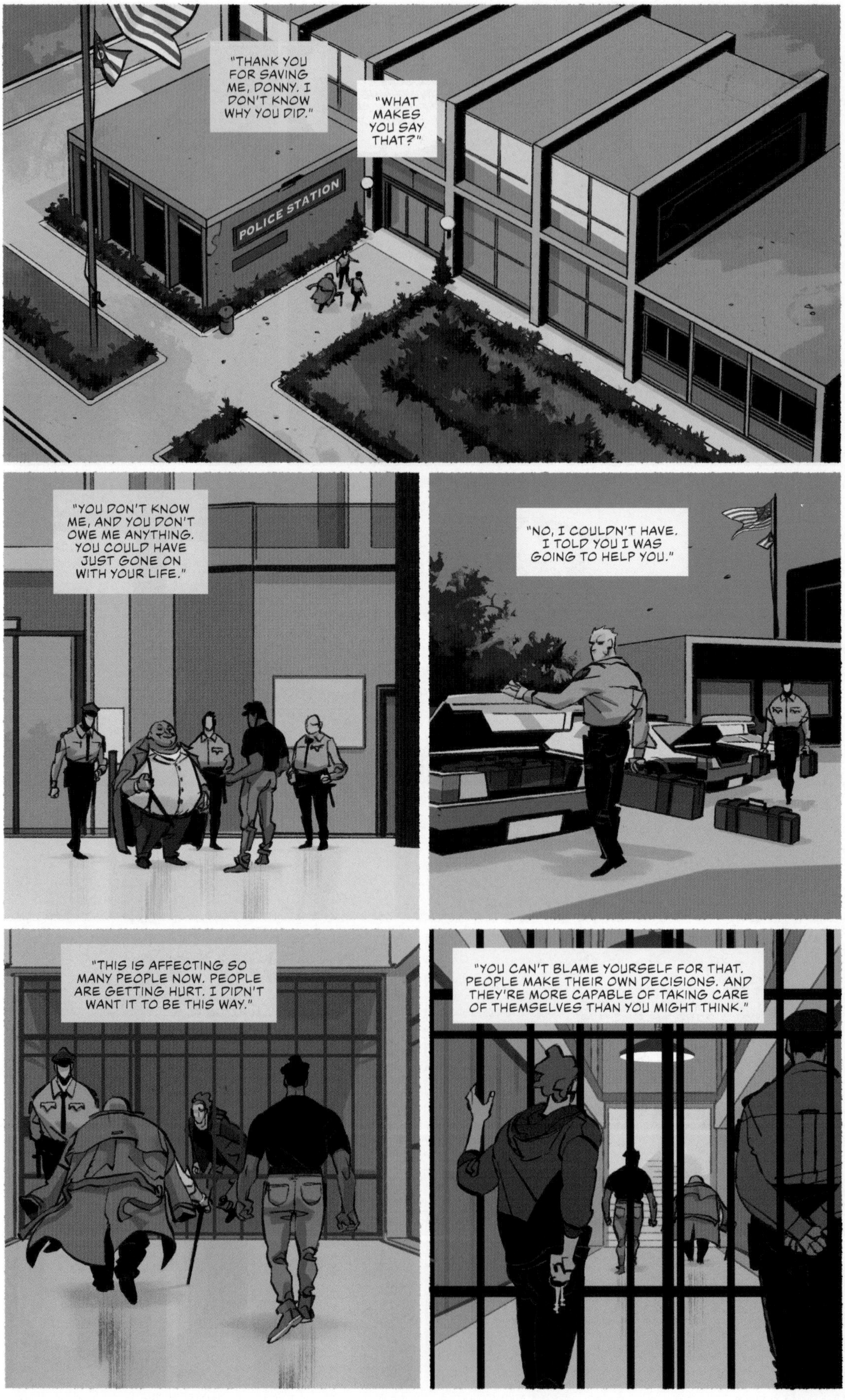
"THANK YOU FOR SAVING ME, DONNY. I DON'T KNOW WHY YOU DID."
"WHAT MAKES YOU SAY THAT?"
POLICE STATION
"YOU DON'T KNOW ME, AND YOU DON'T OWE ME ANYTHING. YOU COULD HAVE JUST GONE ON WITH YOUR LIFE."
"NO, I COULDN'T HAVE. I TOLD YOU I WAS GOING TO HELP YOU."
"THIS IS AFFECTING SO MANY PEOPLE NOW. PEOPLE ARE GETTING HURT. I DIDN'T WANT IT TO BE THIS WAY."
"YOU CAN'T BLAME YOURSELF FOR THAT. PEOPLE MAKE THEIR OWN DECISIONS. AND THEY'RE MORE CAPABLE OF TAKING CARE OF THEMSELVES THAN YOU MIGHT THINK."

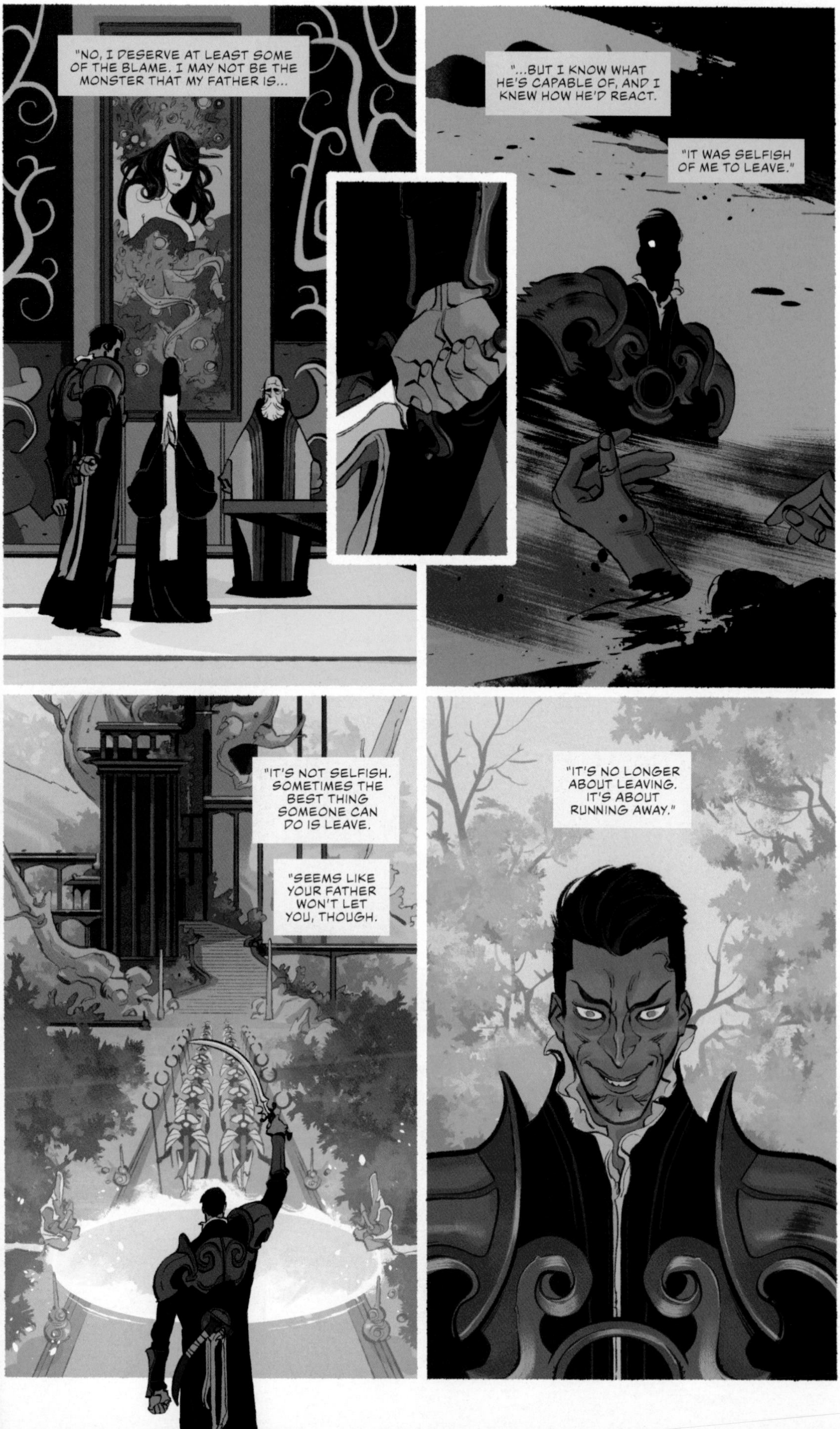
"NO, I DESERVE AT LEAST SOME OF THE BLAME. I MAY NOT BE THE MONSTER THAT MY FATHER IS...
"...BUT I KNOW WHAT HE'S CAPABLE OF, AND I KNEW HOW HE'D REACT.
"IT WAS SELFISH OF ME TO LEAVE."
"IT'S NOT SELFISH. SOMETIMES THE BEST THING SOMEONE CAN DO IS LEAVE.
"SEEMS LIKE YOUR FATHER WON'T LET YOU, THOUGH.
"IT'S NO LONGER ABOUT LEAVING. IT'S ABOUT RUNNING AWAY."

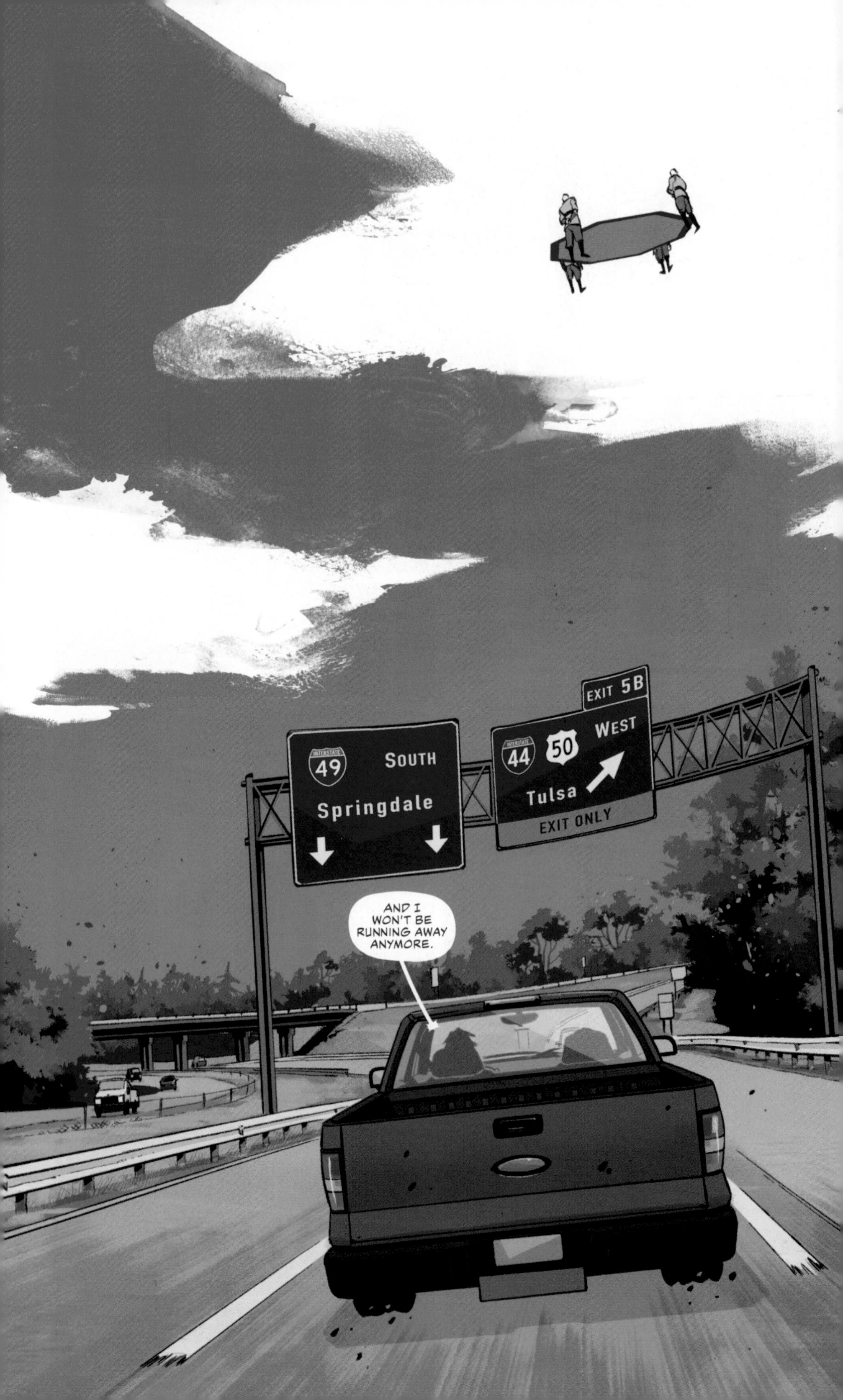

INTERSTATE 49 SOUTH
Springdale
EXIT 5B
INTERSTATE 44 50 WEST
Tulsa
EXIT ONLY
AND I WON'T BE RUNNING AWAY ANYMORE.

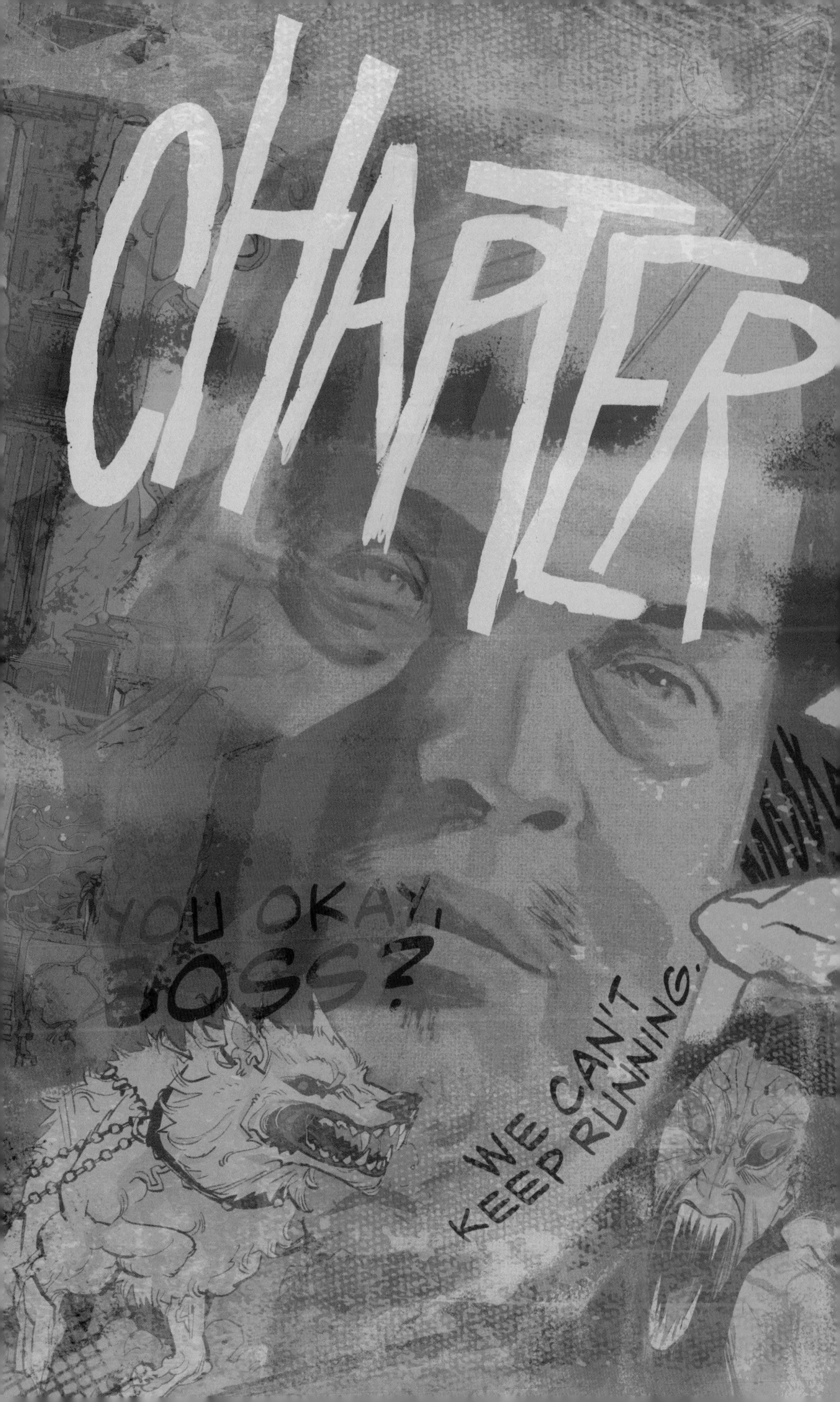
CHAPTER
YOU OKAY, BOSS?
WE CAN'T KEEP RUNNING.

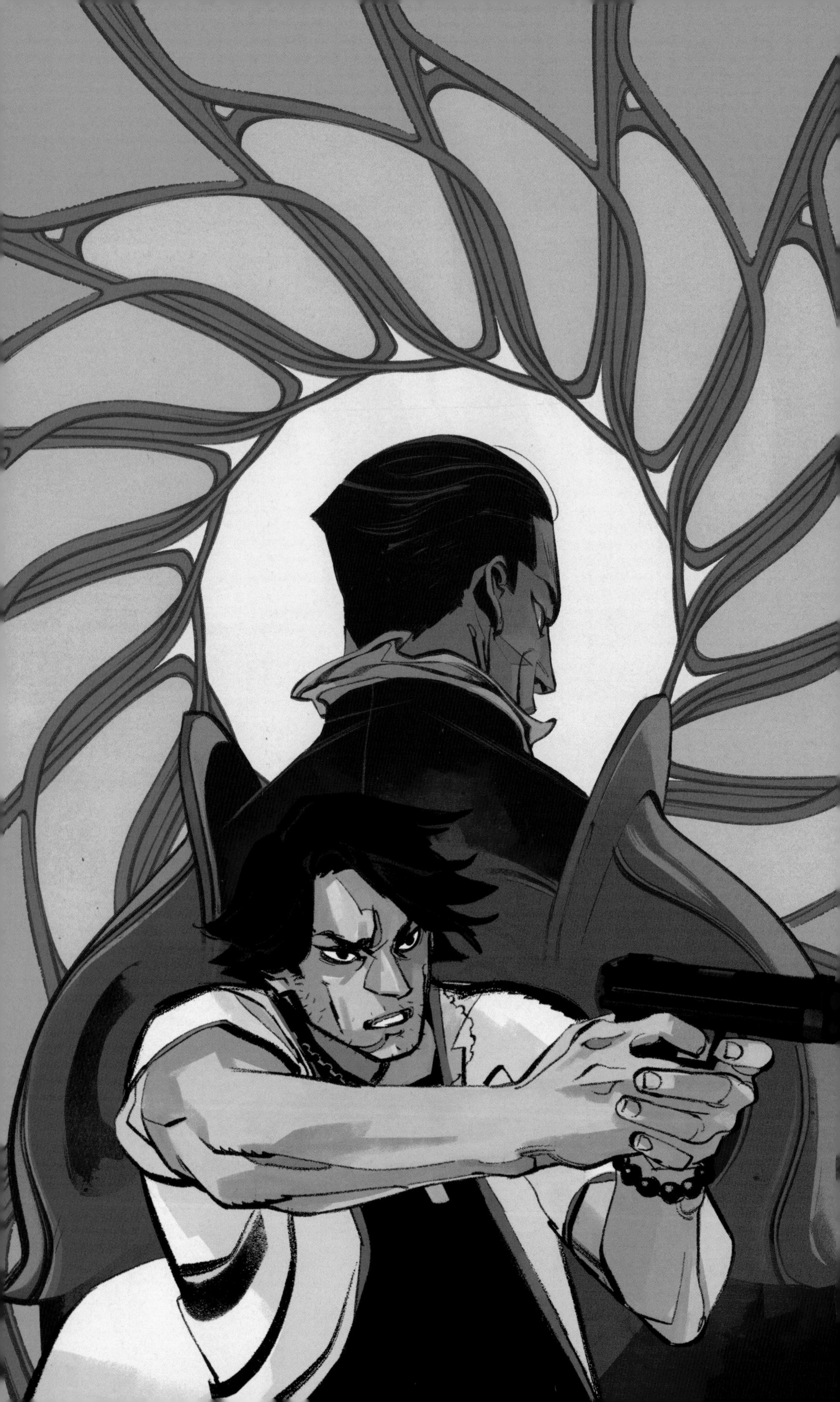

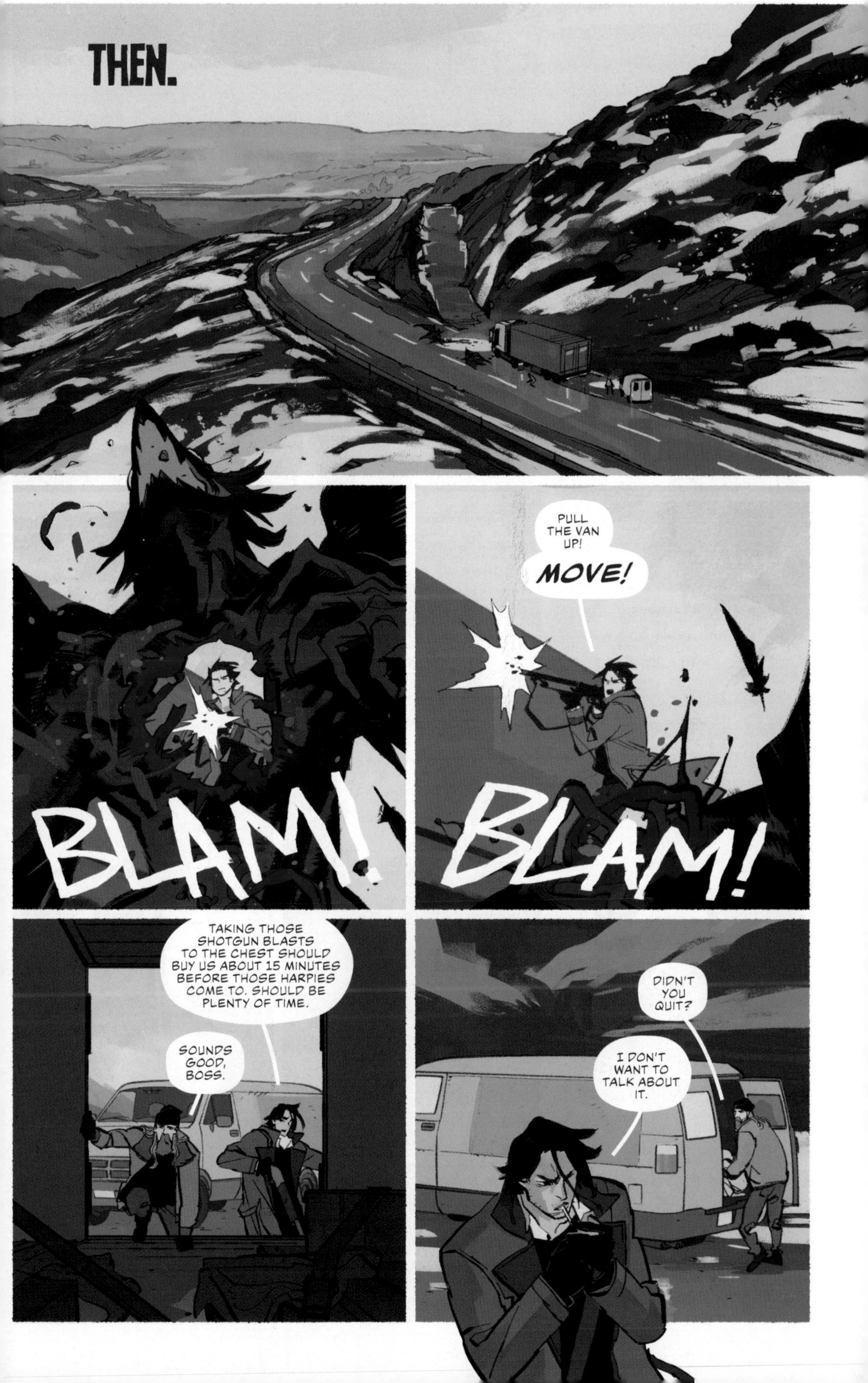
THEN.
BLAM!
PULL THE VAN UP!
MOVE!
BLAM!
TAKING THOSE SHOTGUN BLASTS TO THE CHEST SHOULD BUY US ABOUT 15 MINUTES BEFORE THOSE HARPIES COME TO. SHOULD BE PLENTY OF TIME.
SOUNDS GOOD, BOSS.
DIDN'T YOU QUIT?
I DON'T WANT TO TALK ABOUT IT.

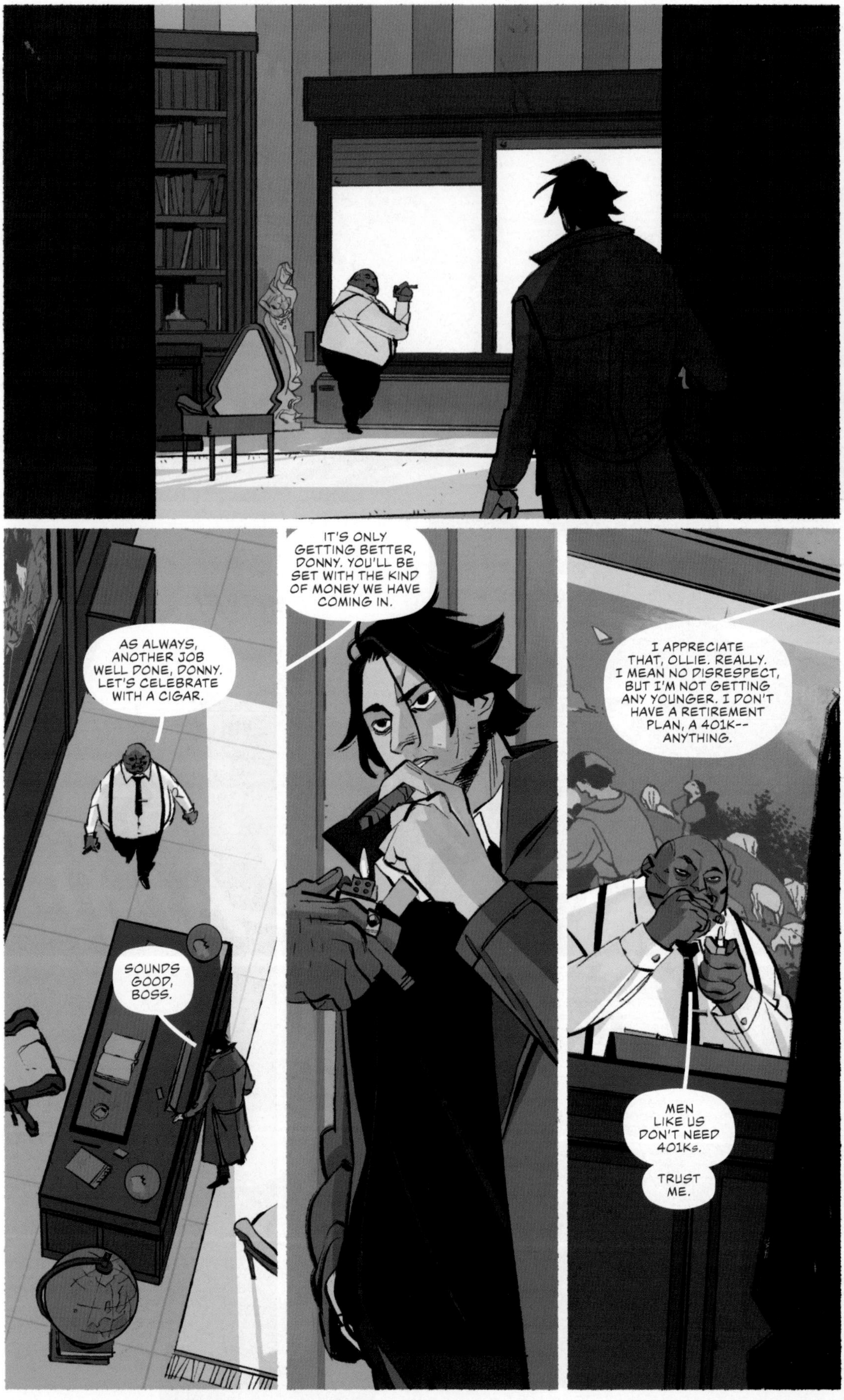
AS ALWAYS, ANOTHER JOB WELL DONE, DONNY. LET'S CELEBRATE WITH A CIGAR.
SOUNDS GOOD, BOSS.
IT'S ONLY GETTING BETTER, DONNY. YOU'LL BE SET WITH THE KIND OF MONEY WE HAVE COMING IN.
I APPRECIATE THAT, OLLIE. REALLY. I MEAN NO DISRESPECT, BUT I'M NOT GETTING ANY YOUNGER. I DON'T HAVE A RETIREMENT PLAN, A 401K-- ANYTHING.
MEN LIKE US DON'T NEED 401Ks.
TRUST ME.

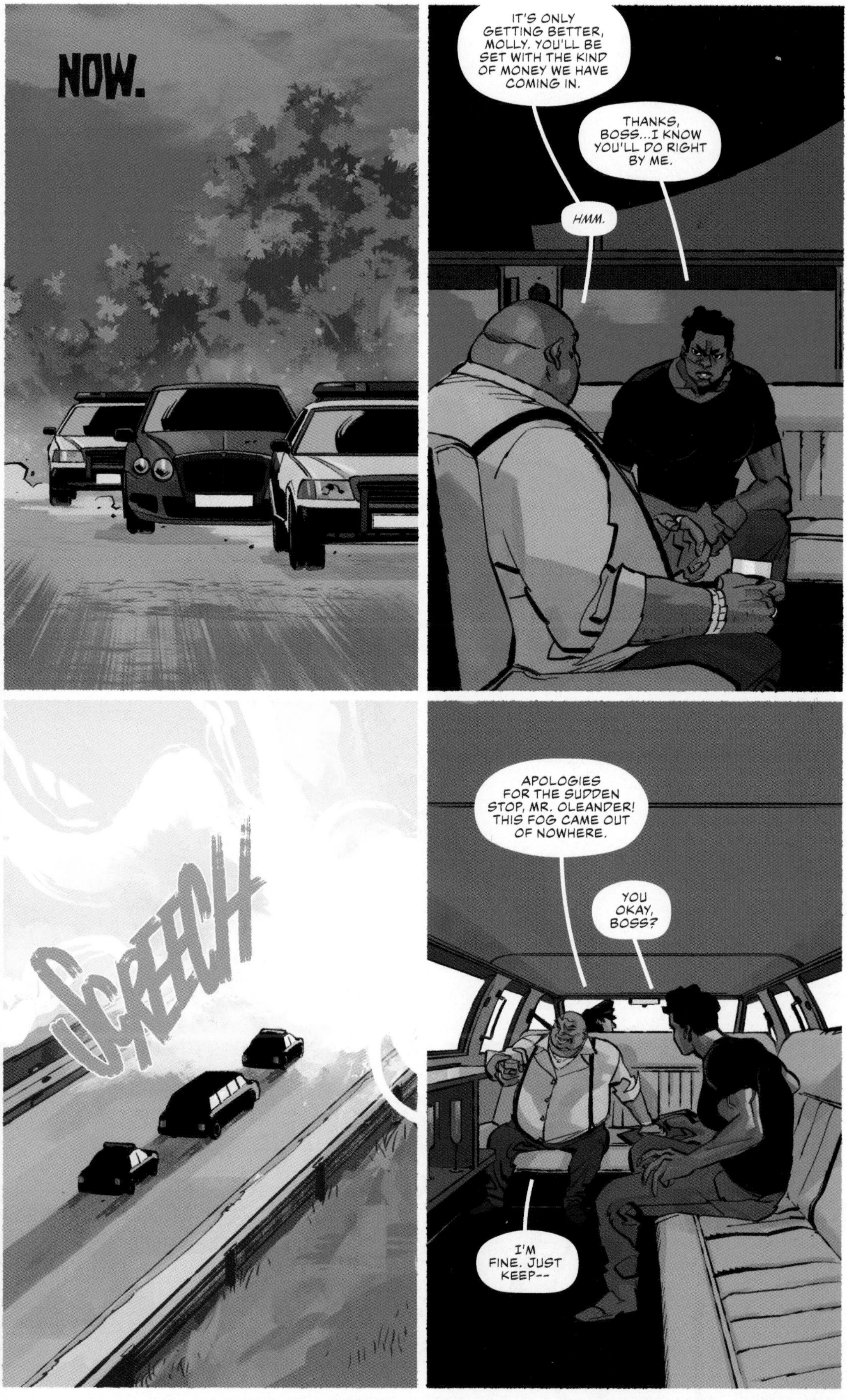
NOW.
IT'S ONLY GETTING BETTER, MOLLY. YOU'LL BE SET WITH THE KIND OF MONEY WE HAVE COMING IN.
THANKS, BOSS...I KNOW YOU'LL DO RIGHT BY ME.
HMM.
SCREECH
APOLOGIES FOR THE SUDDEN STOP, MR. OLEANDER! THIS FOG CAME OUT OF NOWHERE.
YOU OKAY, BOSS?
I'M FINE. JUST KEEP--

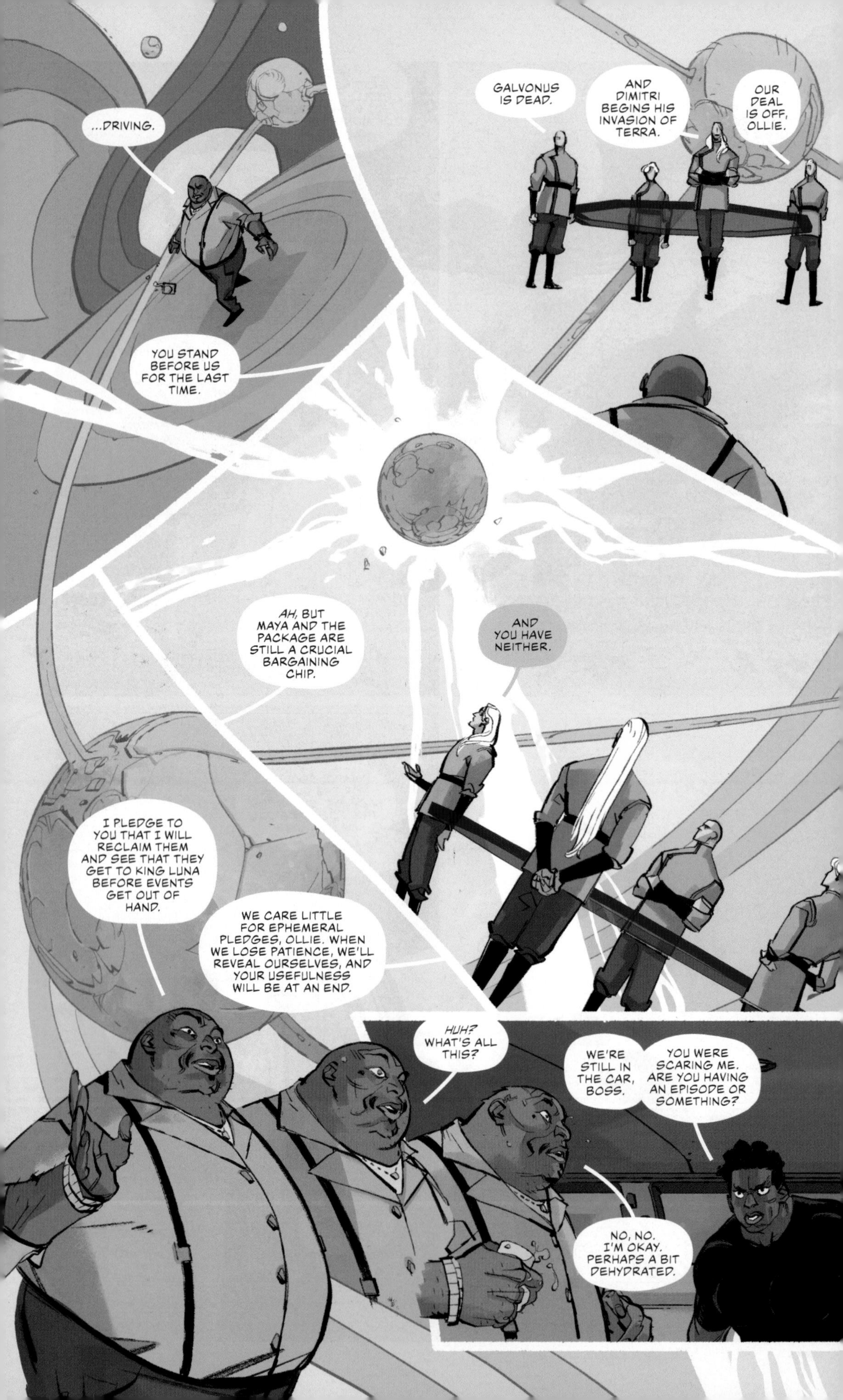
...DRIVING.
GALVONUS IS DEAD.
AND DIMITRI BEGINS HIS INVASION OF TERRA.
OUR DEAL IS OFF, OLLIE.
YOU STAND BEFORE US FOR THE LAST TIME.
AH, BUT MAYA AND THE PACKAGE ARE STILL A CRUCIAL BARGAINING CHIP.
AND YOU HAVE NEITHER.
I PLEDGE TO YOU THAT I WILL RECLAIM THEM AND SEE THAT THEY GET TO KING LUNA BEFORE EVENTS GET OUT OF HAND.
WE CARE LITTLE FOR EPHEMERAL PLEDGES, OLLIE. WHEN WE LOSE PATIENCE, WE'LL REVEAL OURSELVES, AND YOUR USEFULNESS WILL BE AT AN END.
HUH? WHAT'S ALL THIS?
WE'RE STILL IN THE CAR, BOSS.
YOU WERE SCARING ME. ARE YOU HAVING AN EPISODE OR SOMETHING?
NO, NO. I'M OKAY. PERHAPS A BIT DEHYDRATED.

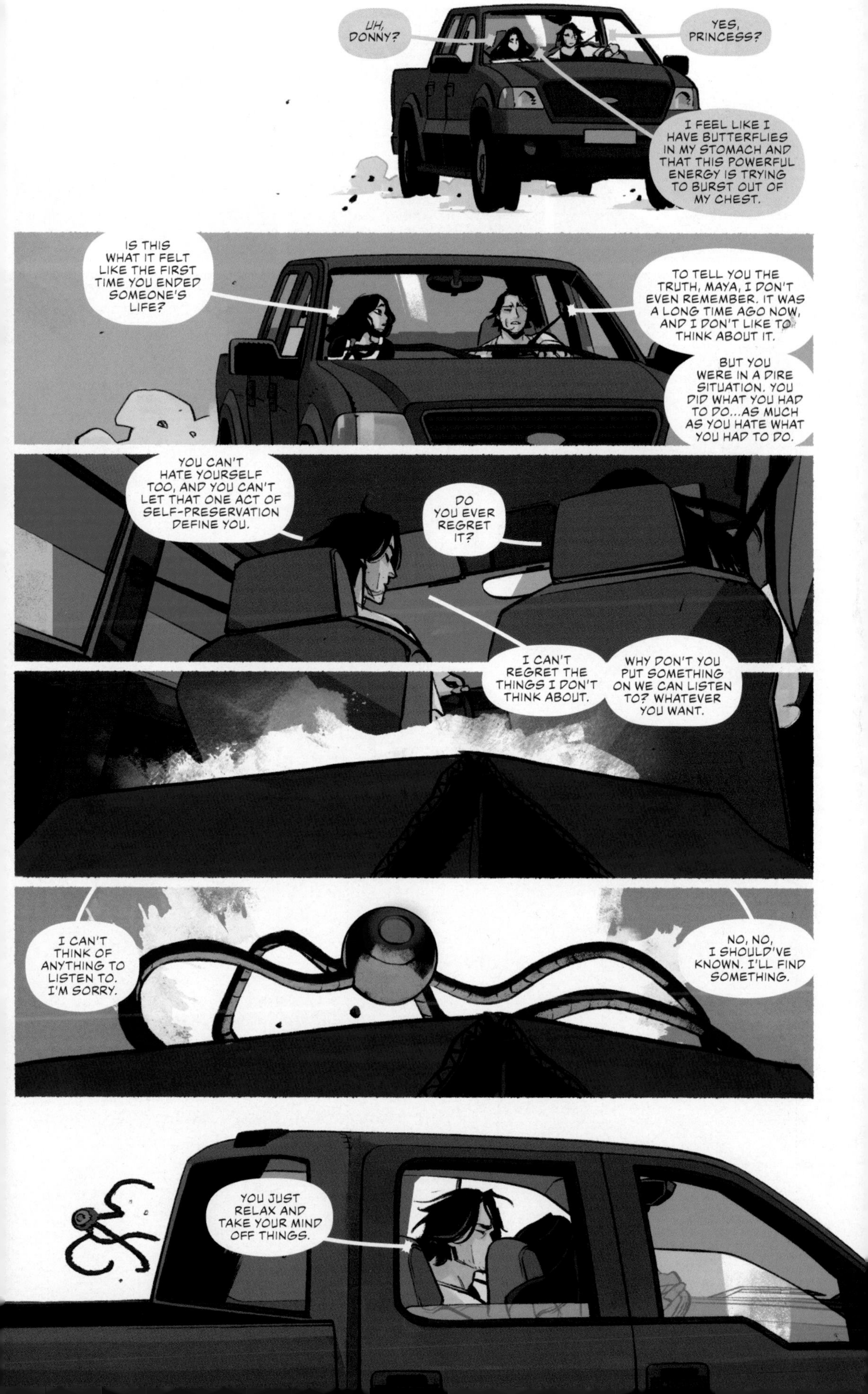
UH, DONNY?
YES, PRINCESS?
I FEEL LIKE I HAVE BUTTERFLIES IN MY STOMACH AND THAT THIS POWERFUL ENERGY IS TRYING TO BURST OUT OF MY CHEST.
IS THIS WHAT IT FELT LIKE THE FIRST TIME YOU ENDED SOMEONE'S LIFE?
TO TELL YOU THE TRUTH, MAYA, I DON'T EVEN REMEMBER. IT WAS A LONG TIME AGO NOW, AND I DON'T LIKE TO THINK ABOUT IT.
BUT YOU WERE IN A DIRE SITUATION. YOU DID WHAT YOU HAD TO DO...AS MUCH AS YOU HATE WHAT YOU HAD TO DO.
YOU CAN'T HATE YOURSELF TOO, AND YOU CAN'T LET THAT ONE ACT OF SELF-PRESERVATION DEFINE YOU.
DO YOU EVER REGRET IT?
I CAN'T REGRET THE THINGS I DON'T THINK ABOUT.
WHY DON'T YOU PUT SOMETHING ON WE CAN LISTEN TO? WHATEVER YOU WANT.
I CAN'T THINK OF ANYTHING TO LISTEN TO. I'M SORRY.
NO, NO, I SHOULD'VE KNOWN. I'LL FIND SOMETHING.
YOU JUST RELAX AND TAKE YOUR MIND OFF THINGS.

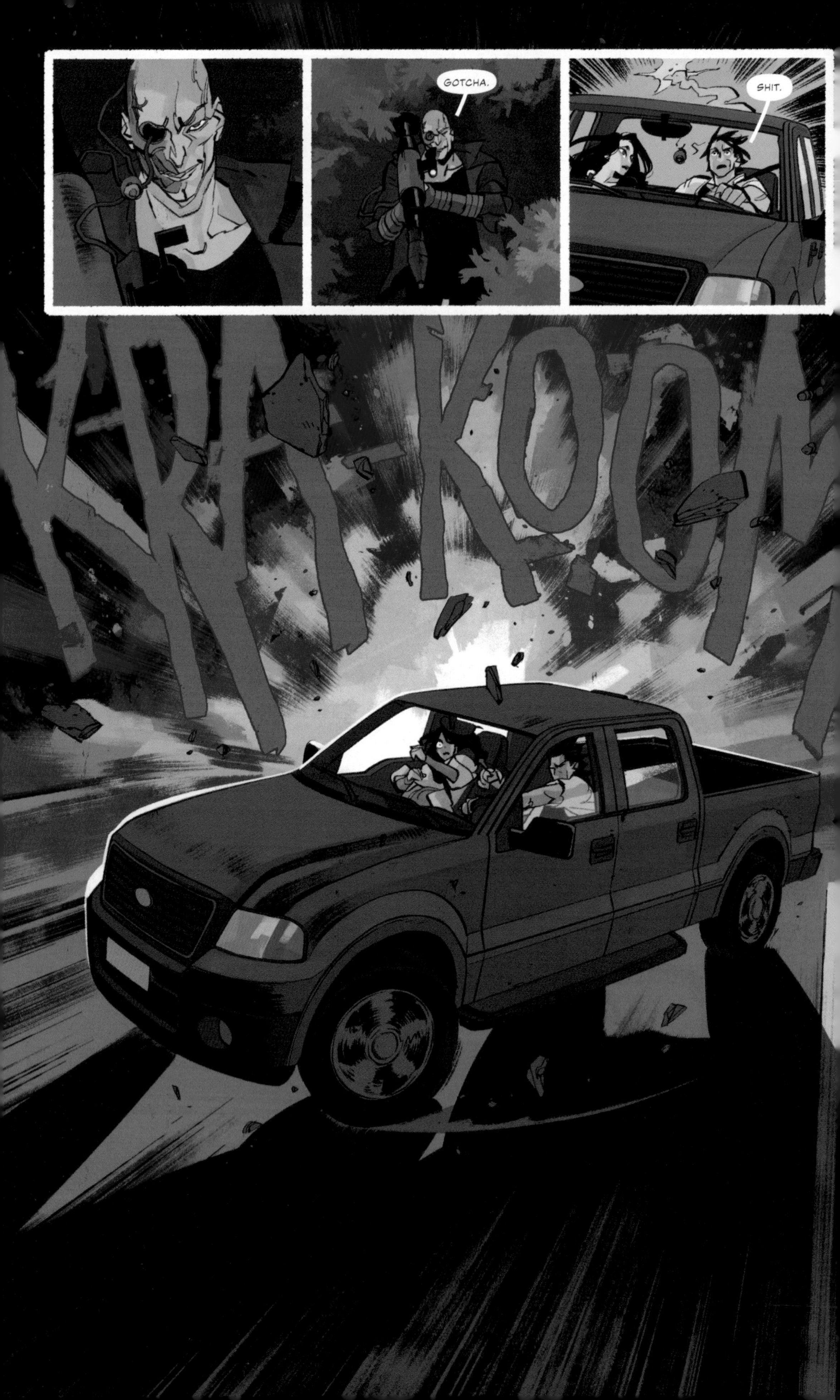
GOTCHA.
SHIT.
KRA-KOOM

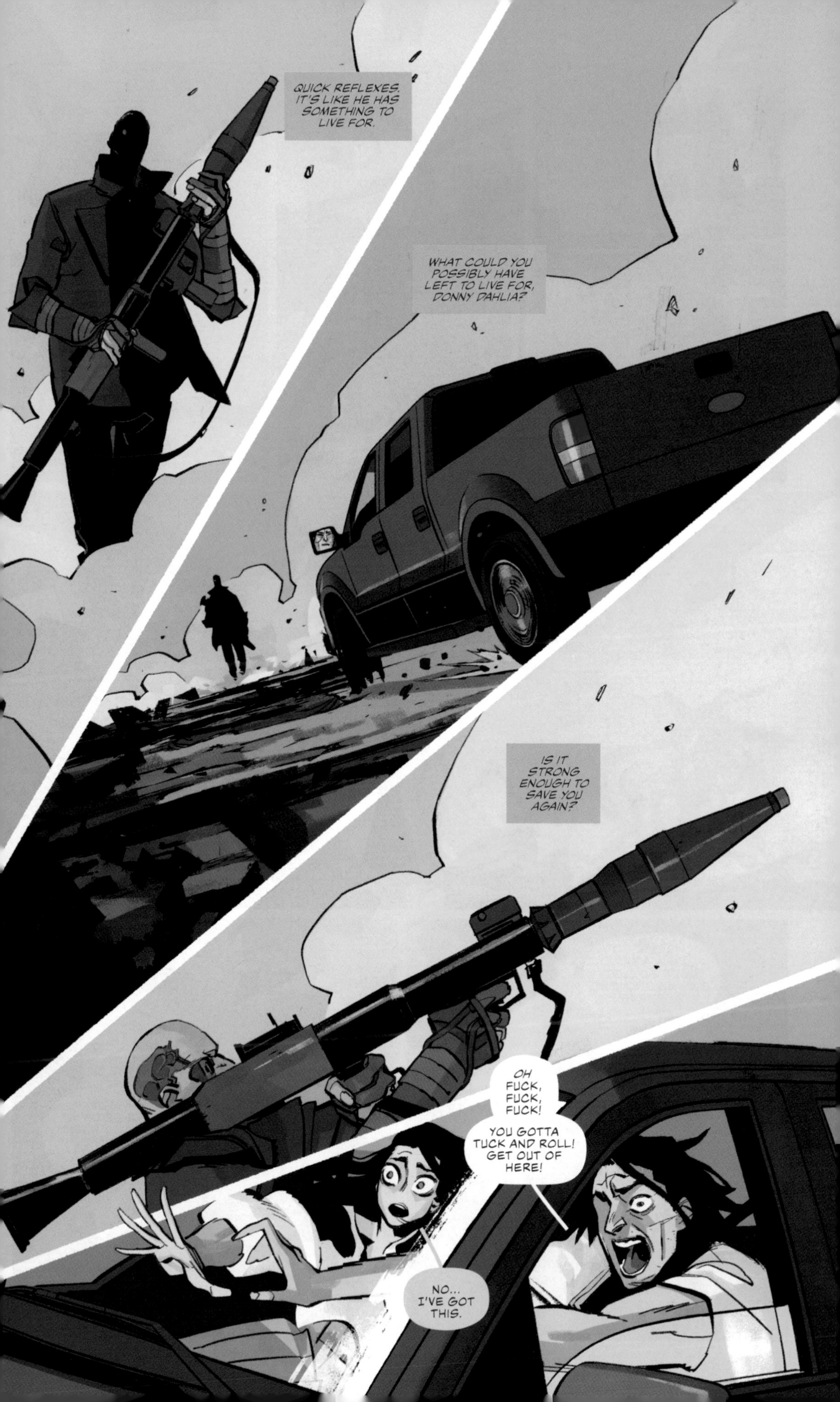
QUICK REFLEXES. IT'S LIKE HE HAS SOMETHING TO LIVE FOR.
WHAT COULD YOU POSSIBLY HAVE LEFT TO LIVE FOR, DONNY DAHLIA?
IS IT STRONG ENOUGH TO SAVE YOU AGAIN?
OH FUCK, FUCK, FUCK!
YOU GOTTA TUCK AND ROLL! GET OUT OF HERE!
NO... I'VE GOT THIS.

OH,
FUCK.

FUCK.

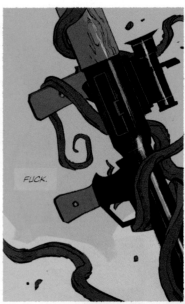

FUCK.

RRRR!

I'VE GOT A HOLD ON RYNE, BUT THEY'RE STRONG. WE *NEED* TO GO. NOW.

NO. I CAN'T. NOT UNTIL I GET SOME ANSWERS.

LOOK, I'M IN A BAD MOOD SO JUST GIVE ME STRAIGHT ANSWERS HERE.

WHY ARE YOU TRYING TO KILL US?

HAHAHA, YOU'RE SERIOUS! SHE REALLY HASN'T TOLD YOU THE WHOLE STORY, HAS SHE?

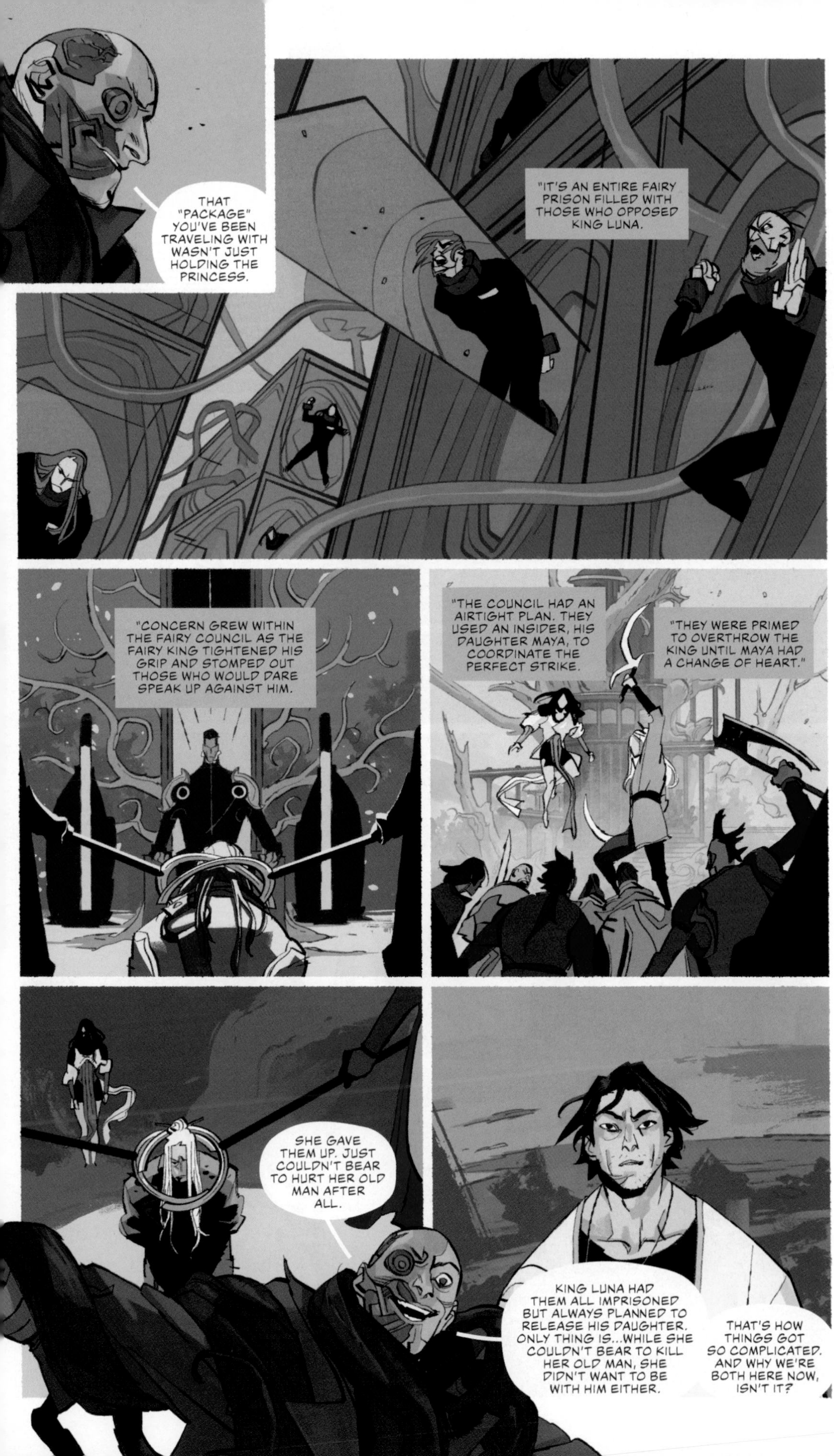
THAT "PACKAGE" YOU'VE BEEN TRAVELING WITH WASN'T JUST HOLDING THE PRINCESS.
"IT'S AN ENTIRE FAIRY PRISON FILLED WITH THOSE WHO OPPOSED KING LUNA.
"CONCERN GREW WITHIN THE FAIRY COUNCIL AS THE FAIRY KING TIGHTENED HIS GRIP AND STOMPED OUT THOSE WHO WOULD DARE SPEAK UP AGAINST HIM.
"THE COUNCIL HAD AN AIRTIGHT PLAN. THEY USED AN INSIDER, HIS DAUGHTER MAYA, TO COORDINATE THE PERFECT STRIKE.
"THEY WERE PRIMED TO OVERTHROW THE KING UNTIL MAYA HAD A CHANGE OF HEART."
SHE GAVE THEM UP. JUST COULDN'T BEAR TO HURT HER OLD MAN AFTER ALL.
KING LUNA HAD THEM ALL IMPRISONED BUT ALWAYS PLANNED TO RELEASE HIS DAUGHTER. ONLY THING IS...WHILE SHE COULDN'T BEAR TO KILL HER OLD MAN, SHE DIDN'T WANT TO BE WITH HIM EITHER.
THAT'S HOW THINGS GOT SO COMPLICATED. AND WHY WE'RE BOTH HERE NOW, ISN'T IT?

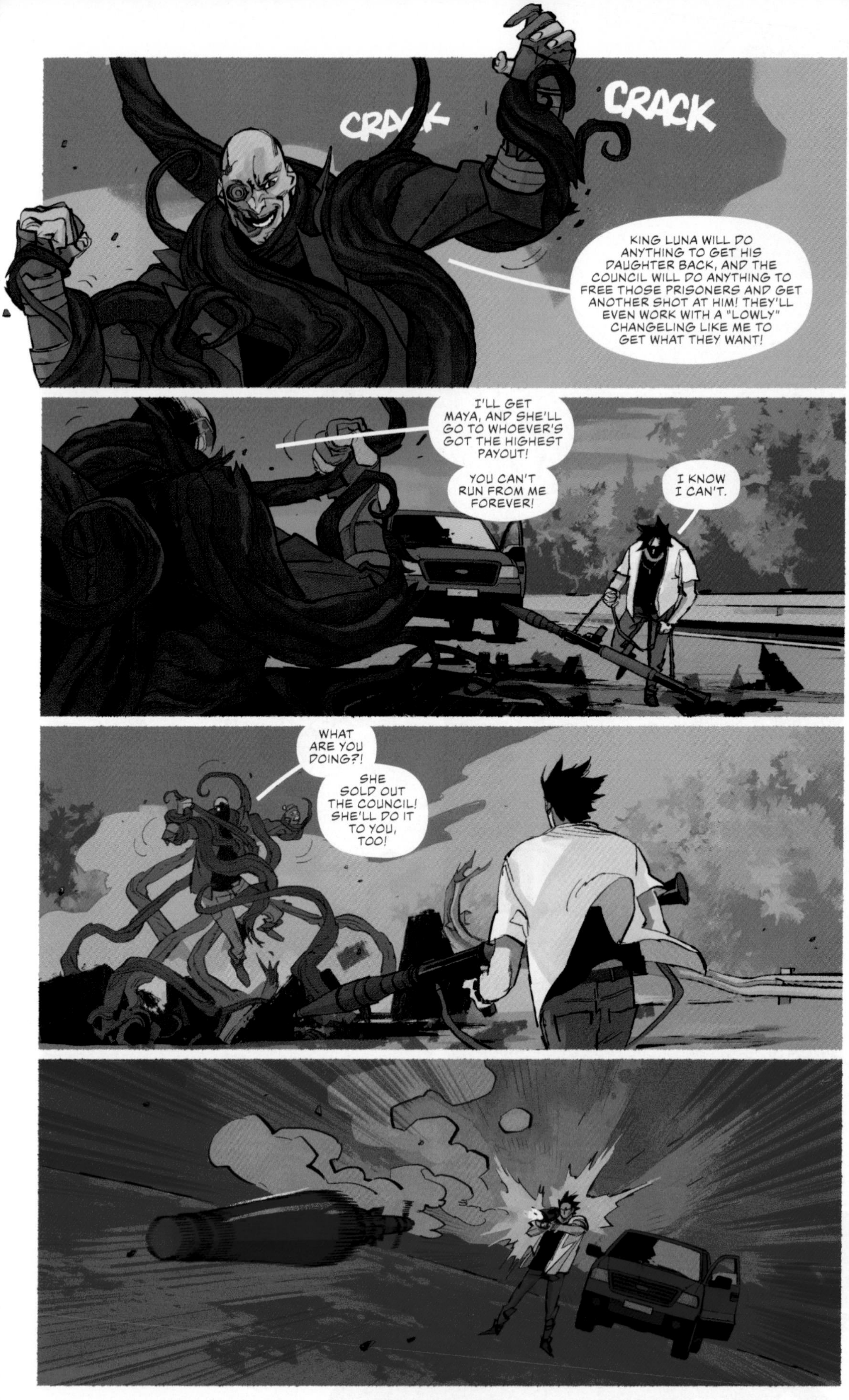
CRACK
CRACK
KING LUNA WILL DO ANYTHING TO GET HIS DAUGHTER BACK, AND THE COUNCIL WILL DO ANYTHING TO FREE THOSE PRISONERS AND GET ANOTHER SHOT AT HIM! THEY'LL EVEN WORK WITH A "LOWLY" CHANGELING LIKE ME TO GET WHAT THEY WANT!
I'LL GET MAYA, AND SHE'LL GO TO WHOEVER'S GOT THE HIGHEST PAYOUT!
YOU CAN'T RUN FROM ME FOREVER!
I KNOW I CAN'T.
WHAT ARE YOU DOING?!
SHE SOLD OUT THE COUNCIL! SHE'LL DO IT TO YOU, TOO!

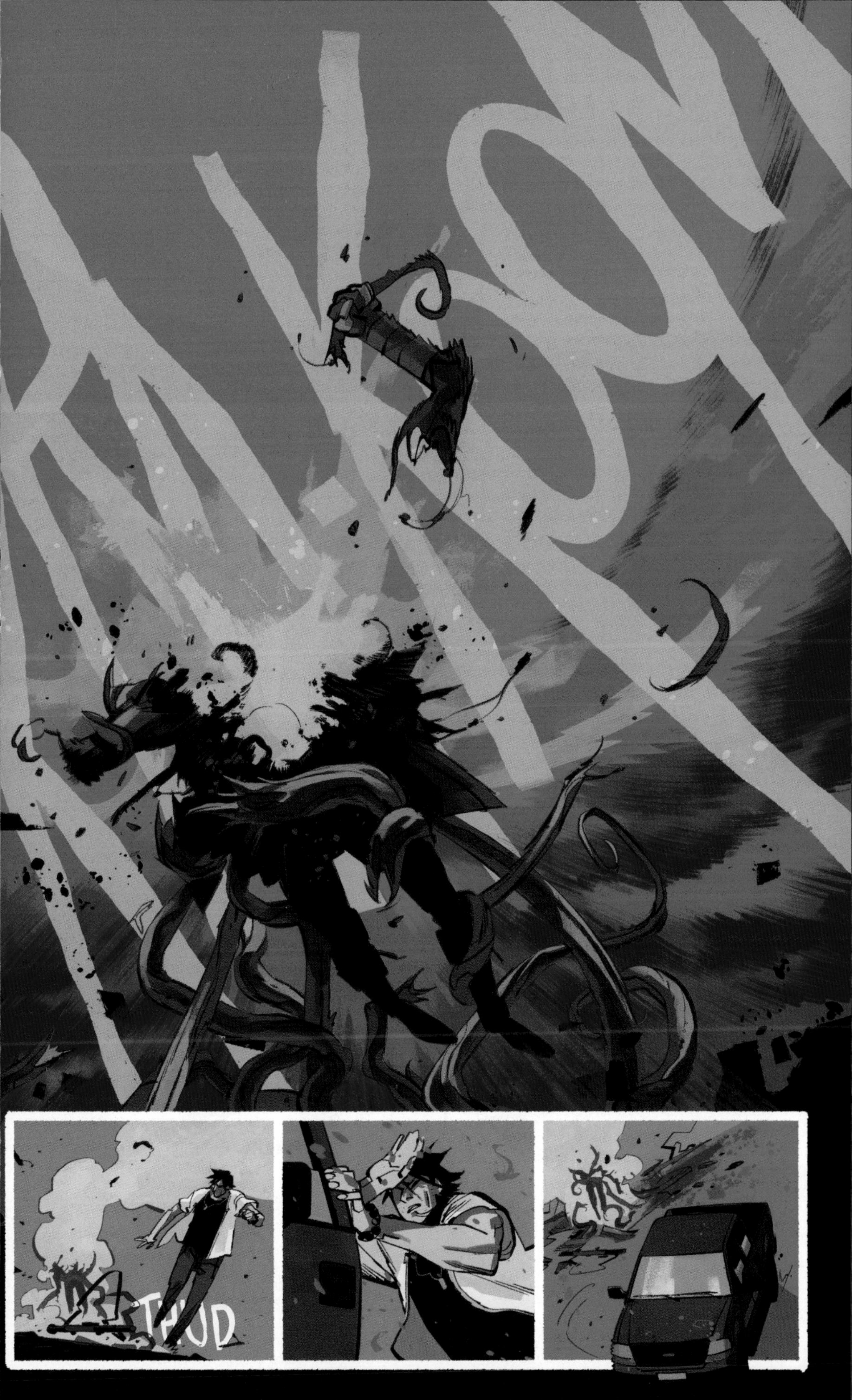
THUD

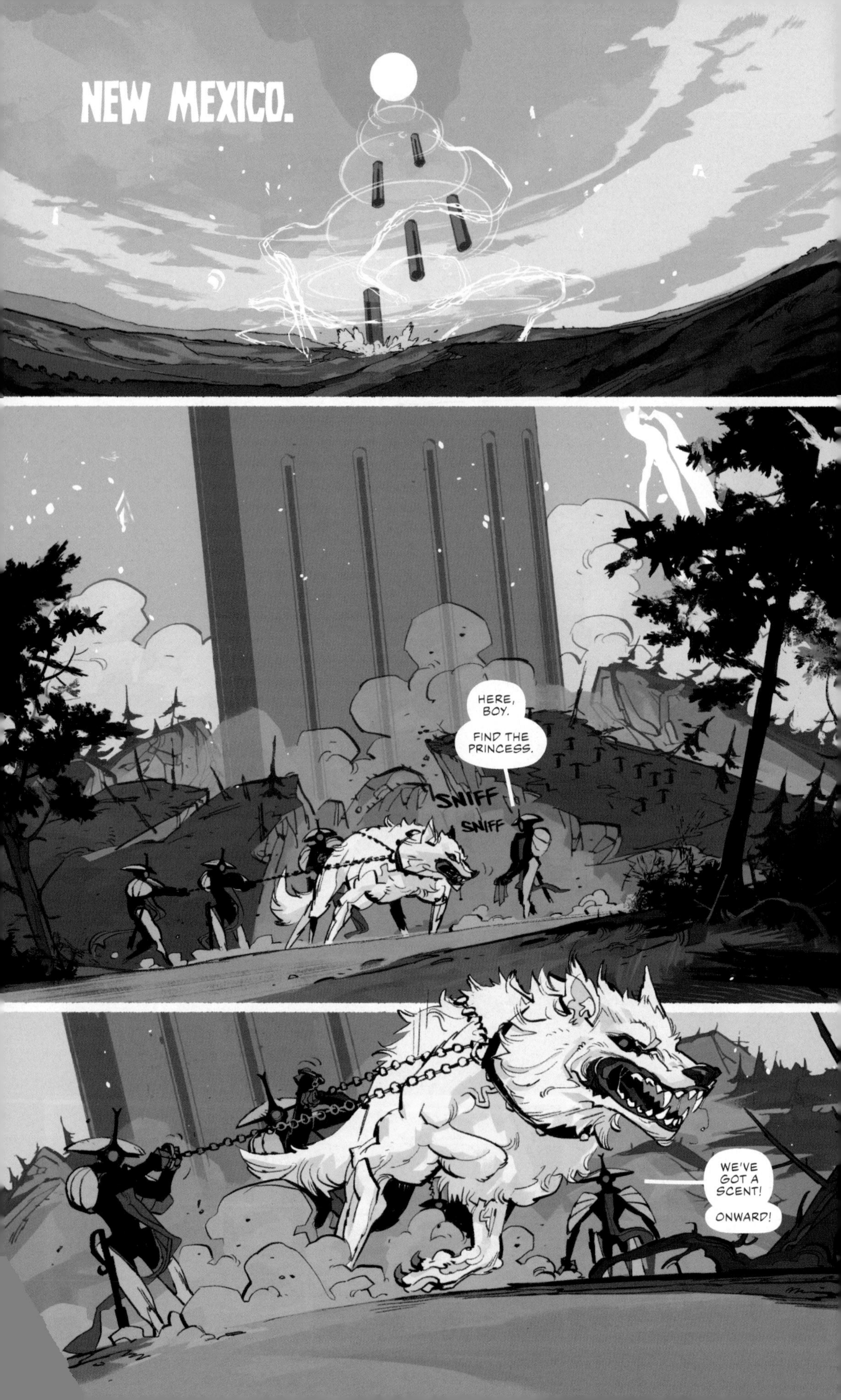
NEW MEXICO.
HERE, BOY.
FIND THE PRINCESS.
SNIFF
SNIFF
WE'VE GOT A SCENT!
ONWARD!

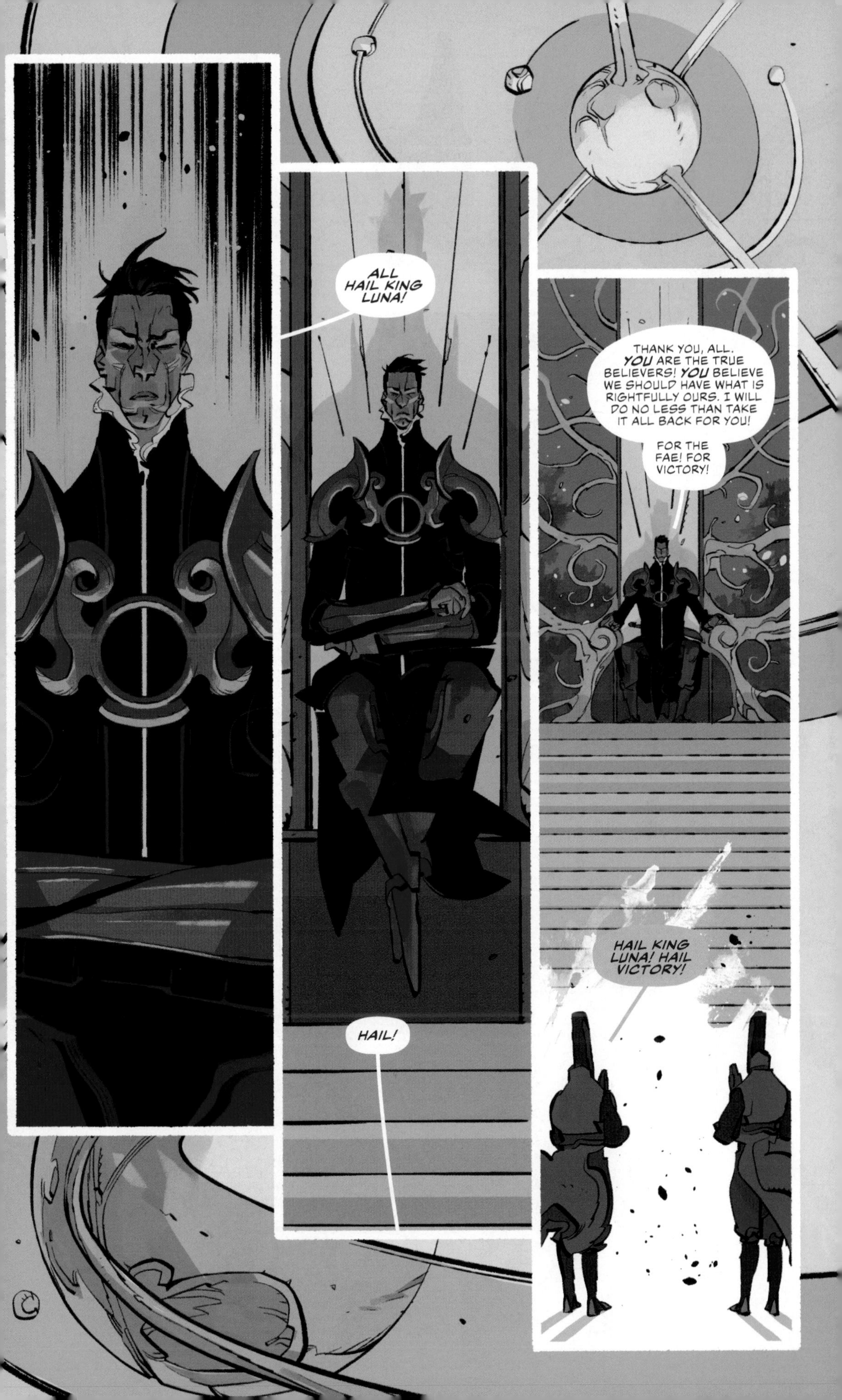
ALL HAIL KING LUNA!
HAIL!
THANK YOU, ALL. YOU ARE THE TRUE BELIEVERS! YOU BELIEVE WE SHOULD HAVE WHAT IS RIGHTFULLY OURS. I WILL DO NO LESS THAN TAKE IT ALL BACK FOR YOU!
FOR THE FAE! FOR VICTORY!
HAIL KING LUNA! HAIL VICTORY!

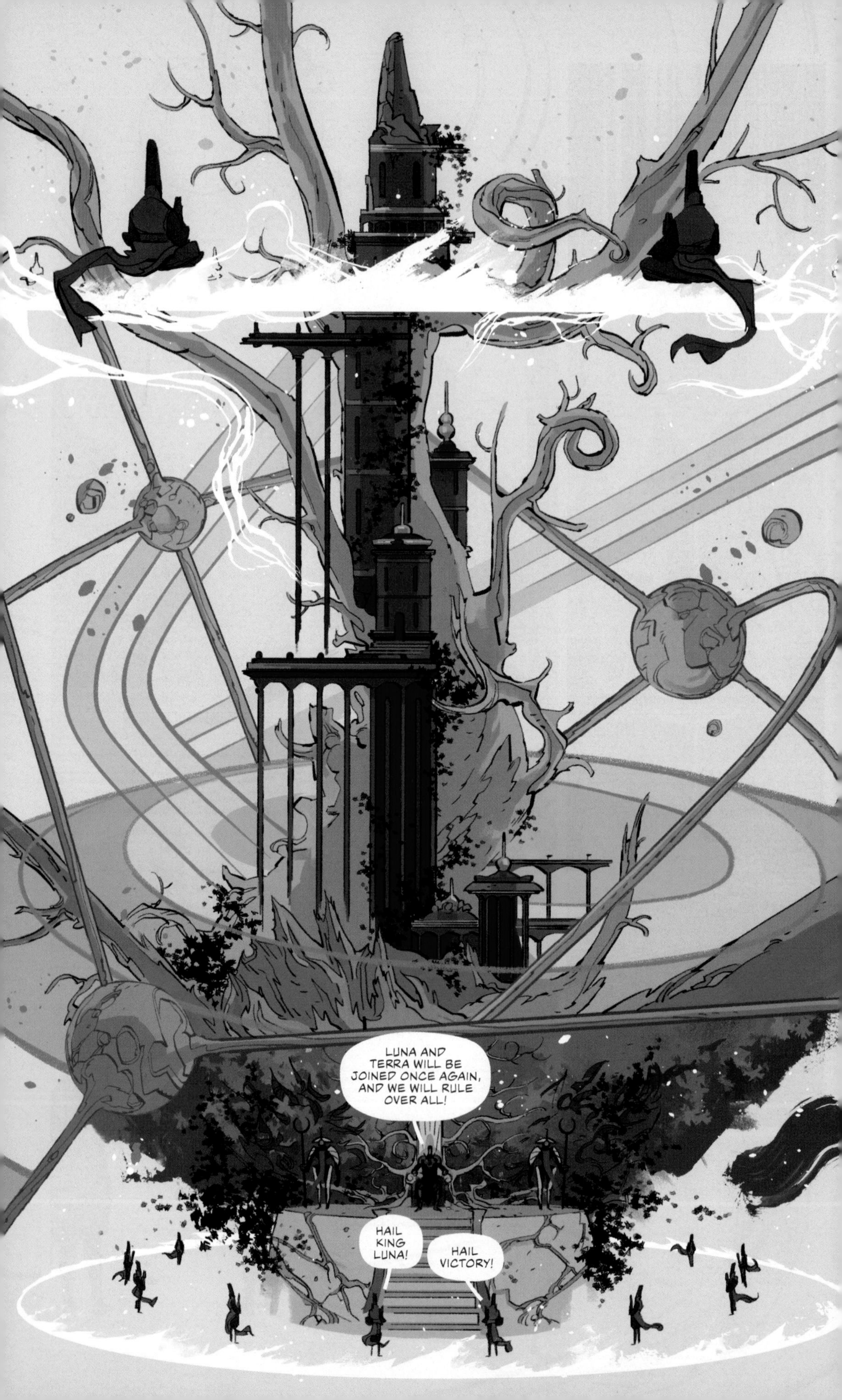
LUNA AND TERRA WILL BE JOINED ONCE AGAIN, AND WE WILL RULE OVER ALL!
HAIL KING LUNA!
HAIL VICTORY!

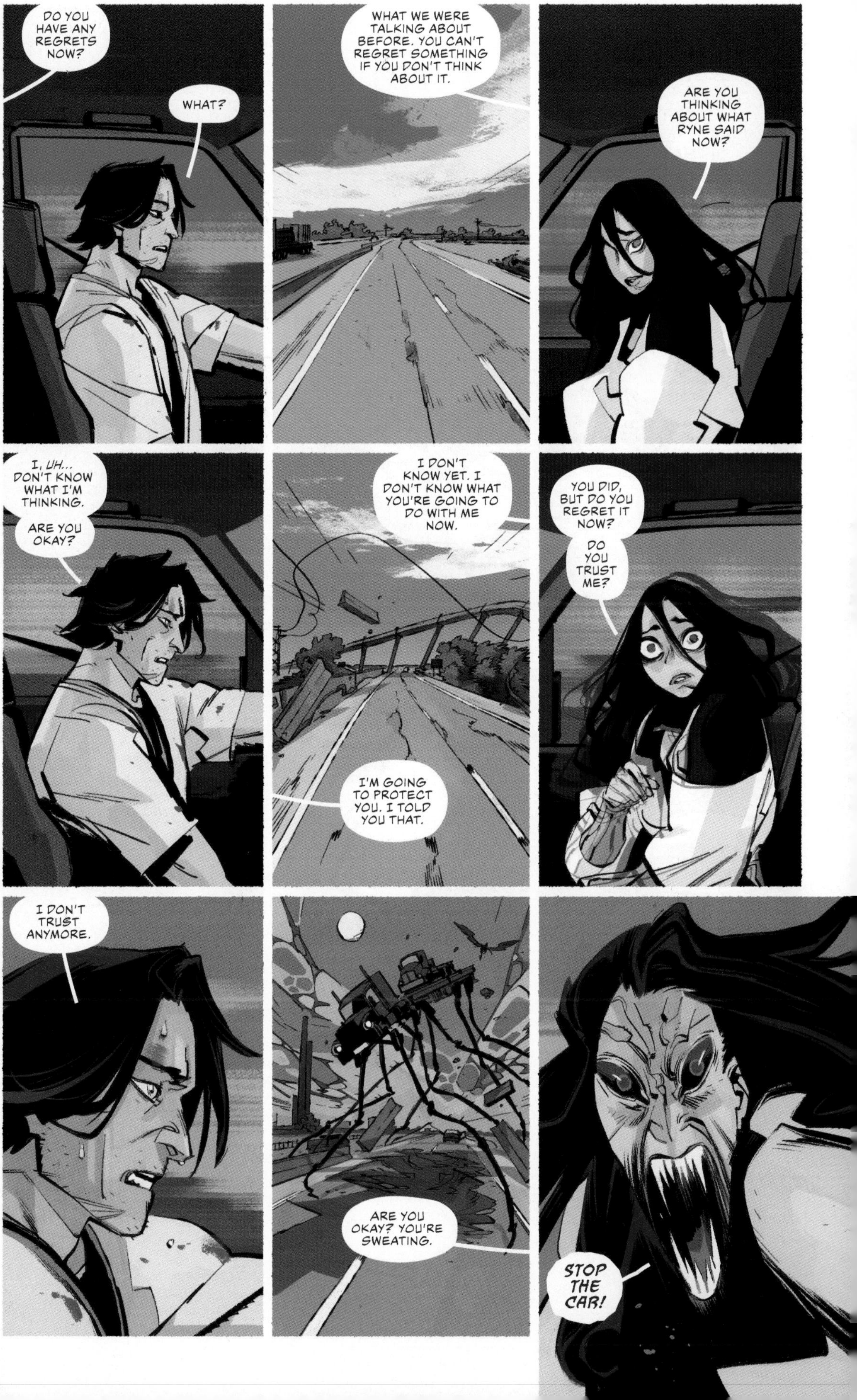
DO YOU HAVE ANY REGRETS NOW?
WHAT?
WHAT WE WERE TALKING ABOUT BEFORE. YOU CAN'T REGRET SOMETHING IF YOU DON'T THINK ABOUT IT.
ARE YOU THINKING ABOUT WHAT RYNE SAID NOW?
I, UH... DON'T KNOW WHAT I'M THINKING.
ARE YOU OKAY?
I DON'T KNOW YET. I DON'T KNOW WHAT YOU'RE GOING TO DO WITH ME NOW.
I'M GOING TO PROTECT YOU. I TOLD YOU THAT.
YOU DID, BUT DO YOU REGRET IT NOW?
DO YOU TRUST ME?
I DON'T TRUST ANYMORE.
ARE YOU OKAY? YOU'RE SWEATING.
STOP THE CAR!

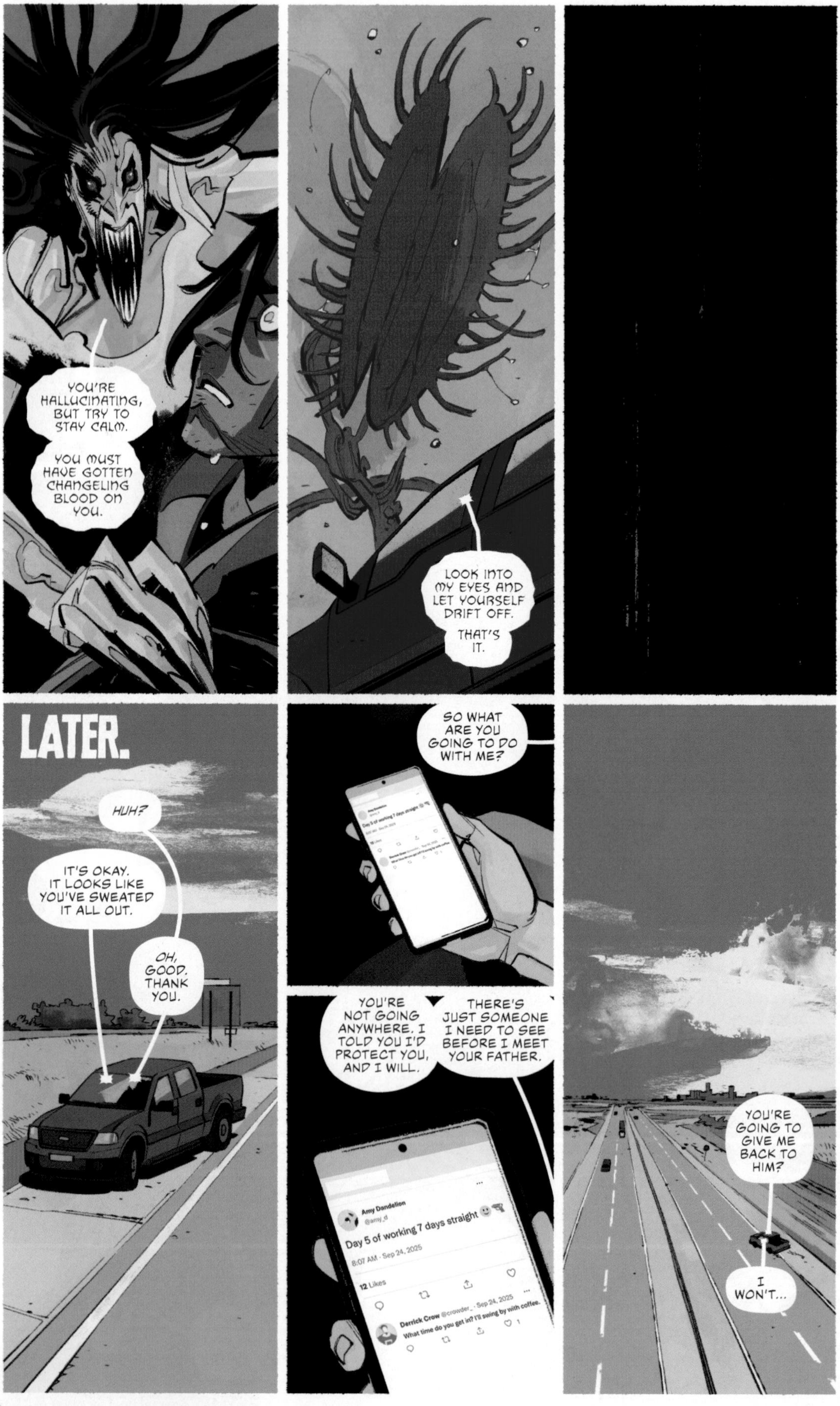
YOU'RE HALLUCINATING, BUT TRY TO STAY CALM.
YOU MUST HAVE GOTTEN CHANGELING BLOOD ON YOU.
LOOK INTO MY EYES AND LET YOURSELF DRIFT OFF.
THAT'S IT.
LATER.
HUH?
IT'S OKAY. IT LOOKS LIKE YOU'VE SWEATED IT ALL OUT.
OH, GOOD. THANK YOU.
SO WHAT ARE YOU GOING TO DO WITH ME?
YOU'RE NOT GOING ANYWHERE. I TOLD YOU I'D PROTECT YOU, AND I WILL.
THERE'S JUST SOMEONE I NEED TO SEE BEFORE I MEET YOUR FATHER.
Amy Dandelion
@amy_d
Day 5 of working 7 days straight
8:07 AM · Sep 24, 2025
12 Likes
Derrick Crow @crowder_ · Sep 24, 2025
What time do you get in? I'll swing by with coffee.
YOU'RE GOING TO GIVE ME BACK TO HIM?
I WON'T...

"...BUT YOUR FATHER ISN'T GOING TO GIVE UP HIS SEARCH FOR YOU OR THE PRISONERS.

"SEEMS LIKE THIS FAIRY COUNCIL WON'T GIVE UP, EITHER.

"I DON'T KNOW EXACTLY WHAT I'M GOING TO DO YET, BUT THERE'S ONE THING I *DO* KNOW.

"WE CAN'T KEEP RUNNING."

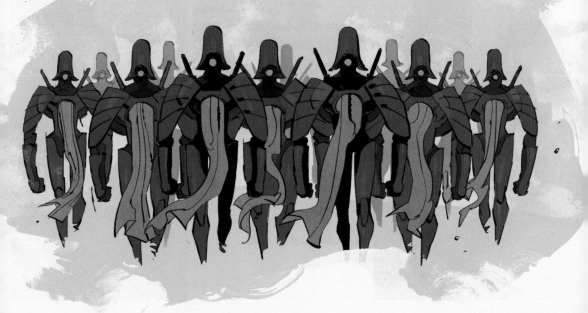

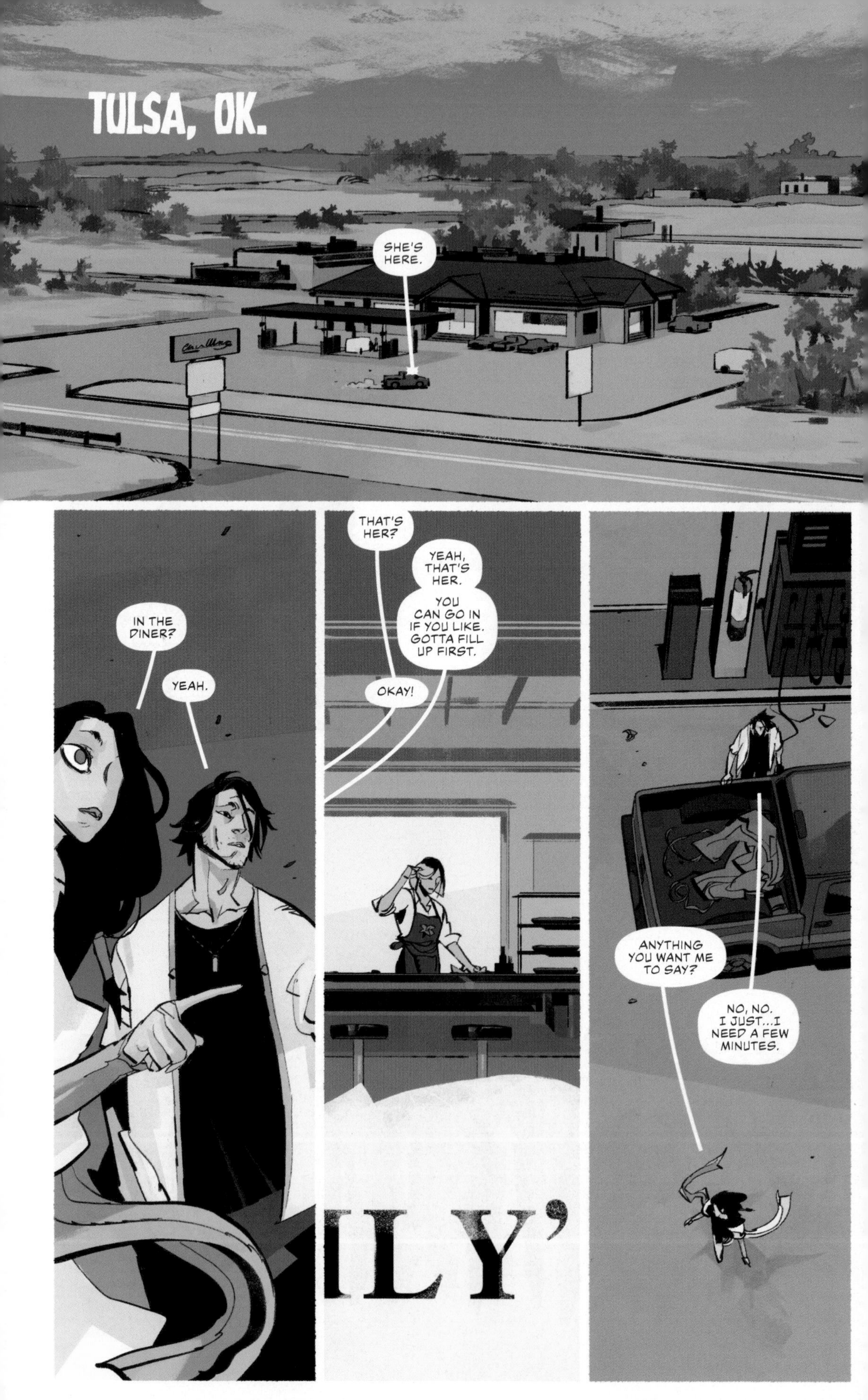
TULSA, OK.
SHE'S HERE.
IN THE DINER?
YEAH.
THAT'S HER?
YEAH, THAT'S HER.
YOU CAN GO IN IF YOU LIKE. GOTTA FILL UP FIRST.
OKAY!
ILY'
ANYTHING YOU WANT ME TO SAY?
NO, NO. I JUST...I NEED A FEW MINUTES.

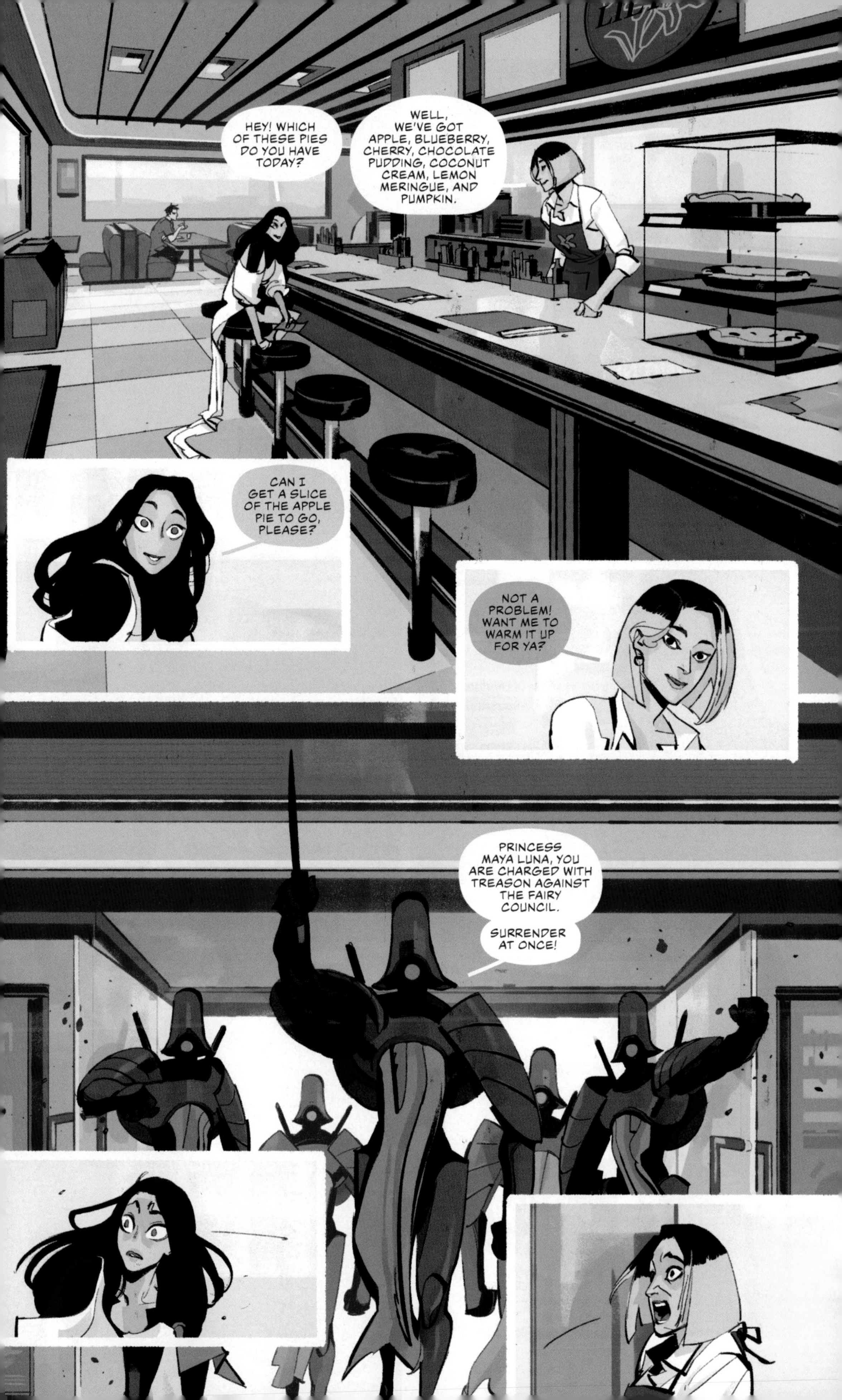
HEY! WHICH OF THESE PIES DO YOU HAVE TODAY?
WELL, WE'VE GOT APPLE, BLUEBERRY, CHERRY, CHOCOLATE PUDDING, COCONUT CREAM, LEMON MERINGUE, AND PUMPKIN.
CAN I GET A SLICE OF THE APPLE PIE TO GO, PLEASE?
NOT A PROBLEM! WANT ME TO WARM IT UP FOR YA?
PRINCESS MAYA LUNA, YOU ARE CHARGED WITH TREASON AGAINST THE FAIRY COUNCIL.
SURRENDER AT ONCE!

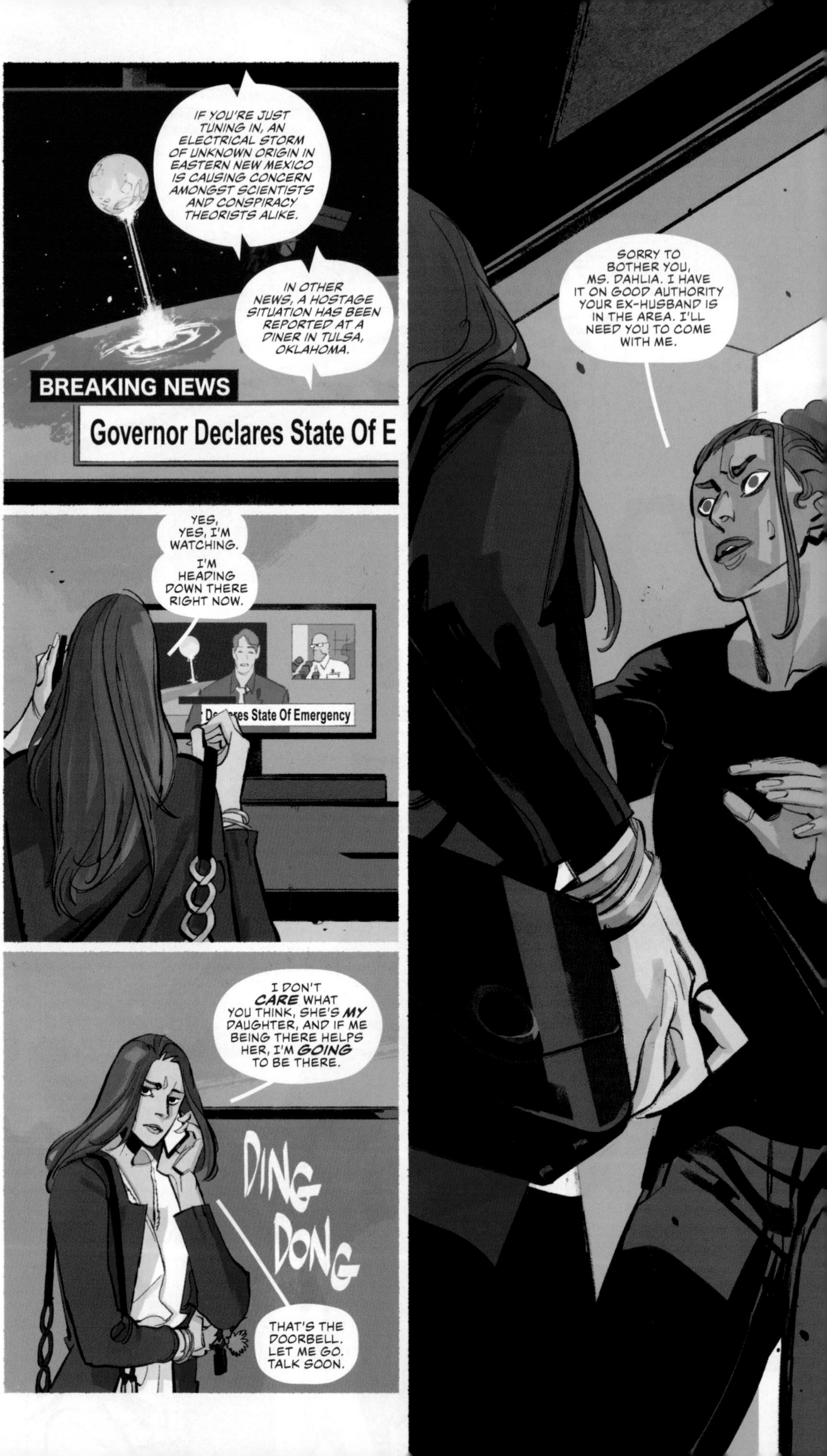
IF YOU'RE JUST TUNING IN, AN ELECTRICAL STORM OF UNKNOWN ORIGIN IN EASTERN NEW MEXICO IS CAUSING CONCERN AMONGST SCIENTISTS AND CONSPIRACY THEORISTS ALIKE.
IN OTHER NEWS, A HOSTAGE SITUATION HAS BEEN REPORTED AT A DINER IN TULSA, OKLAHOMA.
BREAKING NEWS
Governor Declares State Of E
YES, YES, I'M WATCHING.
I'M HEADING DOWN THERE RIGHT NOW.
State Of Emergency
I DON'T CARE WHAT YOU THINK, SHE'S MY DAUGHTER, AND IF ME BEING THERE HELPS HER, I'M GOING TO BE THERE.
DING DONG
THAT'S THE DOORBELL. LET ME GO. TALK SOON.
SORRY TO BOTHER YOU, MS. DAHLIA. I HAVE IT ON GOOD AUTHORITY YOUR EX-HUSBAND IS IN THE AREA. I'LL NEED YOU TO COME WITH ME.

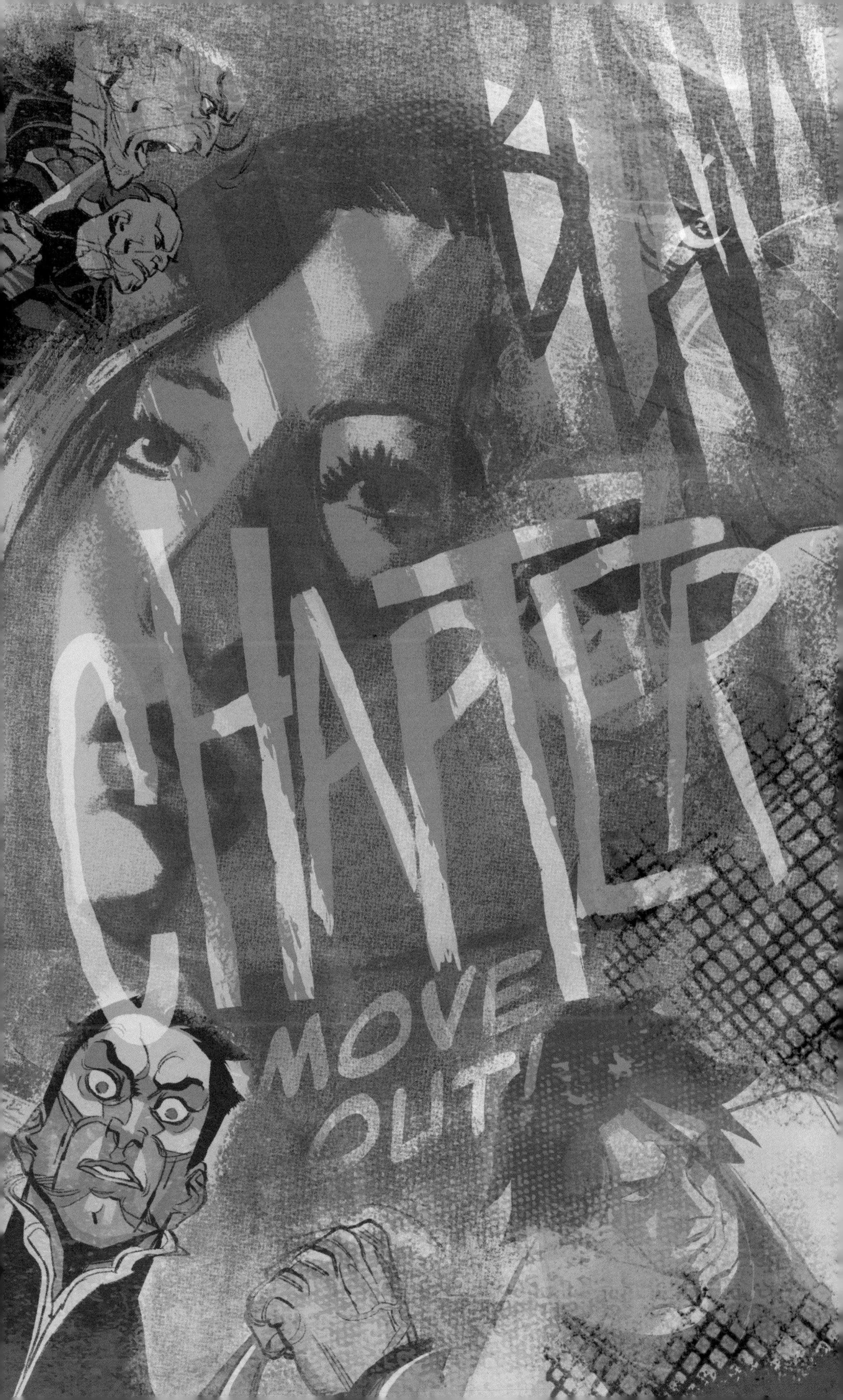
CHAPTER
MOVE OUT!

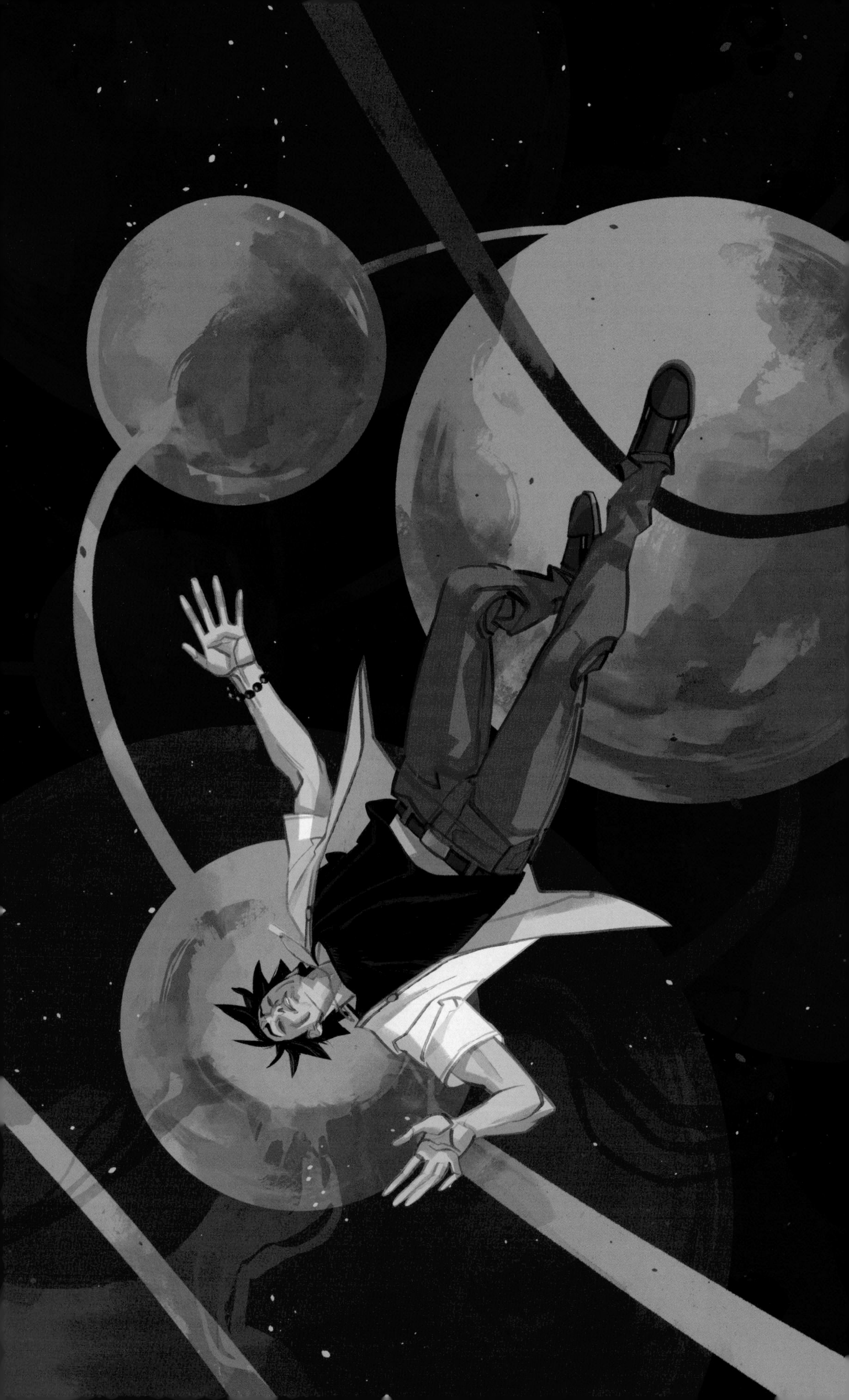

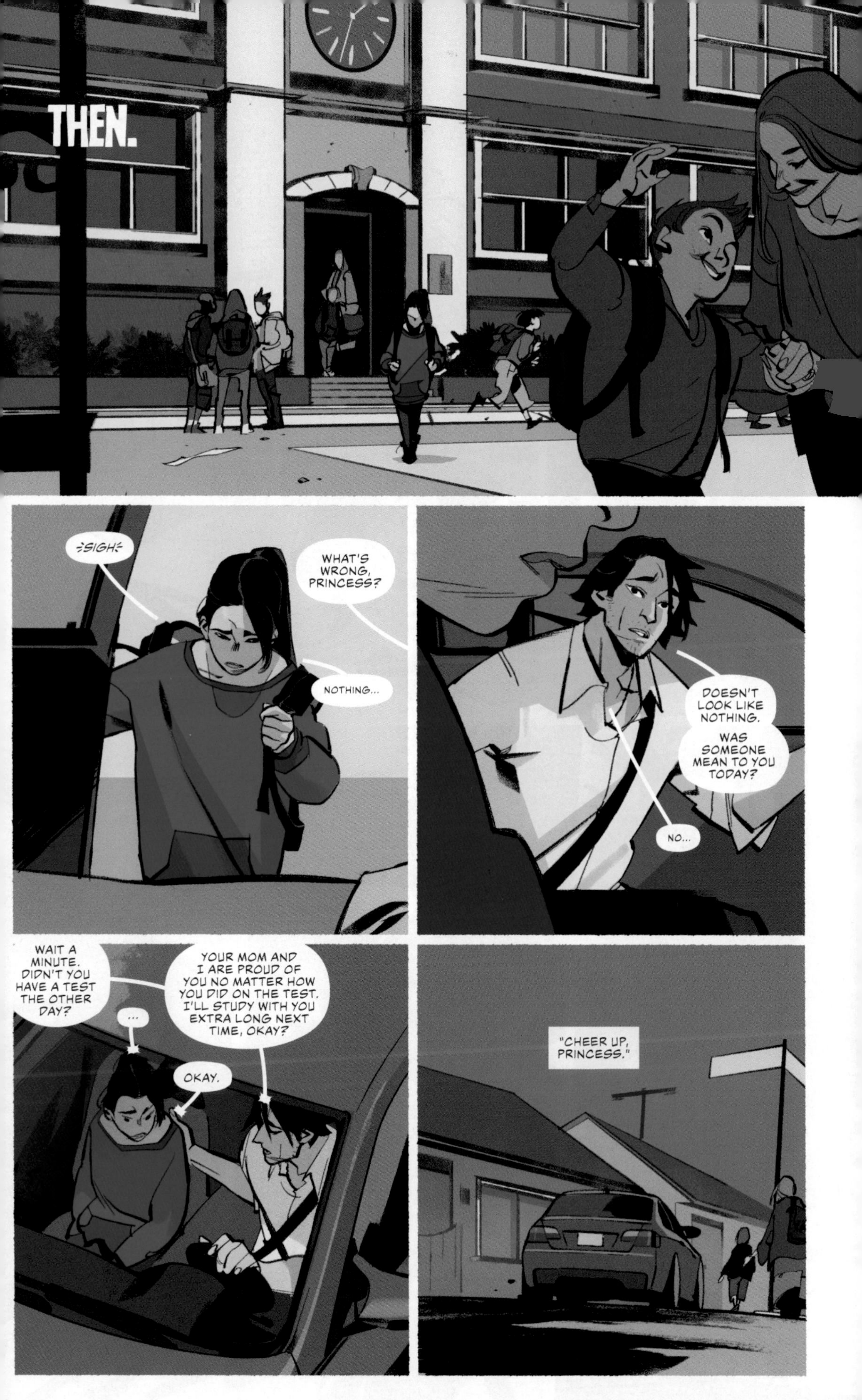
THEN.
-SIGH-
WHAT'S WRONG, PRINCESS?
NOTHING...
DOESN'T LOOK LIKE NOTHING.
WAS SOMEONE MEAN TO YOU TODAY?
NO...
WAIT A MINUTE. DIDN'T YOU HAVE A TEST THE OTHER DAY?
...
YOUR MOM AND I ARE PROUD OF YOU NO MATTER HOW YOU DID ON THE TEST. I'LL STUDY WITH YOU EXTRA LONG NEXT TIME, OKAY?
OKAY.
"CHEER UP, PRINCESS."

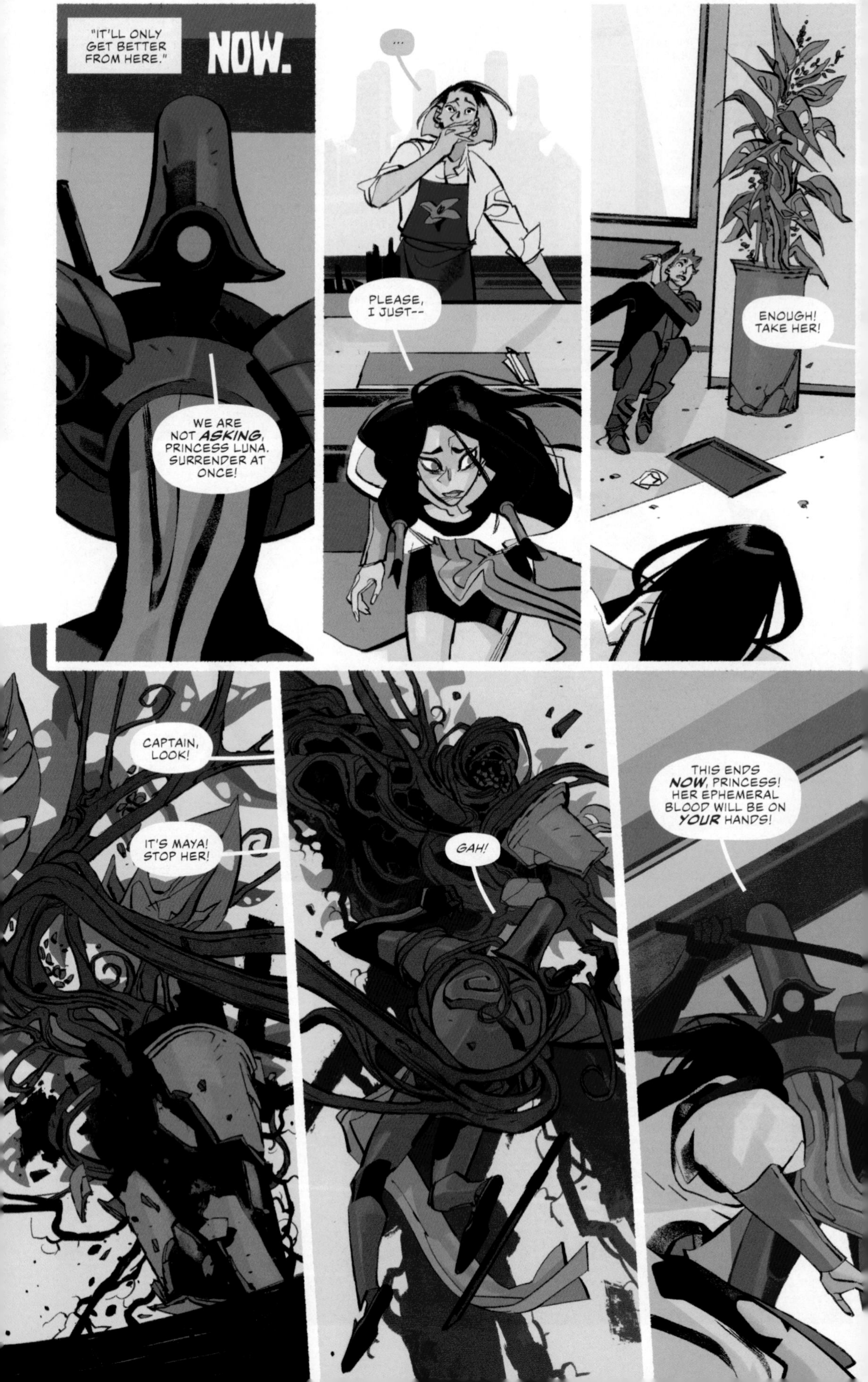
"IT'LL ONLY GET BETTER FROM HERE."
NOW.
WE ARE NOT ASKING, PRINCESS LUNA. SURRENDER AT ONCE!
...
PLEASE, I JUST--
ENOUGH! TAKE HER!
CAPTAIN, LOOK!
IT'S MAYA! STOP HER!
GAH!
THIS ENDS NOW, PRINCESS! HER EPHEMERAL BLOOD WILL BE ON YOUR HANDS!

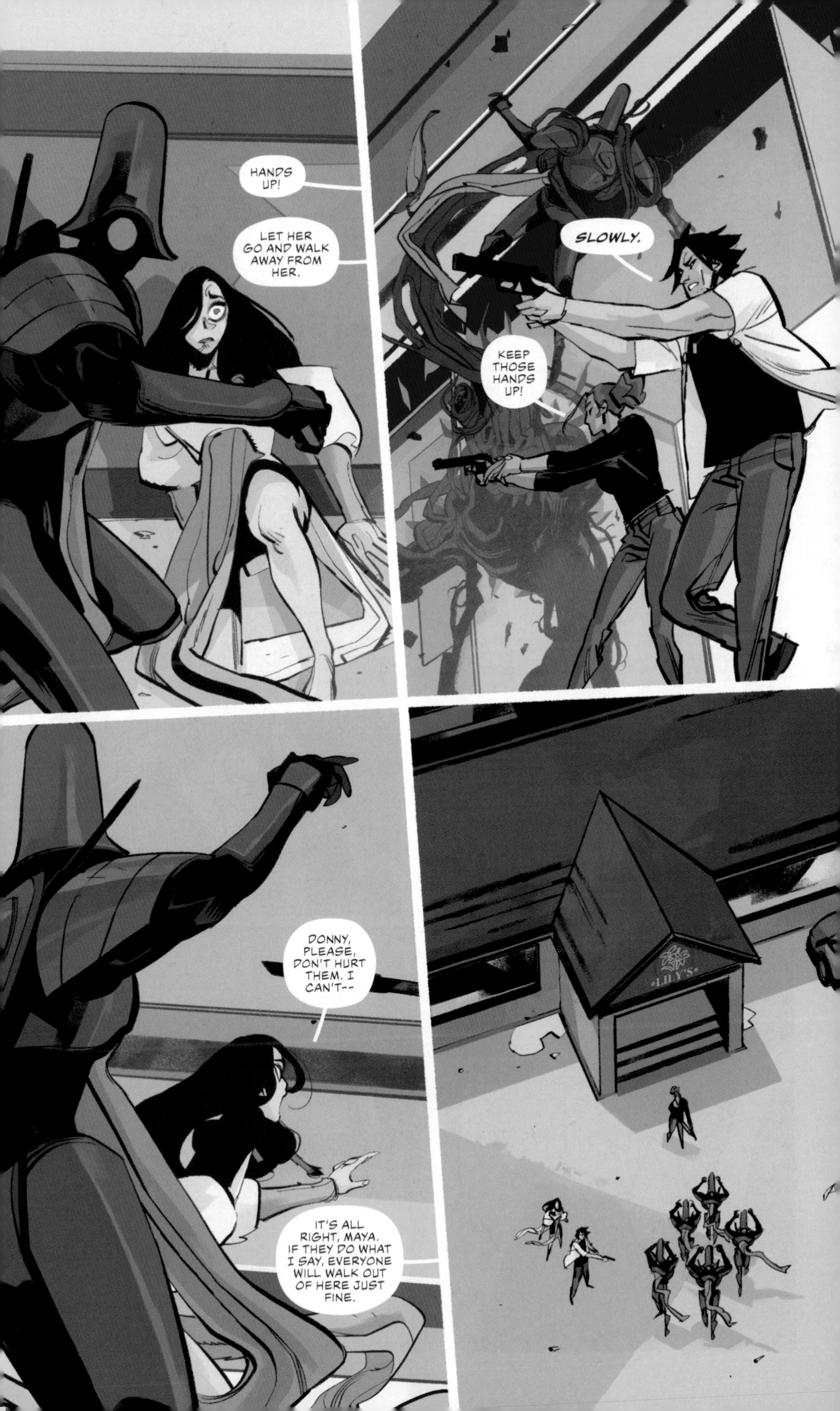
HANDS UP!
LET HER GO AND WALK AWAY FROM HER.
SLOWLY.
KEEP THOSE HANDS UP!
DONNY, PLEASE, DON'T HURT THEM. I CAN'T--
IT'S ALL RIGHT, MAYA. IF THEY DO WHAT I SAY, EVERYONE WILL WALK OUT OF HERE JUST FINE.
LILY'S

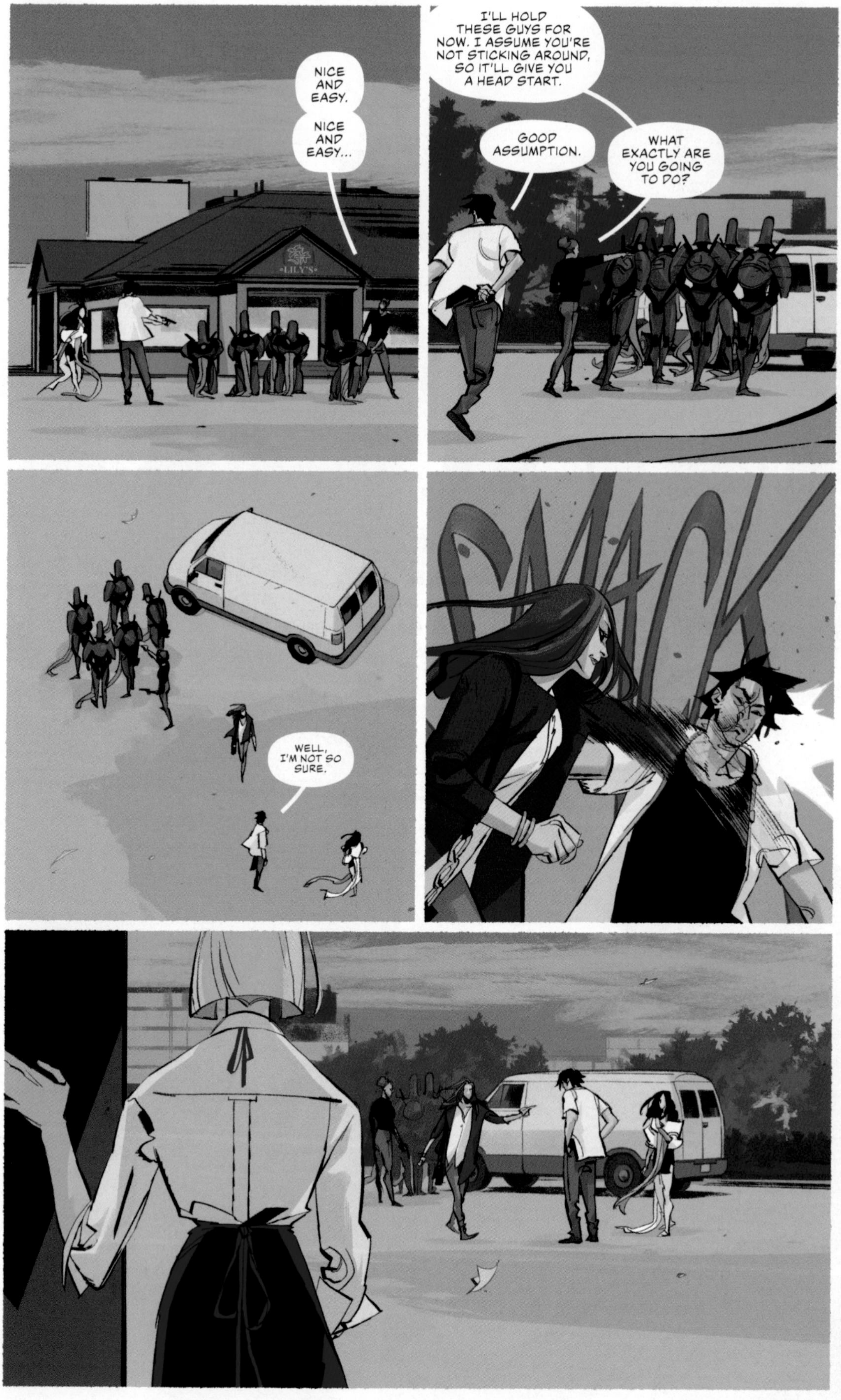
NICE AND EASY.
NICE AND EASY...
I'LL HOLD THESE GUYS FOR NOW. I ASSUME YOU'RE NOT STICKING AROUND, SO IT'LL GIVE YOU A HEAD START.
GOOD ASSUMPTION.
WHAT EXACTLY ARE YOU GOING TO DO?
WELL, I'M NOT SO SURE.
SMACK

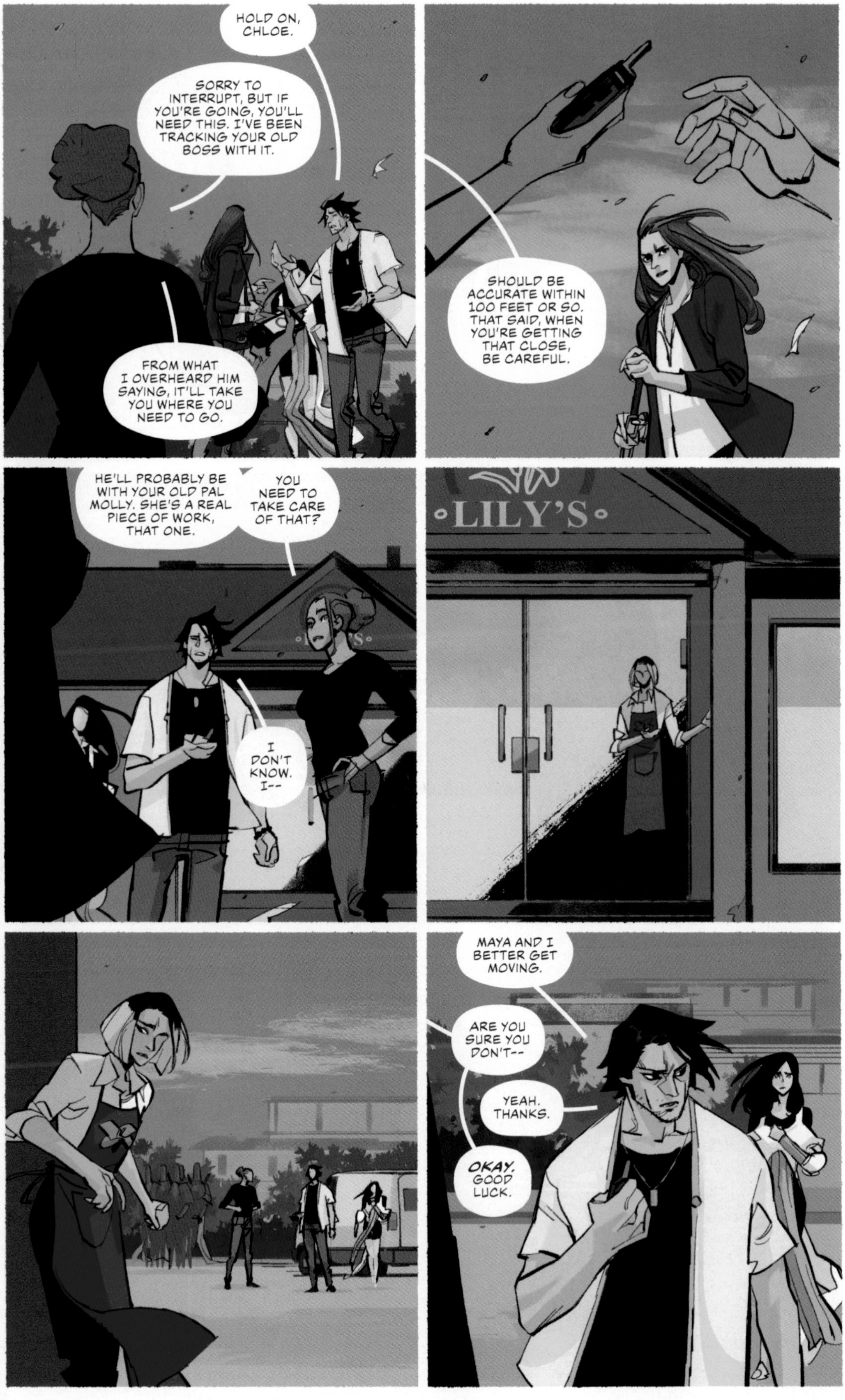
HOLD ON, CHLOE.
SORRY TO INTERRUPT, BUT IF YOU'RE GOING, YOU'LL NEED THIS. I'VE BEEN TRACKING YOUR OLD BOSS WITH IT.
FROM WHAT I OVERHEARD HIM SAYING, IT'LL TAKE YOU WHERE YOU NEED TO GO.
SHOULD BE ACCURATE WITHIN 100 FEET OR SO. THAT SAID, WHEN YOU'RE GETTING THAT CLOSE, BE CAREFUL.
HE'LL PROBABLY BE WITH YOUR OLD PAL MOLLY. SHE'S A REAL PIECE OF WORK, THAT ONE.
YOU NEED TO TAKE CARE OF THAT?
I DON'T KNOW. I--
LILY'S
MAYA AND I BETTER GET MOVING.
ARE YOU SURE YOU DON'T--
YEAH. THANKS.
OKAY. GOOD LUCK.

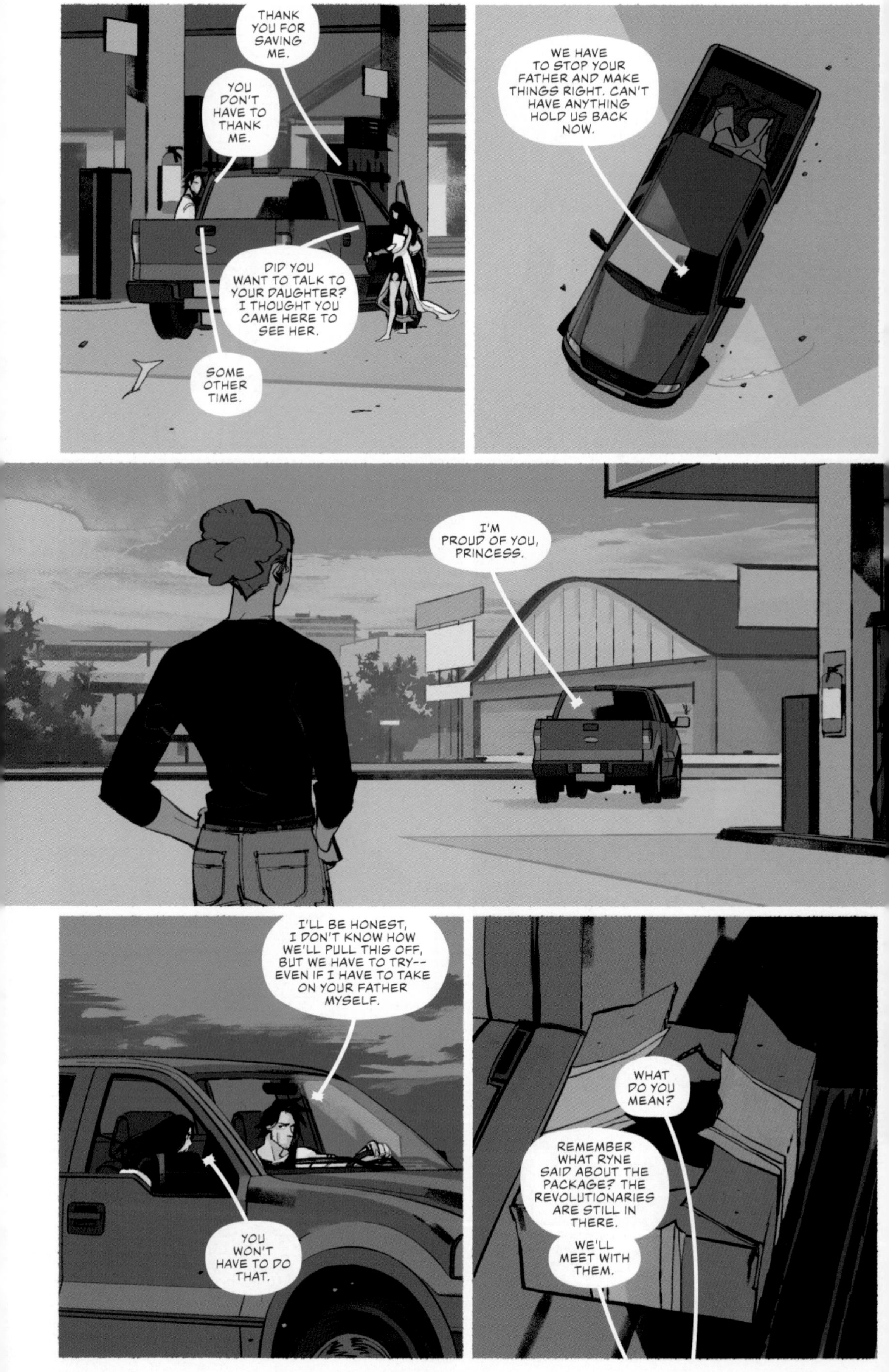
THANK YOU FOR SAVING ME.
YOU DON'T HAVE TO THANK ME.
DID YOU WANT TO TALK TO YOUR DAUGHTER? I THOUGHT YOU CAME HERE TO SEE HER.
SOME OTHER TIME.
WE HAVE TO STOP YOUR FATHER AND MAKE THINGS RIGHT. CAN'T HAVE ANYTHING HOLD US BACK NOW.
I'M PROUD OF YOU, PRINCESS.
I'LL BE HONEST, I DON'T KNOW HOW WE'LL PULL THIS OFF, BUT WE HAVE TO TRY-- EVEN IF I HAVE TO TAKE ON YOUR FATHER MYSELF.
YOU WON'T HAVE TO DO THAT.
WHAT DO YOU MEAN?
REMEMBER WHAT RYNE SAID ABOUT THE PACKAGE? THE REVOLUTIONARIES ARE STILL IN THERE.
WE'LL MEET WITH THEM.

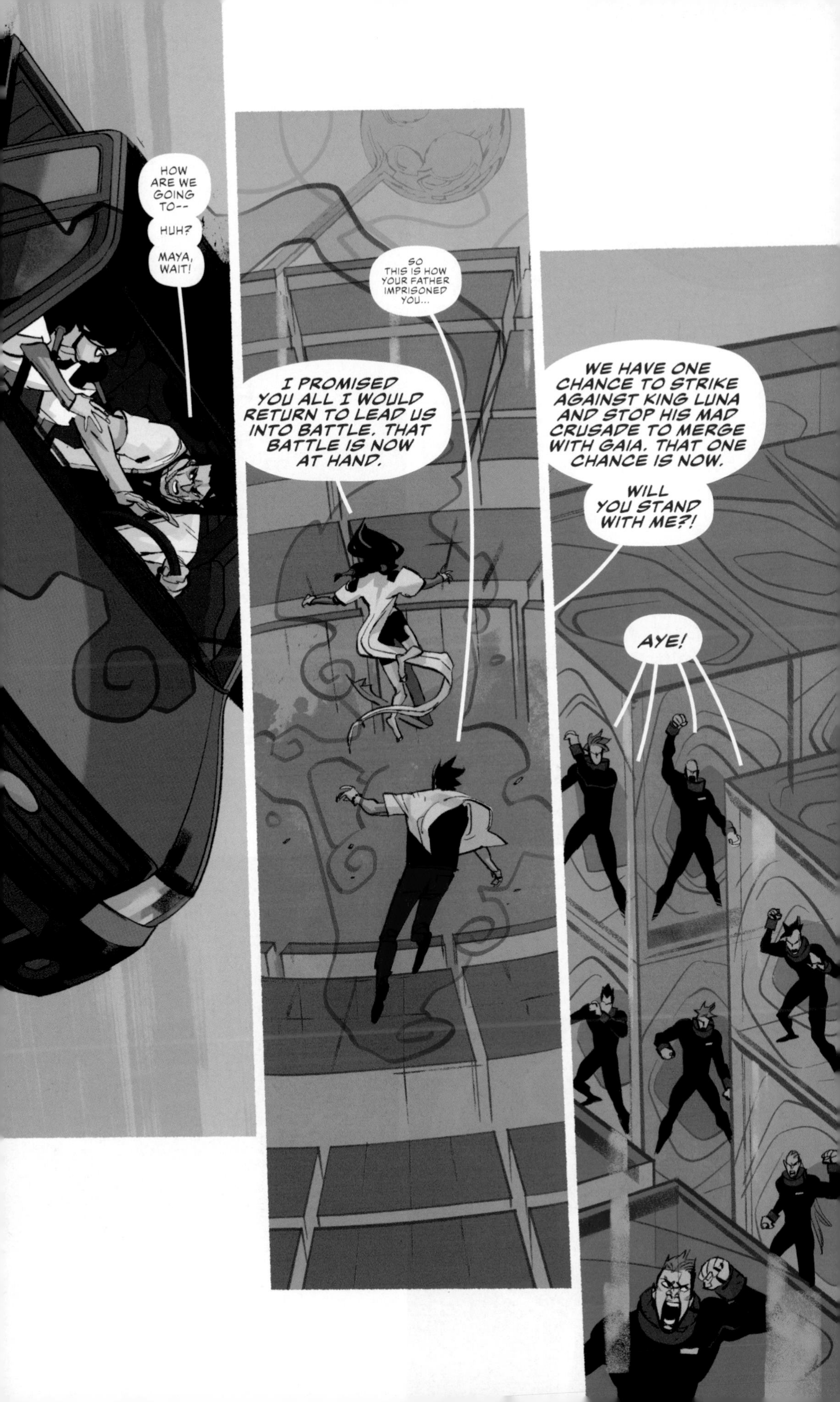

HOW ARE WE GOING TO--
HUH?
MAYA, WAIT!
SO THIS IS HOW YOUR FATHER IMPRISONED YOU...
I PROMISED YOU ALL I WOULD RETURN TO LEAD US INTO BATTLE. THAT BATTLE IS NOW AT HAND.
WE HAVE ONE CHANCE TO STRIKE AGAINST KING LUNA AND STOP HIS MAD CRUSADE TO MERGE WITH GAIA. THAT ONE CHANCE IS NOW.
WILL YOU STAND WITH ME?!
AYE!

MEANWHILE.

HMMM, I SEE YOU HAVE ONE FINAL, DESPERATE PLAN TO PUT INTO MOTION, DON'T YOU?

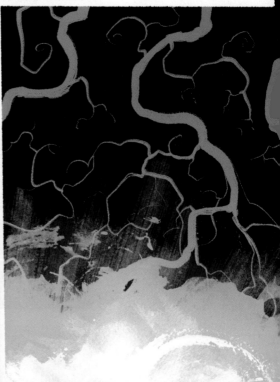

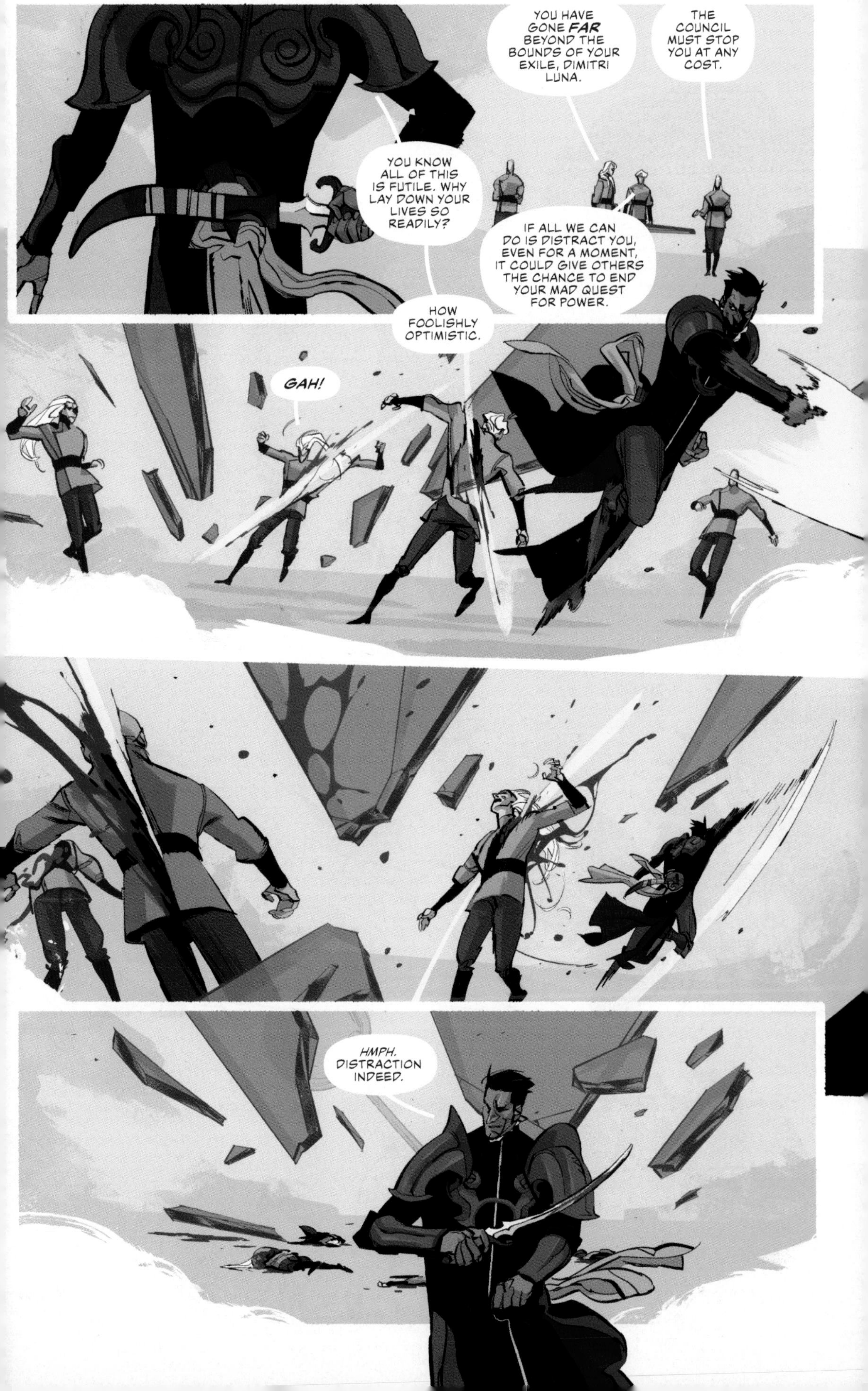
YOU HAVE GONE FAR BEYOND THE BOUNDS OF YOUR EXILE, DIMITRI LUNA.
THE COUNCIL MUST STOP YOU AT ANY COST.
YOU KNOW ALL OF THIS IS FUTILE. WHY LAY DOWN YOUR LIVES SO READILY?
IF ALL WE CAN DO IS DISTRACT YOU, EVEN FOR A MOMENT, IT COULD GIVE OTHERS THE CHANCE TO END YOUR MAD QUEST FOR POWER.
HOW FOOLISHLY OPTIMISTIC.
GAH!
HMPH. DISTRACTION INDEED.

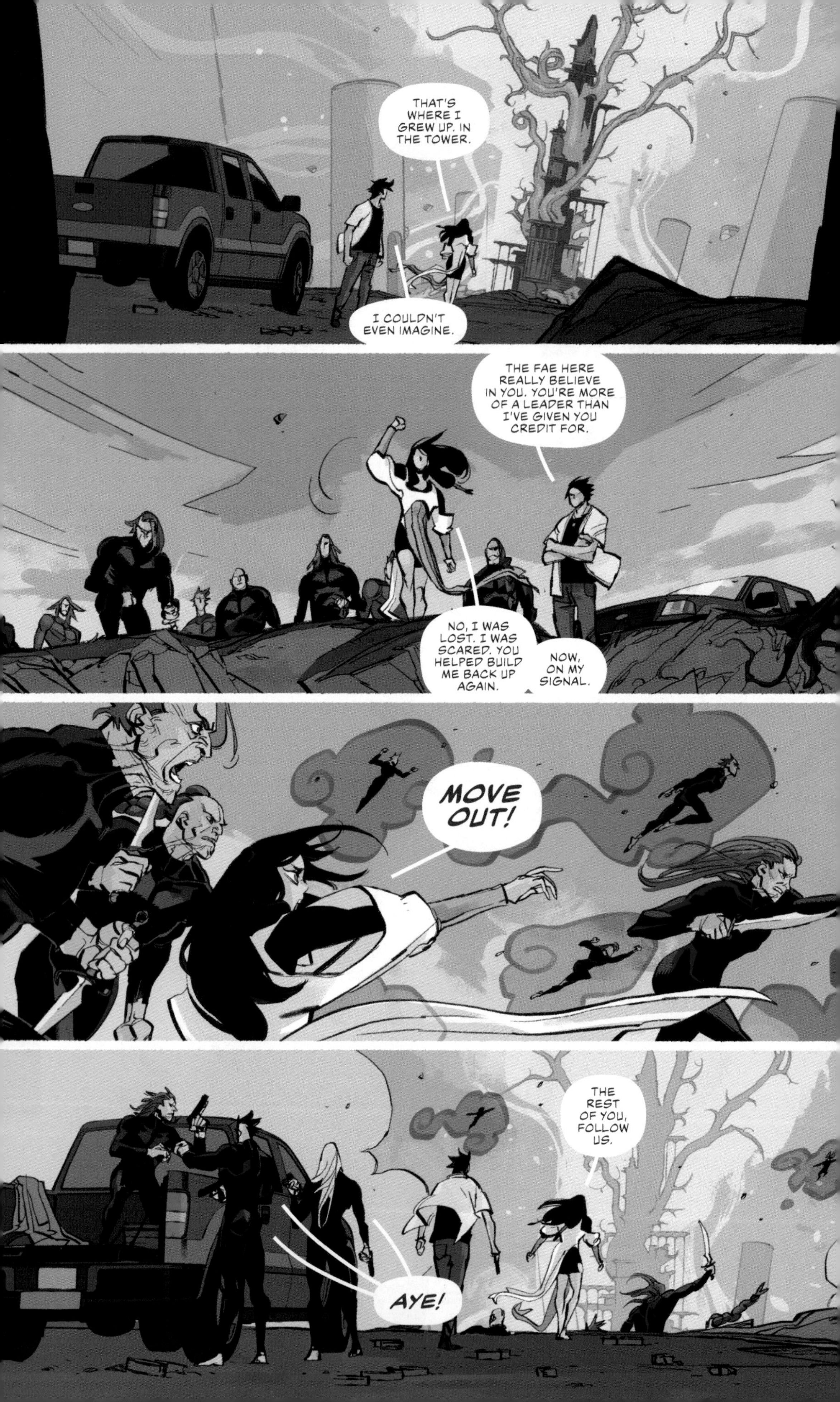
THAT'S WHERE I GREW UP. IN THE TOWER.
I COULDN'T EVEN IMAGINE.
THE FAE HERE REALLY BELIEVE IN YOU. YOU'RE MORE OF A LEADER THAN I'VE GIVEN YOU CREDIT FOR.
NO, I WAS LOST. I WAS SCARED. YOU HELPED BUILD ME BACK UP AGAIN.
NOW, ON MY SIGNAL.
MOVE OUT!
THE REST OF YOU, FOLLOW US.
AYE!

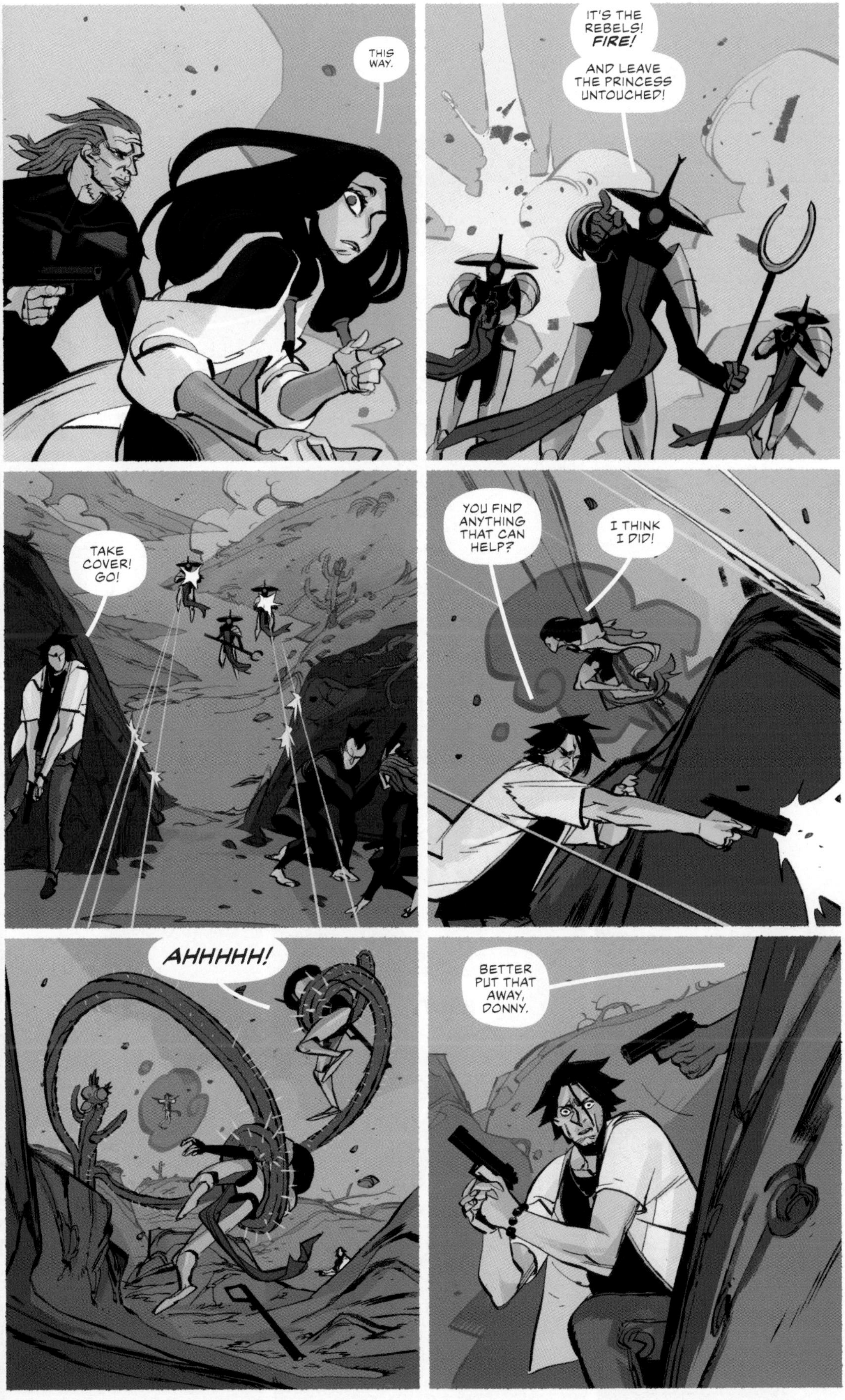
THIS WAY.
IT'S THE REBELS! FIRE!
AND LEAVE THE PRINCESS UNTOUCHED!
TAKE COVER! GO!
YOU FIND ANYTHING THAT CAN HELP?
I THINK I DID!
AHHHHH!
BETTER PUT THAT AWAY, DONNY.

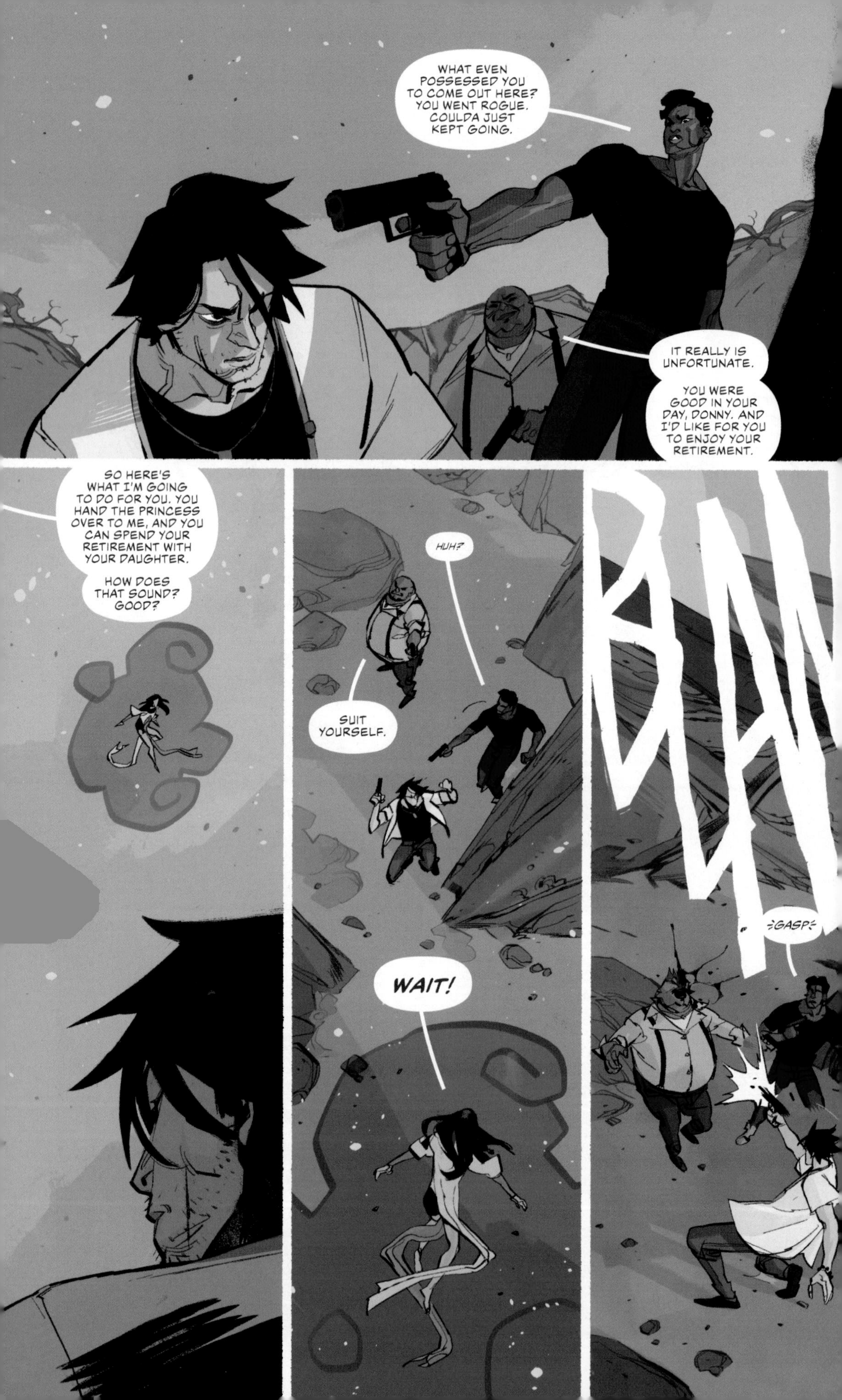

WHAT EVEN POSSESSED YOU TO COME OUT HERE? YOU WENT ROGUE. COULDA JUST KEPT GOING.
IT REALLY IS UNFORTUNATE.
YOU WERE GOOD IN YOUR DAY, DONNY. AND I'D LIKE FOR YOU TO ENJOY YOUR RETIREMENT.
SO HERE'S WHAT I'M GOING TO DO FOR YOU. YOU HAND THE PRINCESS OVER TO ME, AND YOU CAN SPEND YOUR RETIREMENT WITH YOUR DAUGHTER.
HOW DOES THAT SOUND? GOOD?
HUH?
SUIT YOURSELF.
WAIT!
BLAM
GASP

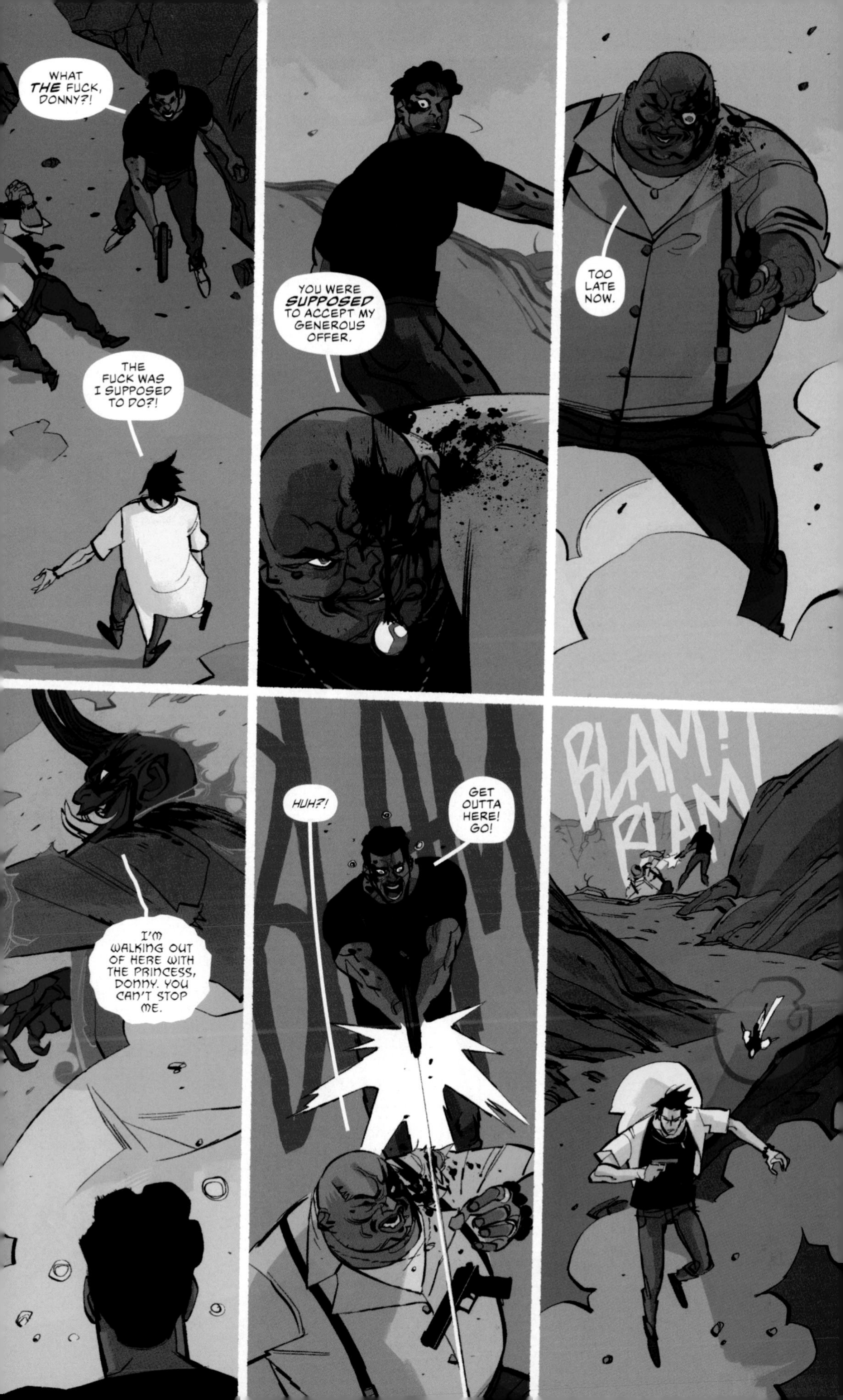
WHAT THE FUCK, DONNY?!
THE FUCK WAS I SUPPOSED TO DO?!
YOU WERE SUPPOSED TO ACCEPT MY GENEROUS OFFER.
TOO LATE NOW.
I'M WALKING OUT OF HERE WITH THE PRINCESS, DONNY. YOU CAN'T STOP ME.
HUH?!
GET OUTTA HERE! GO!
BLAM! BLAM!

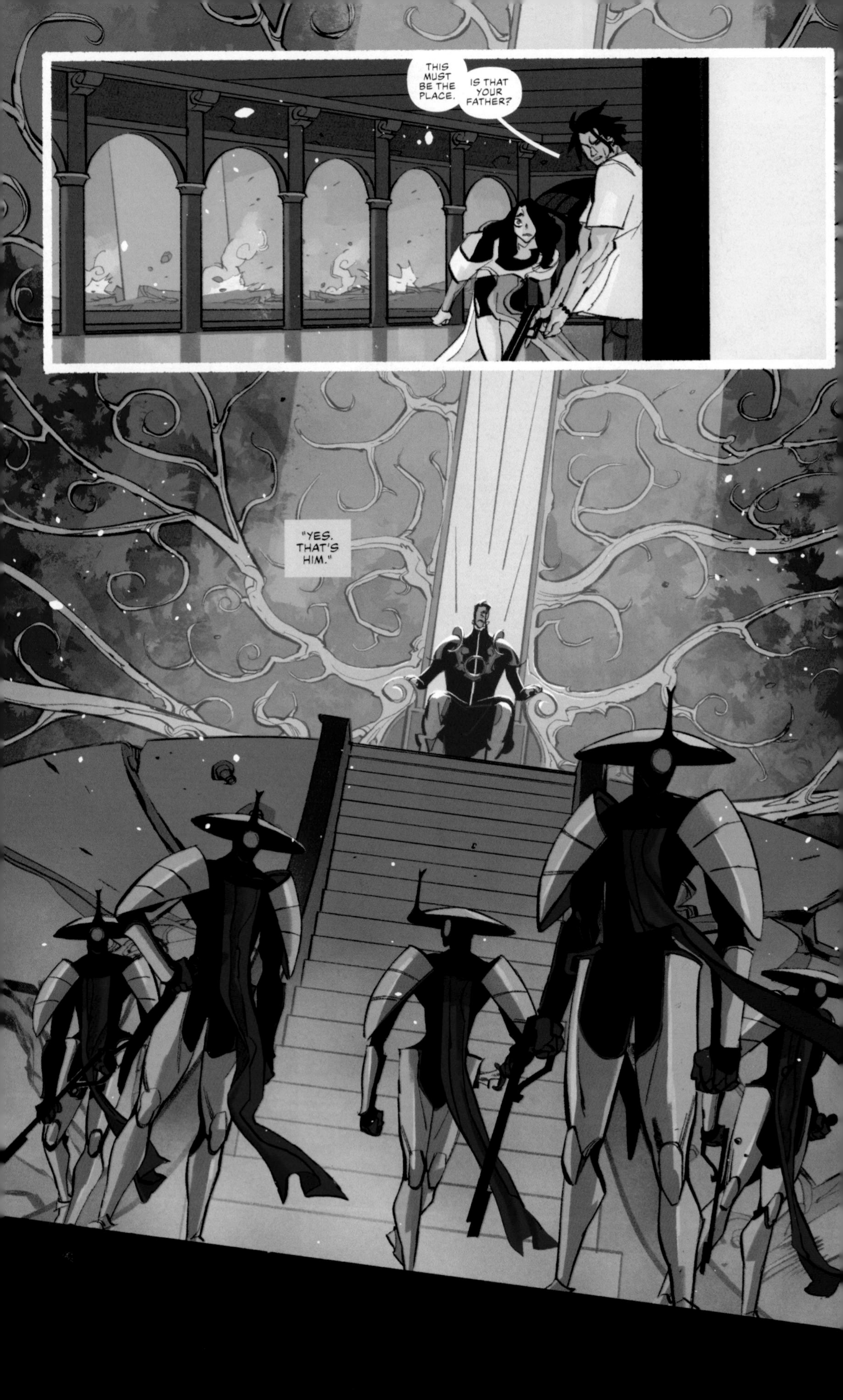
THIS MUST BE THE PLACE.
IS THAT YOUR FATHER?
"YES. THAT'S HIM."

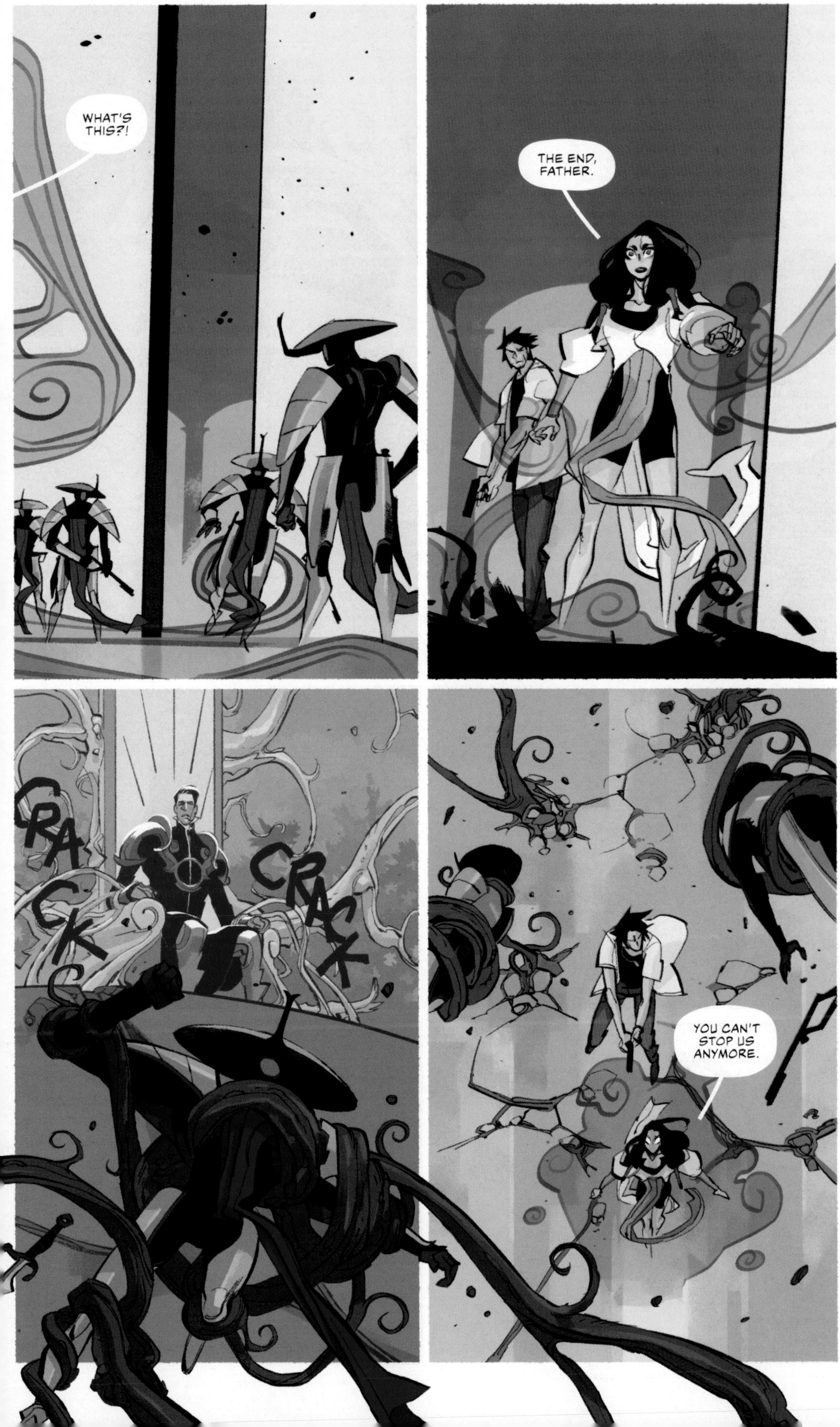
WHAT'S THIS?!
THE END, FATHER.
CRACK
CRACK
YOU CAN'T STOP US ANYMORE.

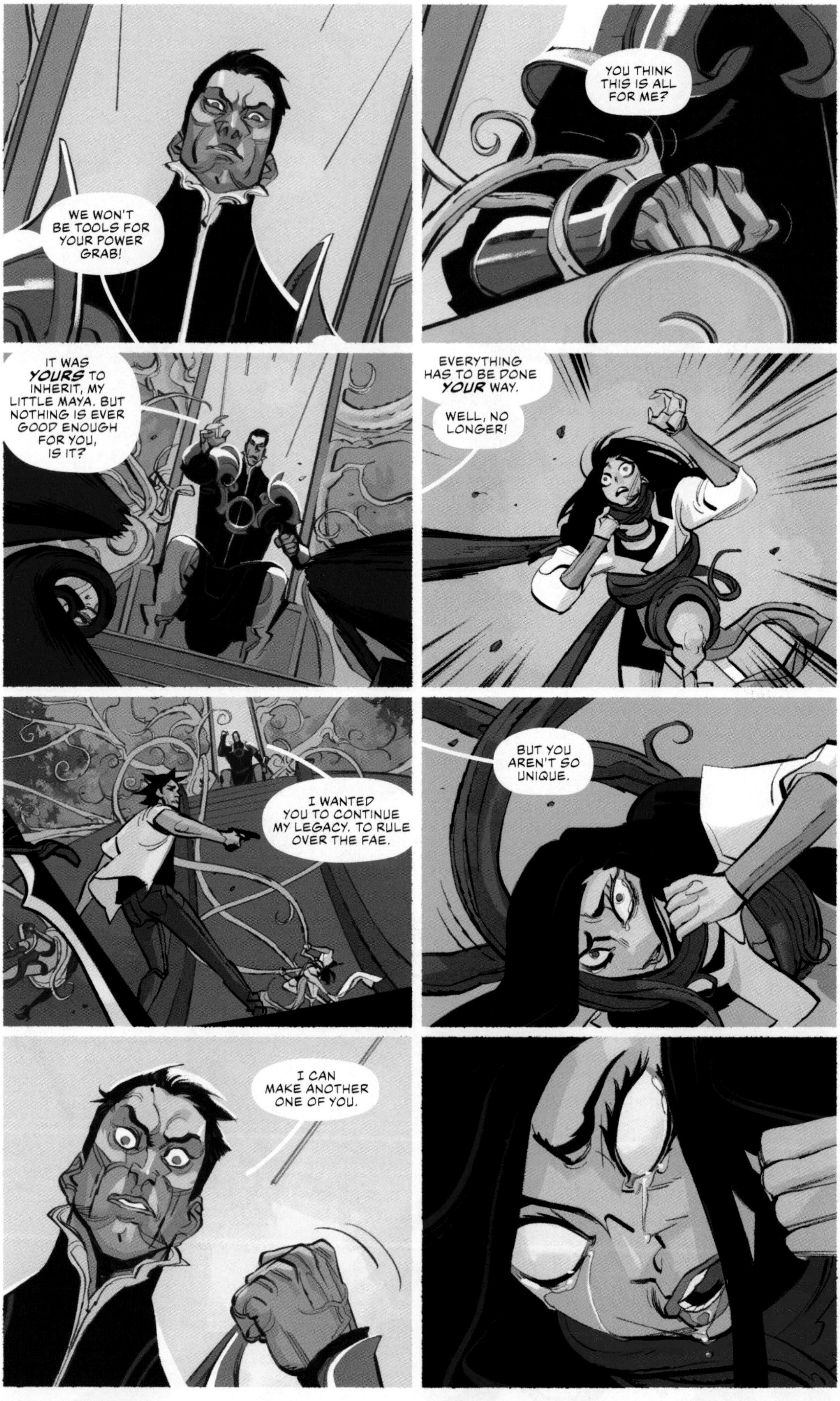
WE WON'T BE TOOLS FOR YOUR POWER GRAB!
YOU THINK THIS IS ALL FOR ME?
IT WAS *YOURS* TO INHERIT, MY LITTLE MAYA. BUT NOTHING IS EVER GOOD ENOUGH FOR YOU, IS IT?
EVERYTHING HAS TO BE DONE *YOUR* WAY.
WELL, NO LONGER!
I WANTED YOU TO CONTINUE MY LEGACY. TO RULE OVER THE FAE.
BUT YOU AREN'T SO UNIQUE.
I CAN MAKE ANOTHER ONE OF YOU.

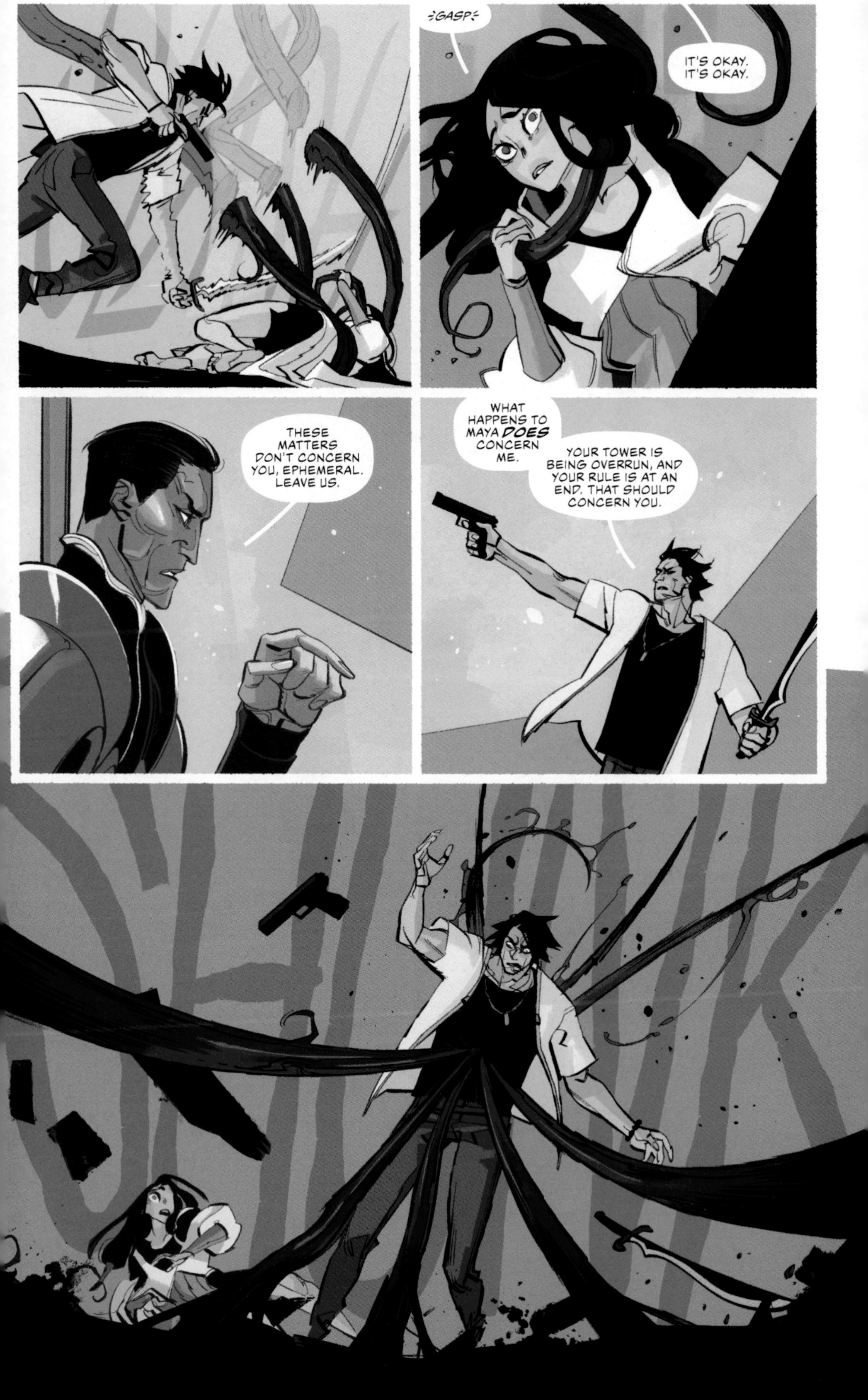

GASP
IT'S OKAY. IT'S OKAY.
THESE MATTERS DON'T CONCERN YOU, EPHEMERAL. LEAVE US.
WHAT HAPPENS TO MAYA DOES CONCERN ME.
YOUR TOWER IS BEING OVERRUN, AND YOUR RULE IS AT AN END. THAT SHOULD CONCERN YOU.

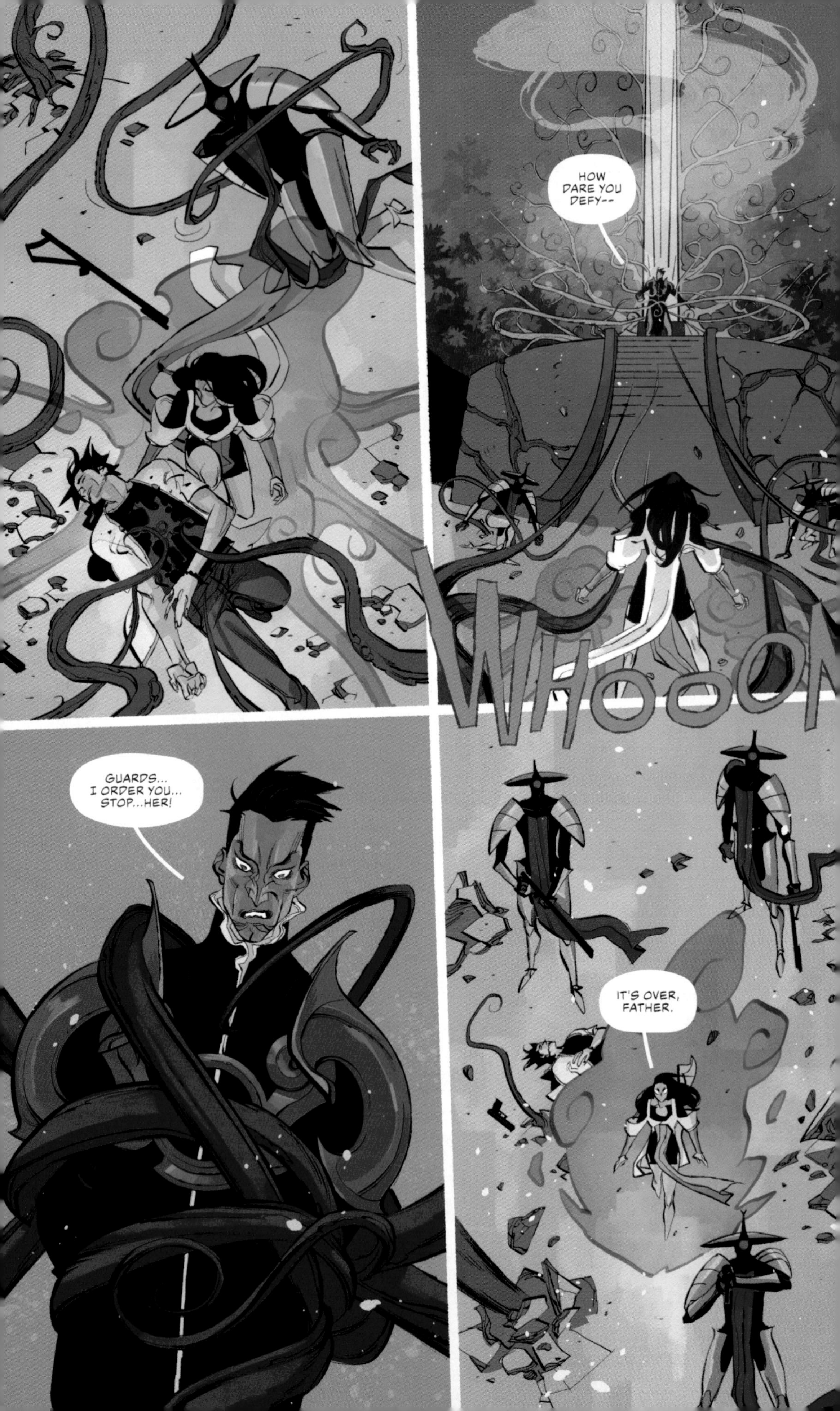
HOW DARE YOU DEFY--
WHOOOM
GUARDS... I ORDER YOU... STOP...HER!
IT'S OVER, FATHER.

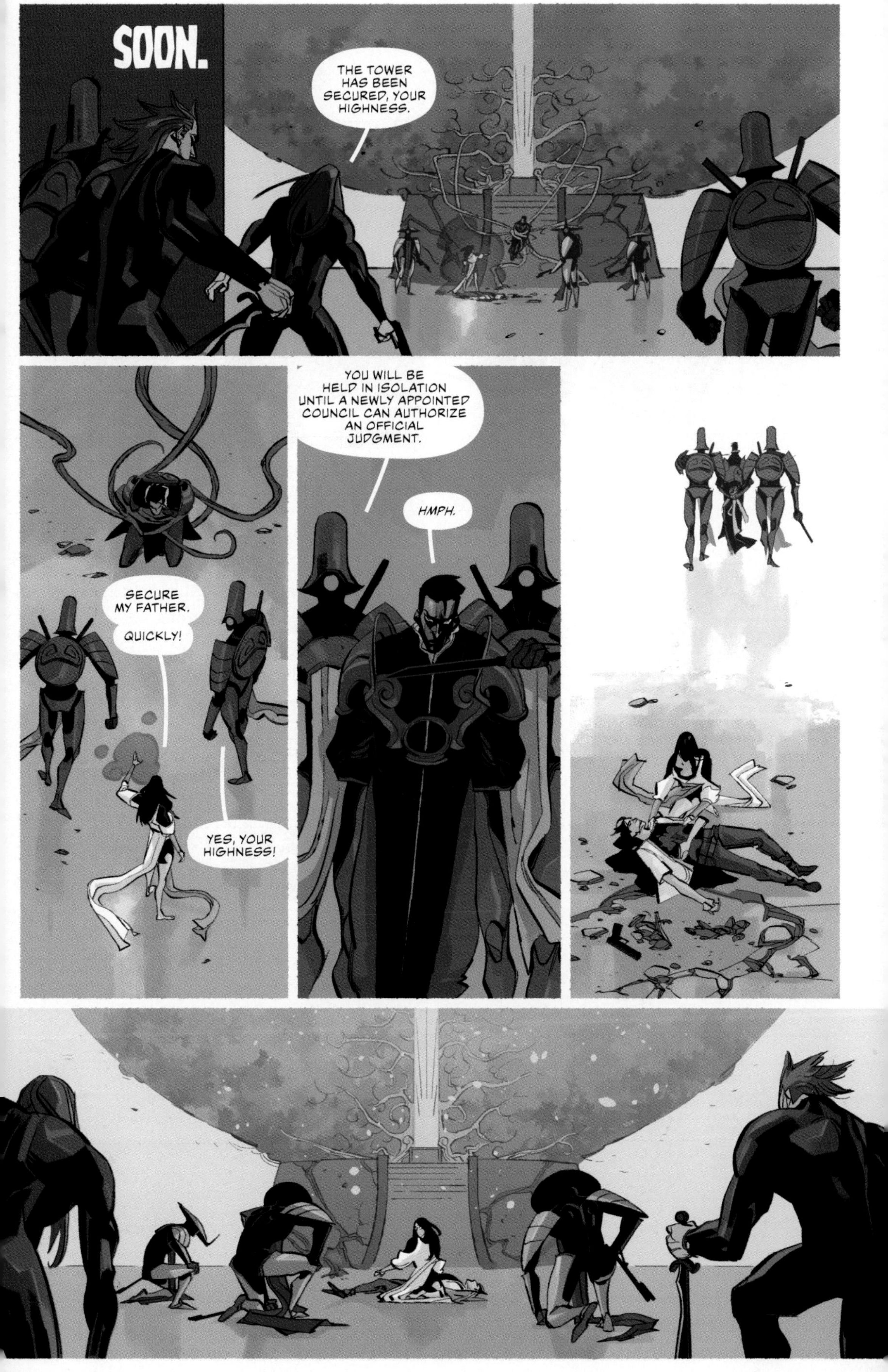
SOON.
THE TOWER HAS BEEN SECURED, YOUR HIGHNESS.
SECURE MY FATHER.
QUICKLY!
YES, YOUR HIGHNESS!
YOU WILL BE HELD IN ISOLATION UNTIL A NEWLY APPOINTED COUNCIL CAN AUTHORIZE AN OFFICIAL JUDGMENT.
HMPH.

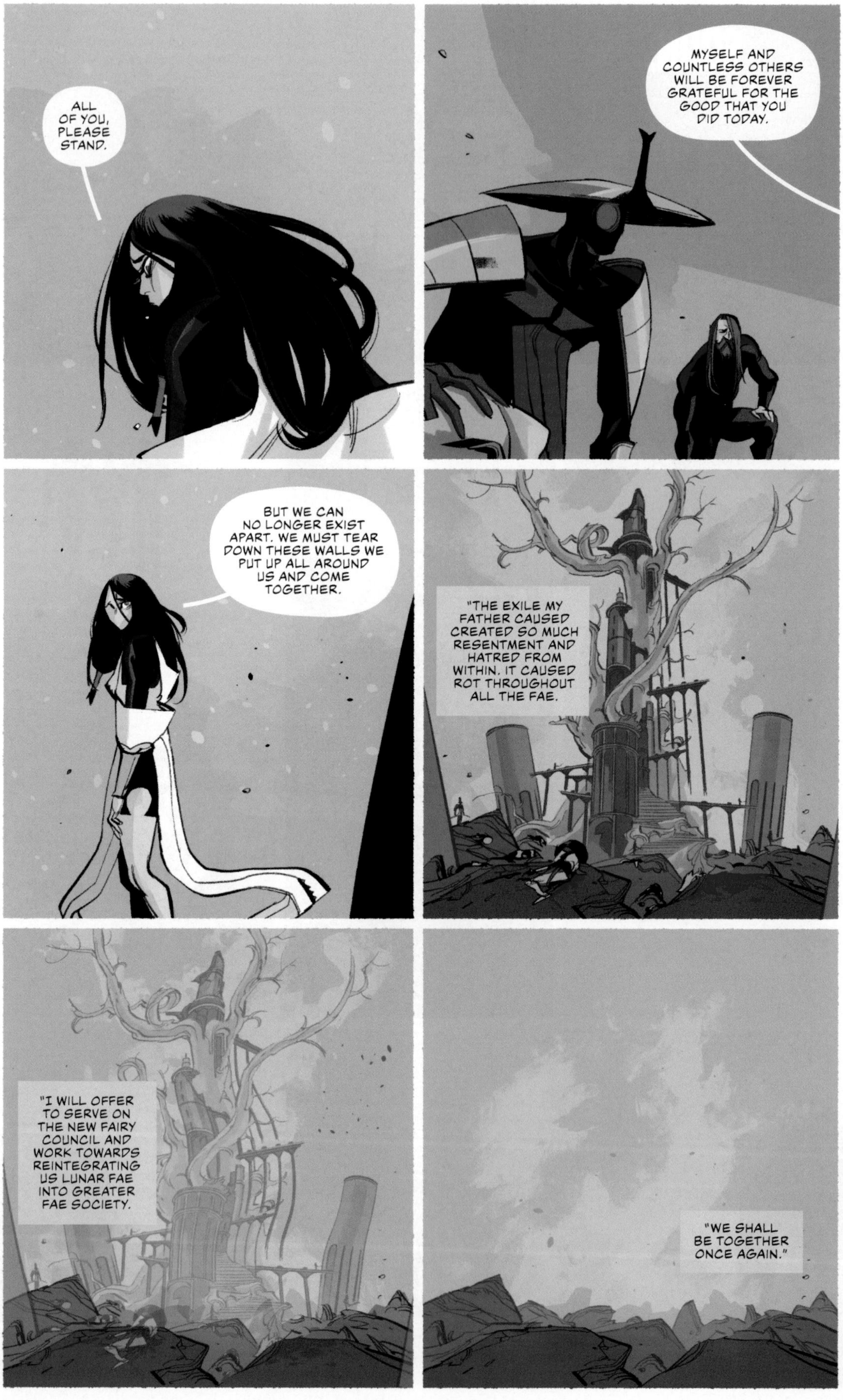
ALL OF YOU, PLEASE STAND.
MYSELF AND COUNTLESS OTHERS WILL BE FOREVER GRATEFUL FOR THE GOOD THAT YOU DID TODAY.
BUT WE CAN NO LONGER EXIST APART. WE MUST TEAR DOWN THESE WALLS WE PUT UP ALL AROUND US AND COME TOGETHER.
"THE EXILE MY FATHER CAUSED CREATED SO MUCH RESENTMENT AND HATRED FROM WITHIN. IT CAUSED ROT THROUGHOUT ALL THE FAE.
"I WILL OFFER TO SERVE ON THE NEW FAIRY COUNCIL AND WORK TOWARDS REINTEGRATING US LUNAR FAE INTO GREATER FAE SOCIETY.
"WE SHALL BE TOGETHER ONCE AGAIN."

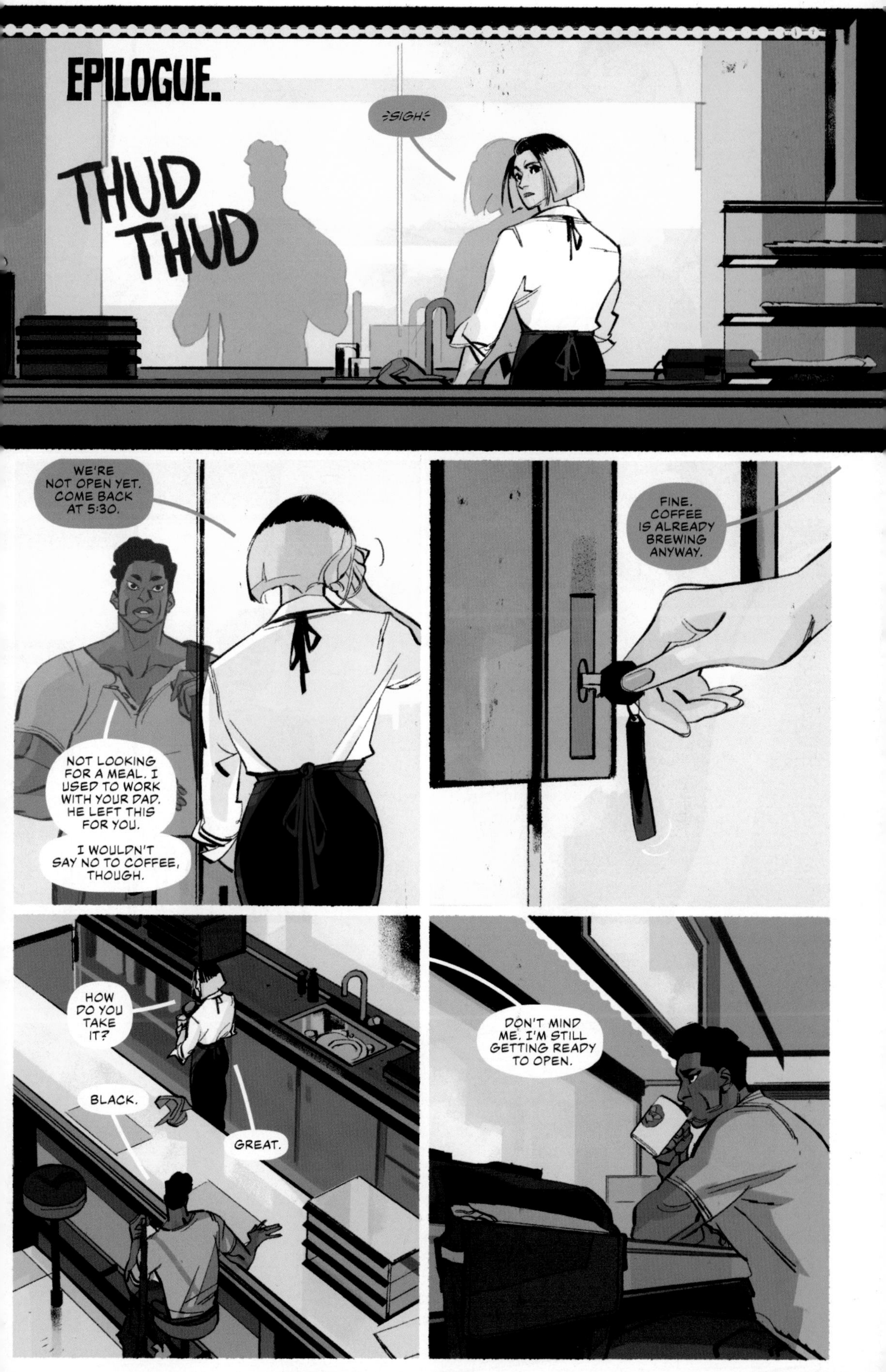
EPILOGUE.
THUD THUD
≈SIGH≈
WE'RE NOT OPEN YET. COME BACK AT 5:30.
NOT LOOKING FOR A MEAL. I USED TO WORK WITH YOUR DAD. HE LEFT THIS FOR YOU.
I WOULDN'T SAY NO TO COFFEE, THOUGH.
FINE. COFFEE IS ALREADY BREWING ANYWAY.
HOW DO YOU TAKE IT?
BLACK.
GREAT.
DON'T MIND ME. I'M STILL GETTING READY TO OPEN.

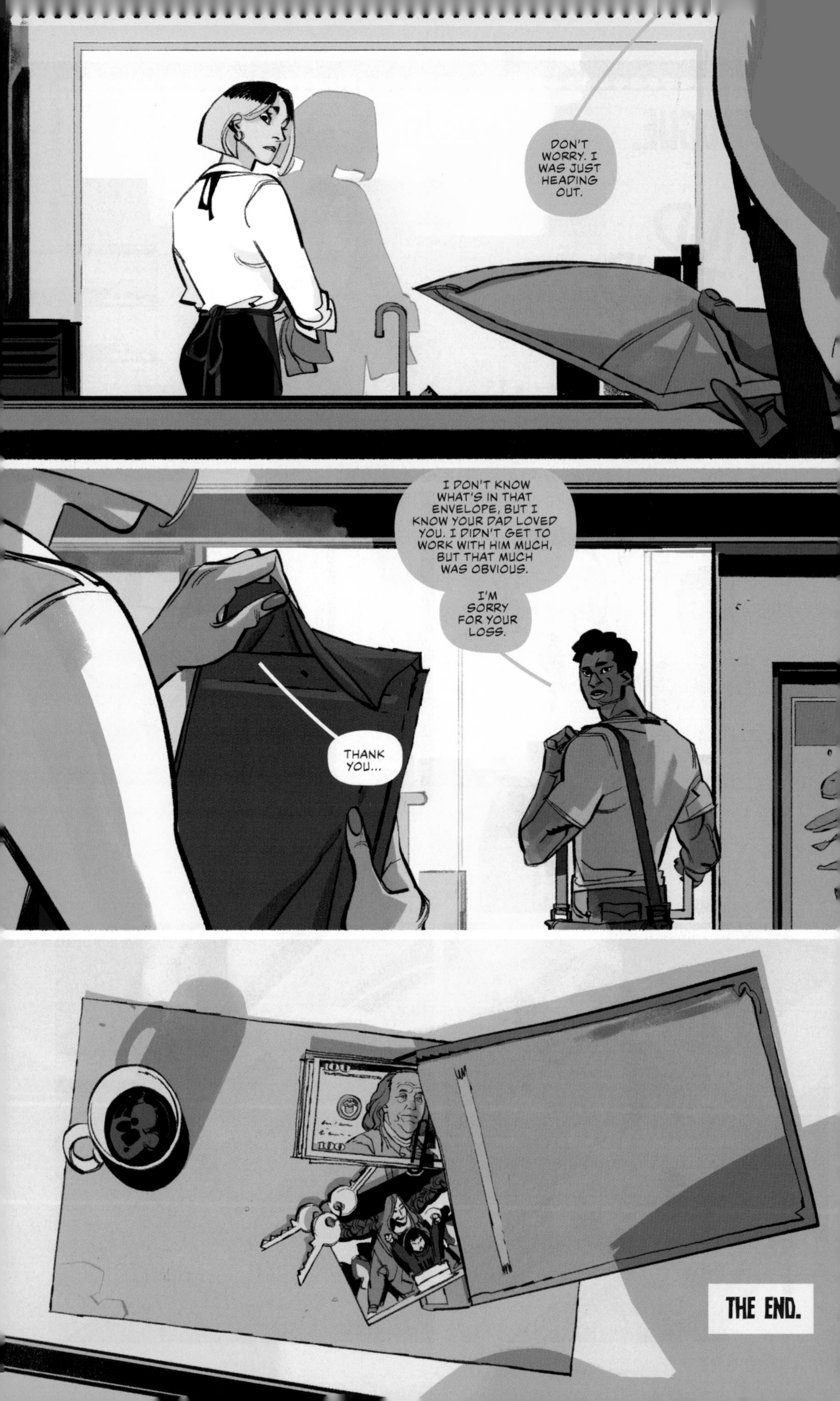
DON'T WORRY. I WAS JUST HEADING OUT.
I DON'T KNOW WHAT'S IN THAT ENVELOPE, BUT I KNOW YOUR DAD LOVED YOU. I DIDN'T GET TO WORK WITH HIM MUCH, BUT THAT MUCH WAS OBVIOUS.
I'M SORRY FOR YOUR LOSS.
THANK YOU...
THE END.

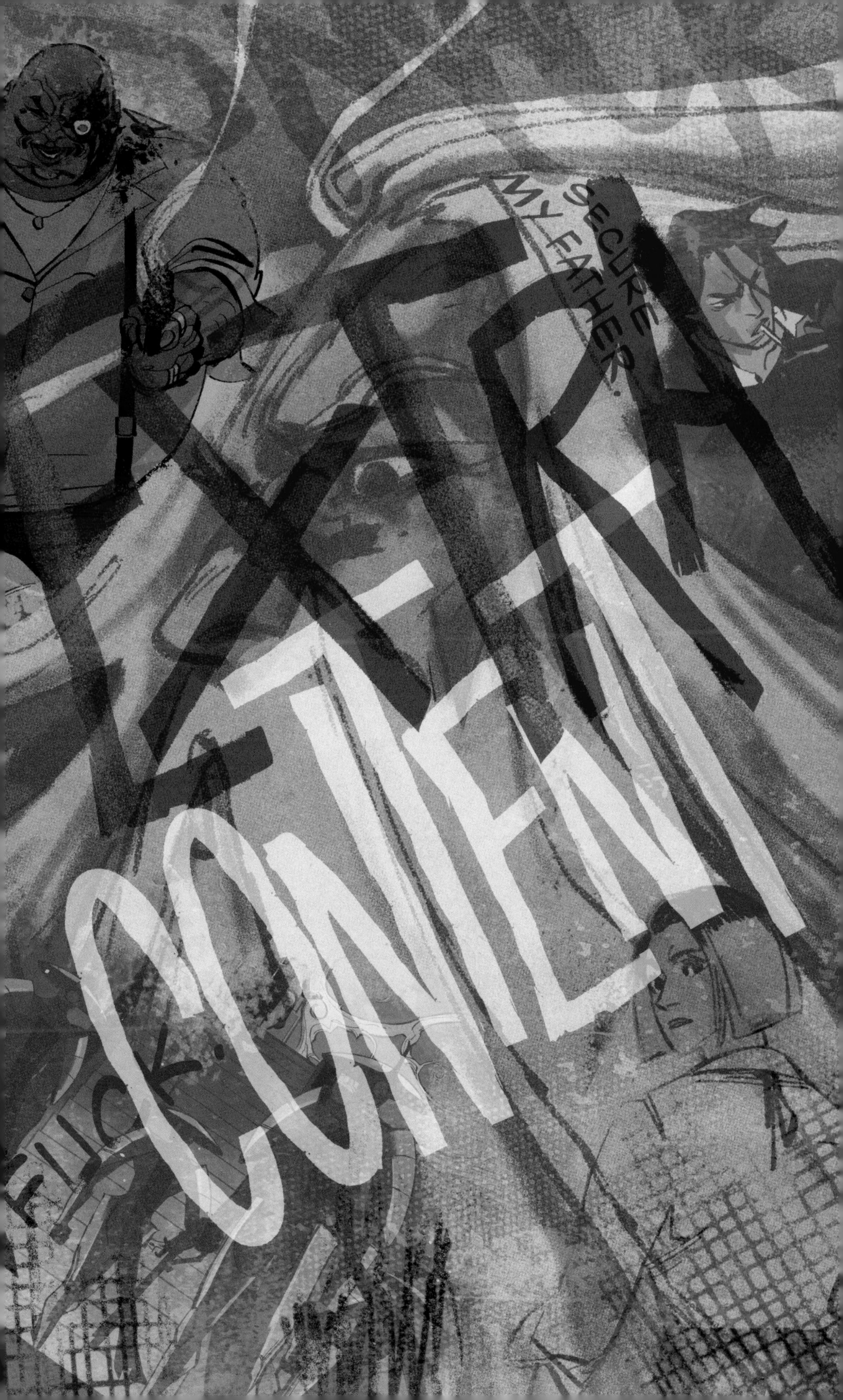
EXTRA
CONTENT
SECURE MY FATHER.
FLICK

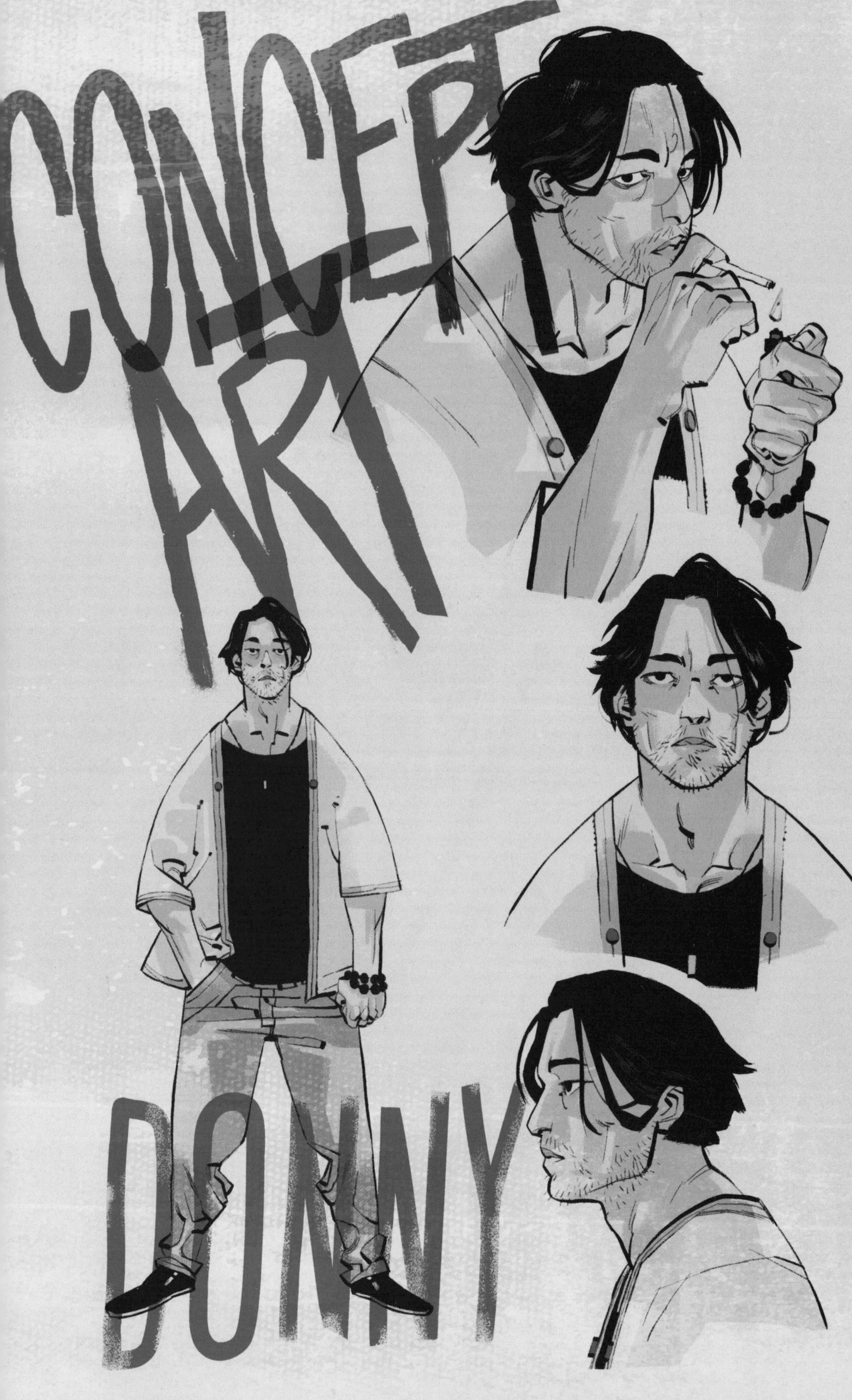
CONCEPT ART
DONNY

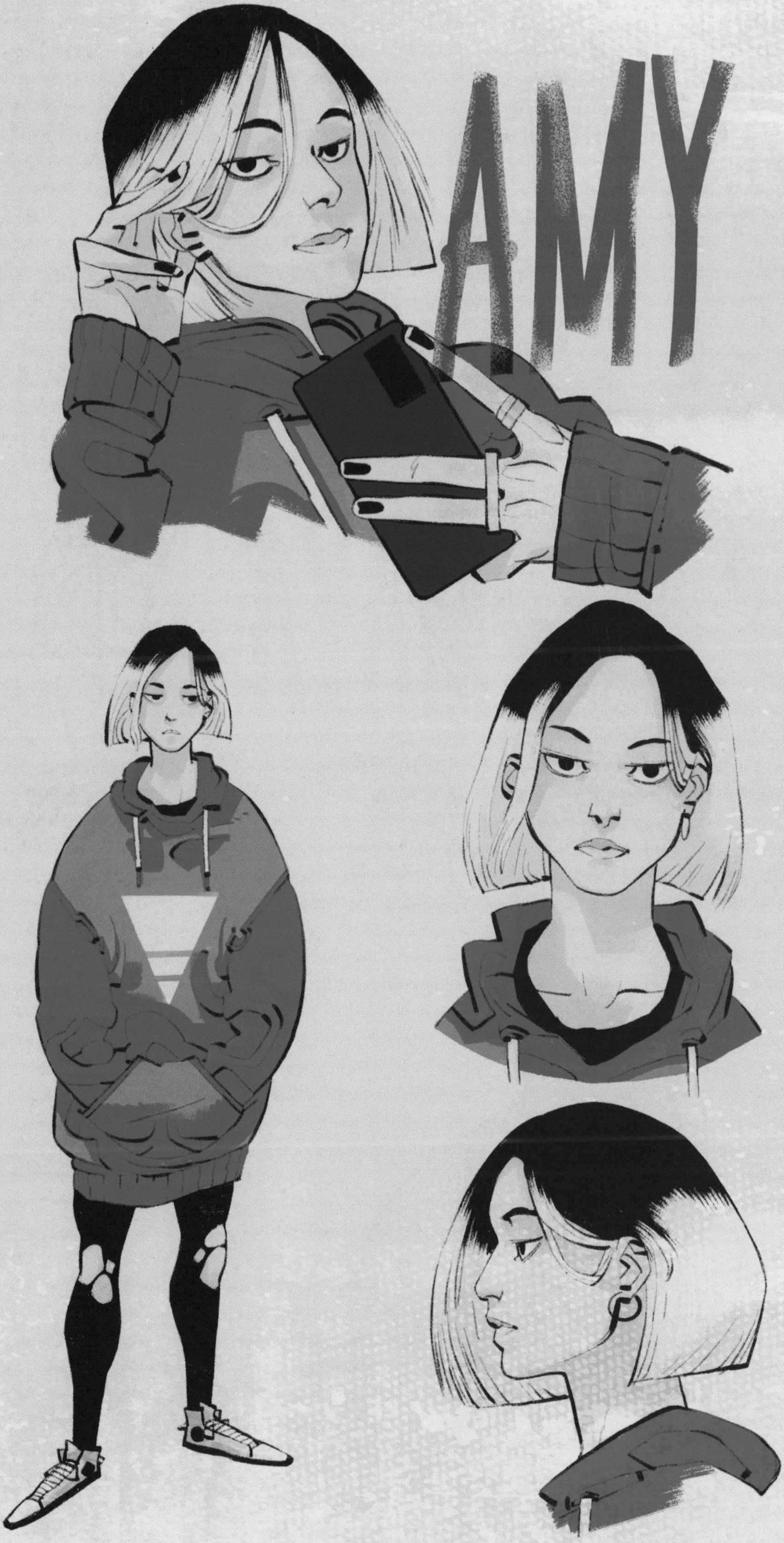
AMY

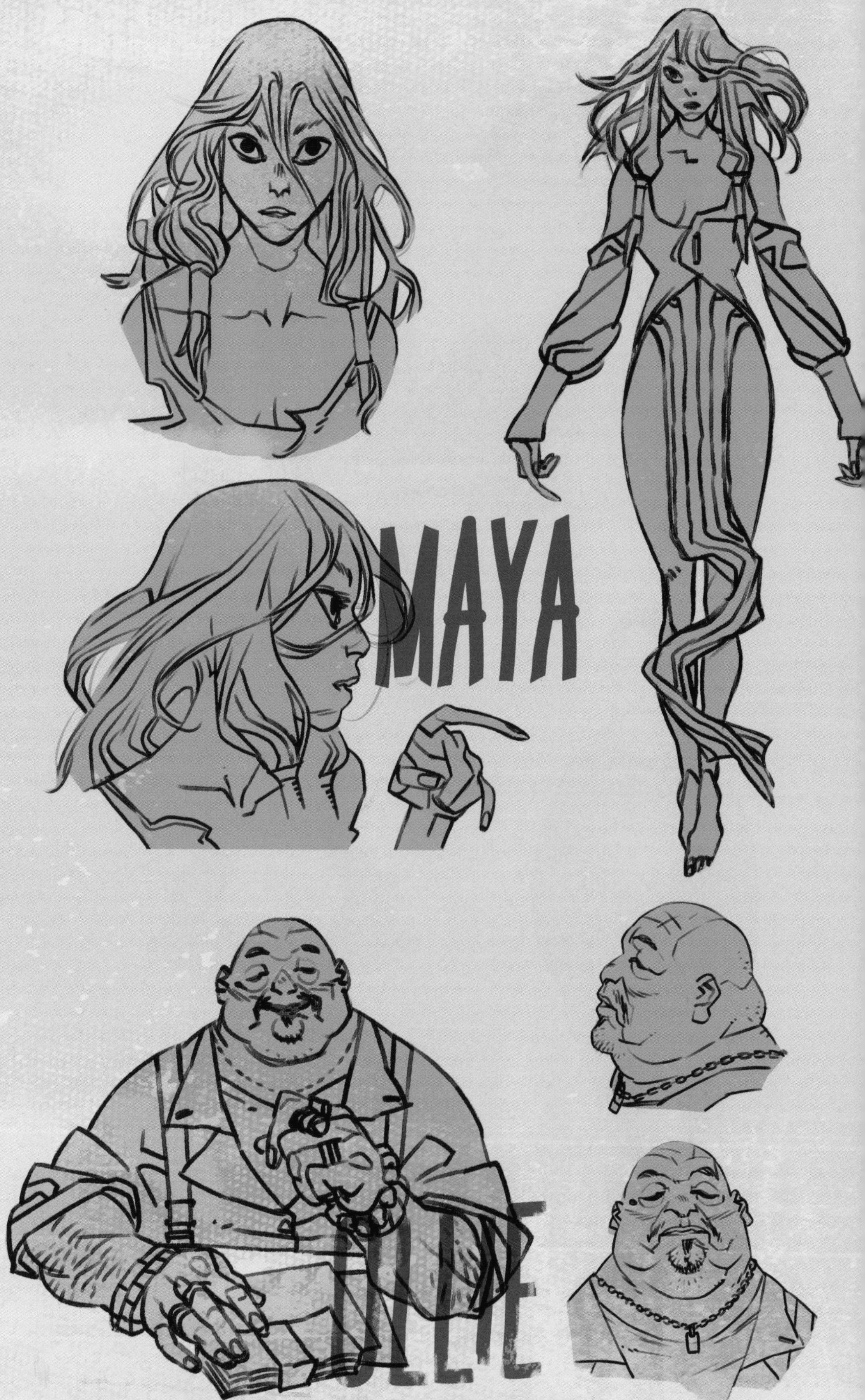
MAYA
OLLIE

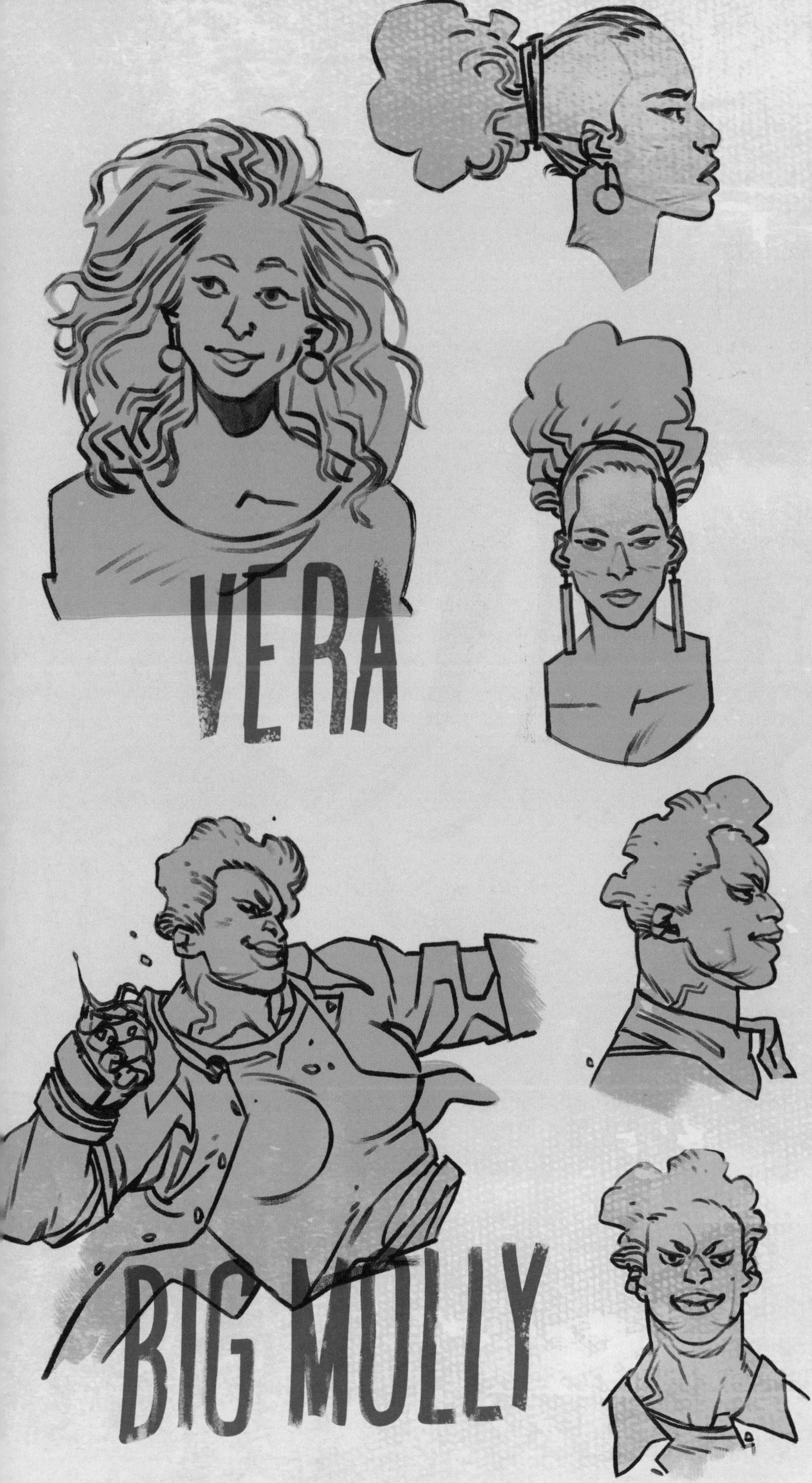
VERA
BIG MOLLY

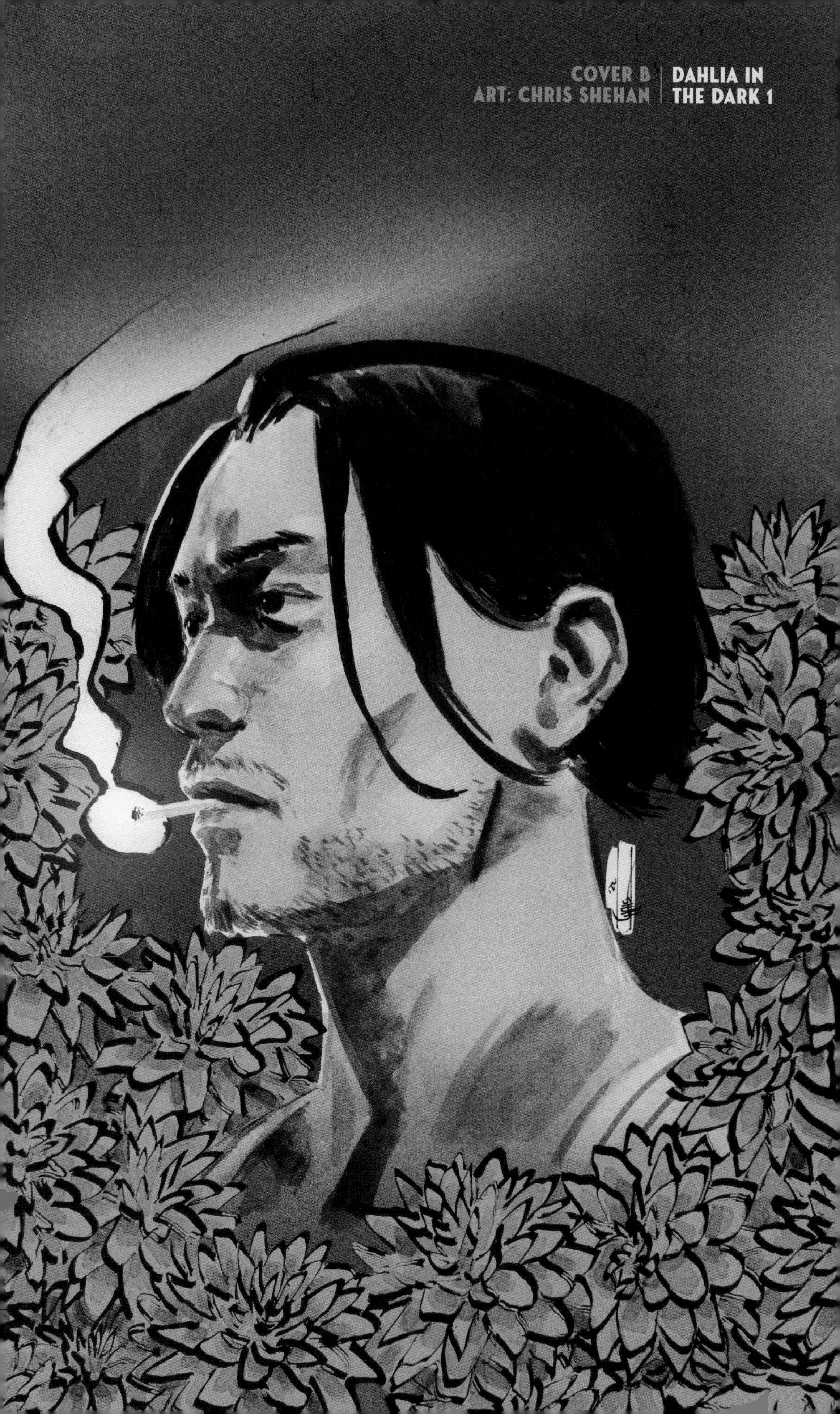
COVER B
ART: CHRIS SHEHAN
DAHLIA IN THE DARK 1

COVER B | DAHLIA IN THE DARK 2
ART: CHRIS SHEHAN

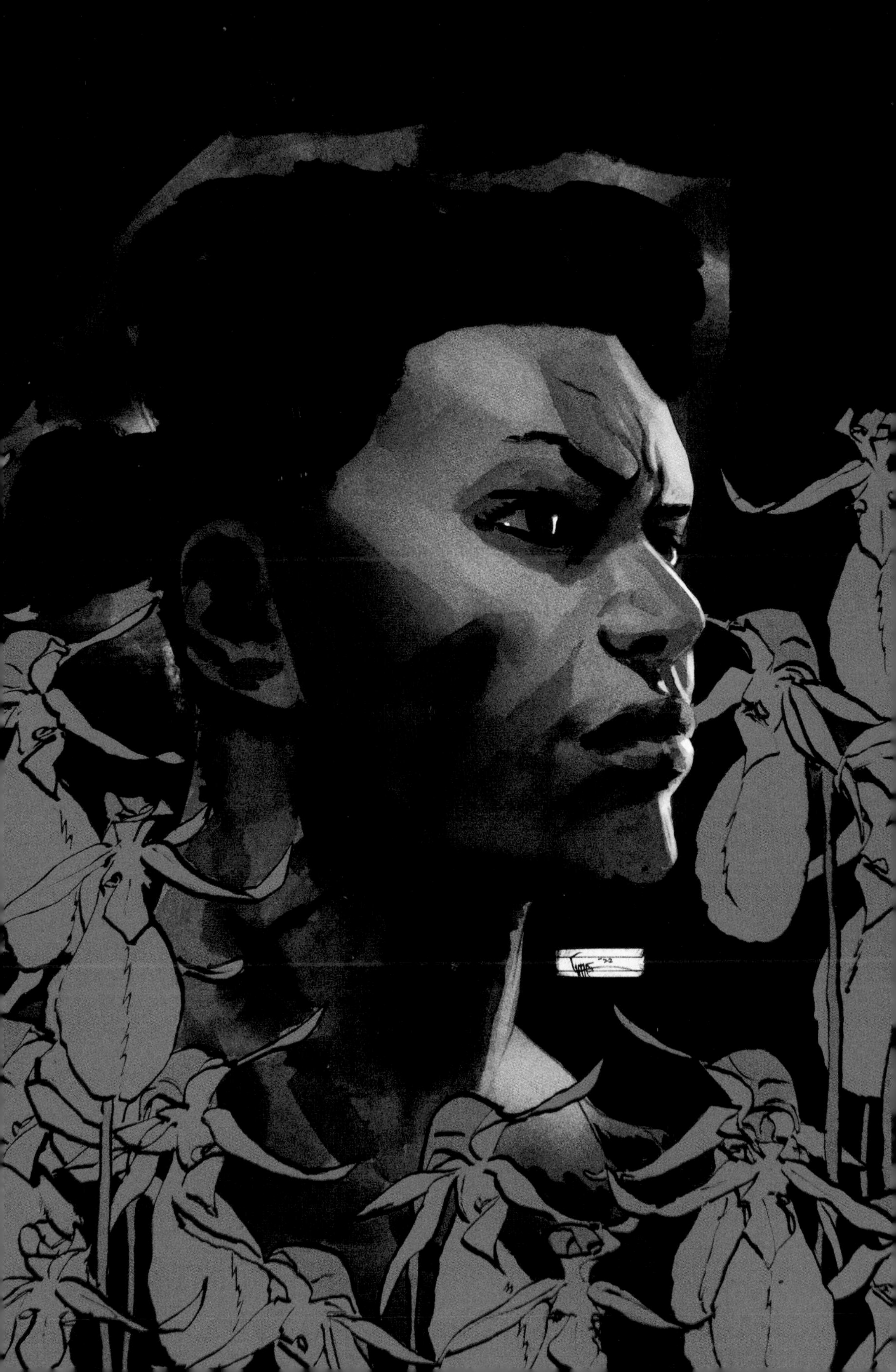

COVER B | ART: CHRIS SHEHAN | DAHLIA IN THE DARK 3

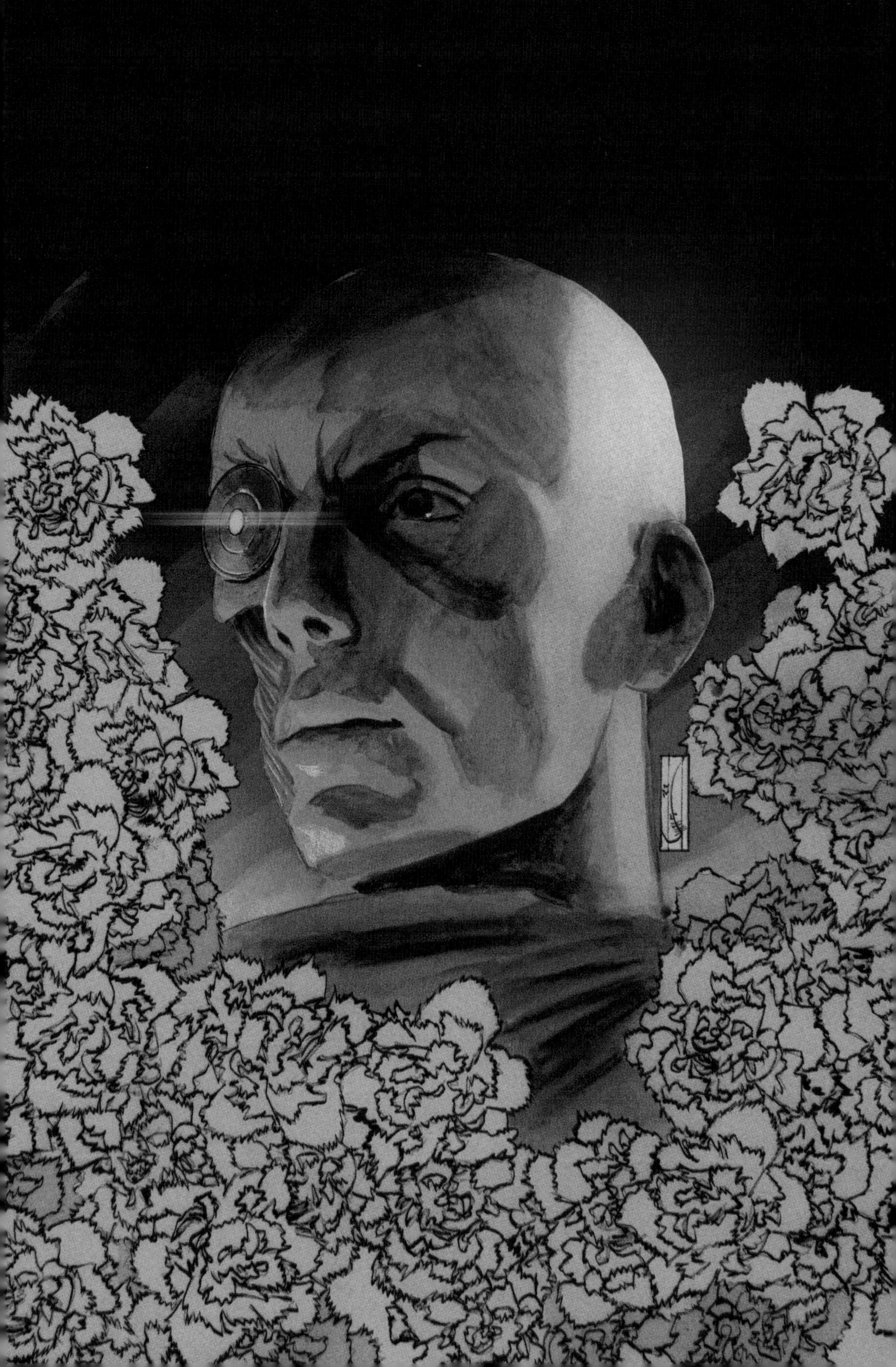

COVER B
ART: CHRIS SHEHAN

DAHLIA IN
THE DARK 4

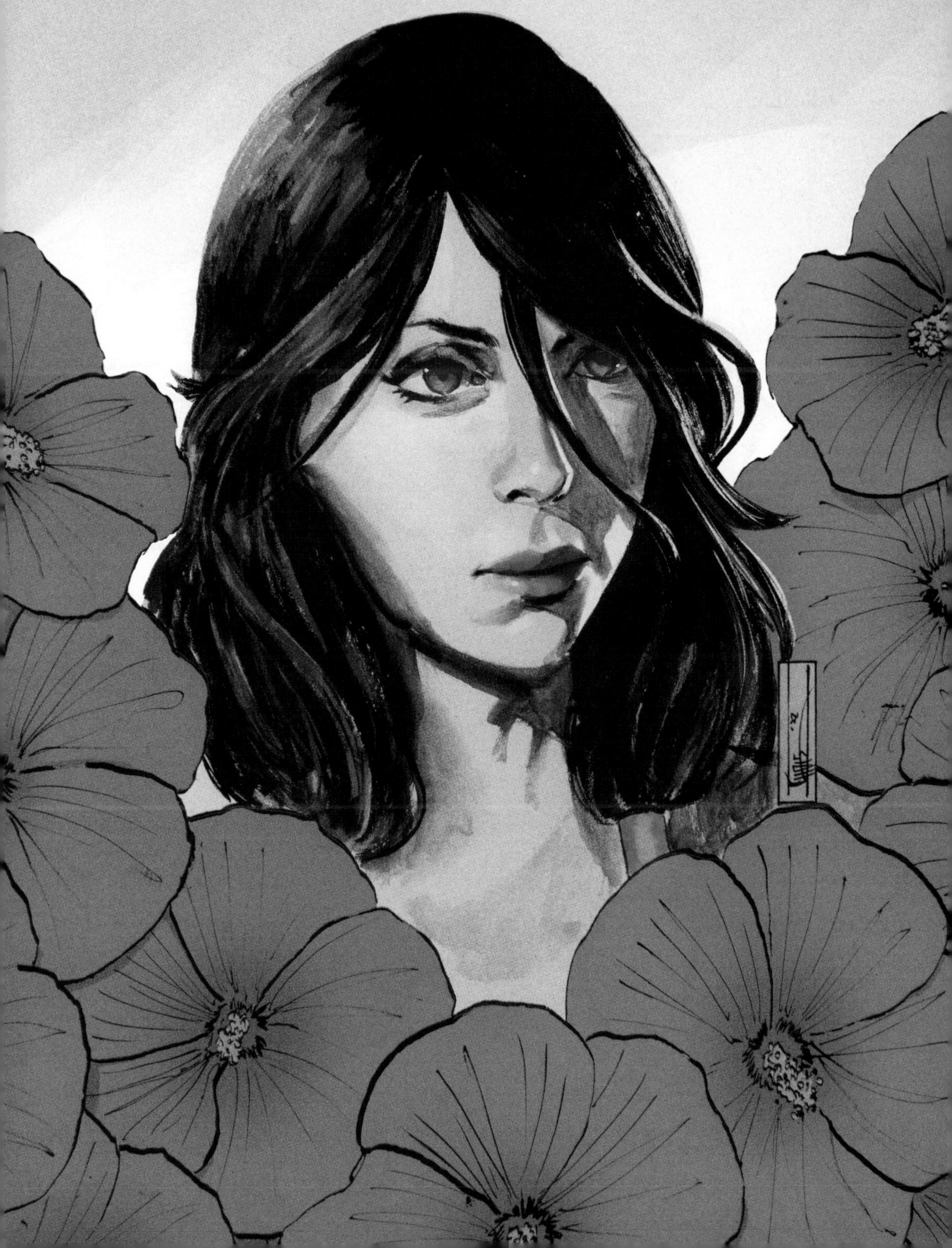

COVER B | DAHLIA IN
ART: CHRIS SHEHAN | THE DARK 5

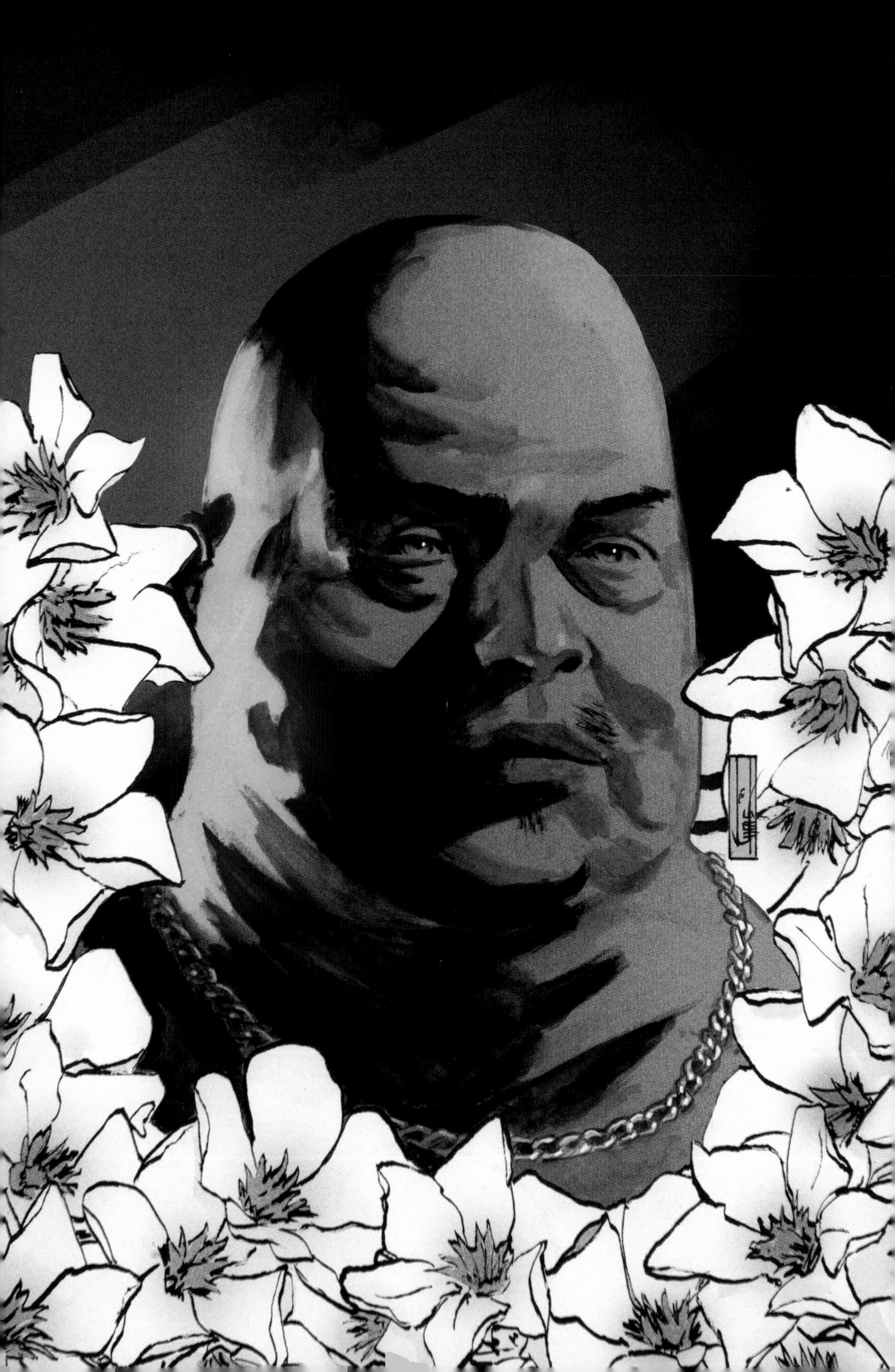

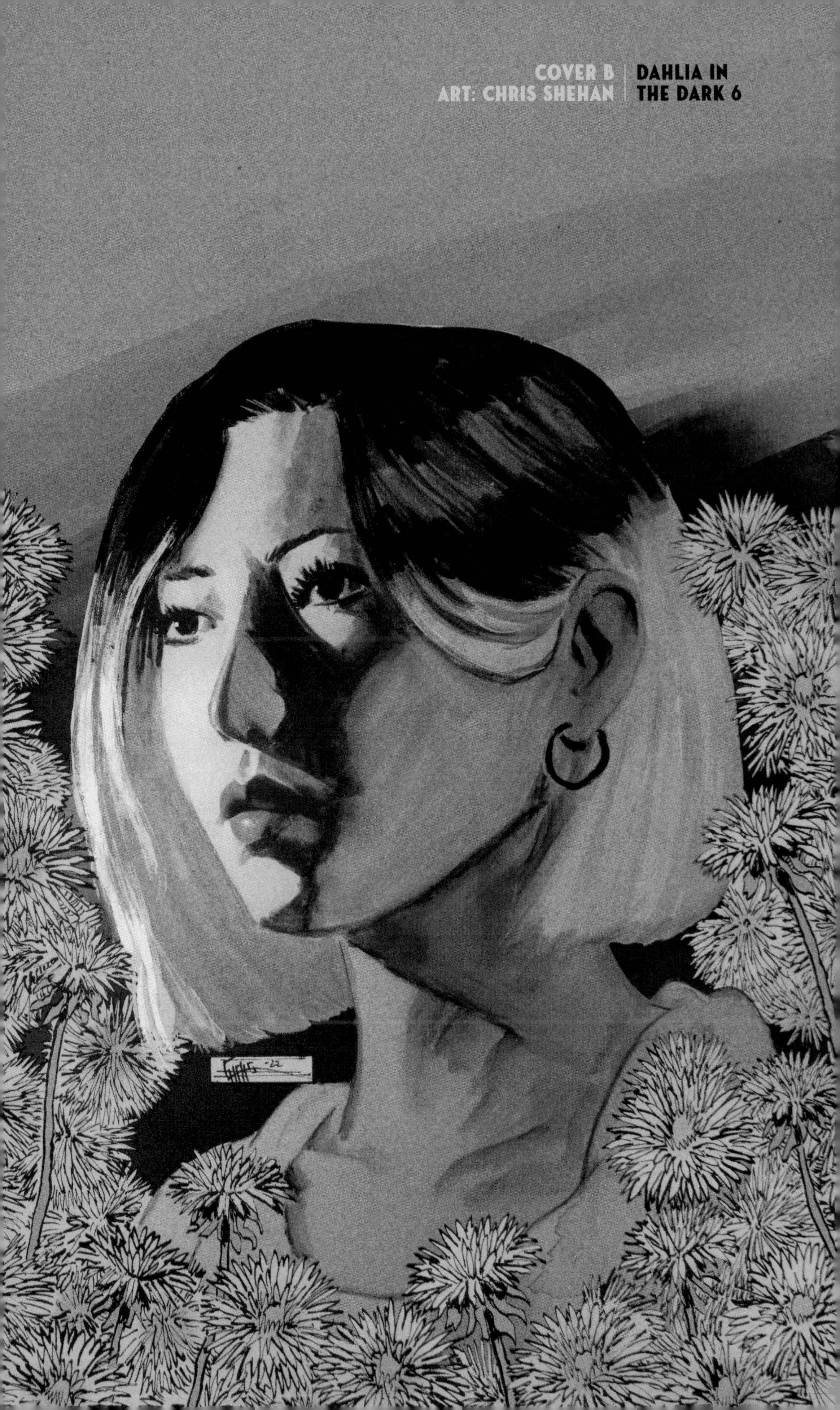

COVER B
ART: CHRIS SHEHAN
DAHLIA IN THE DARK 6

MCS EXCLUSIVE | DAHLIA IN THE DARK 1
ART: FRANCINE DELGADO

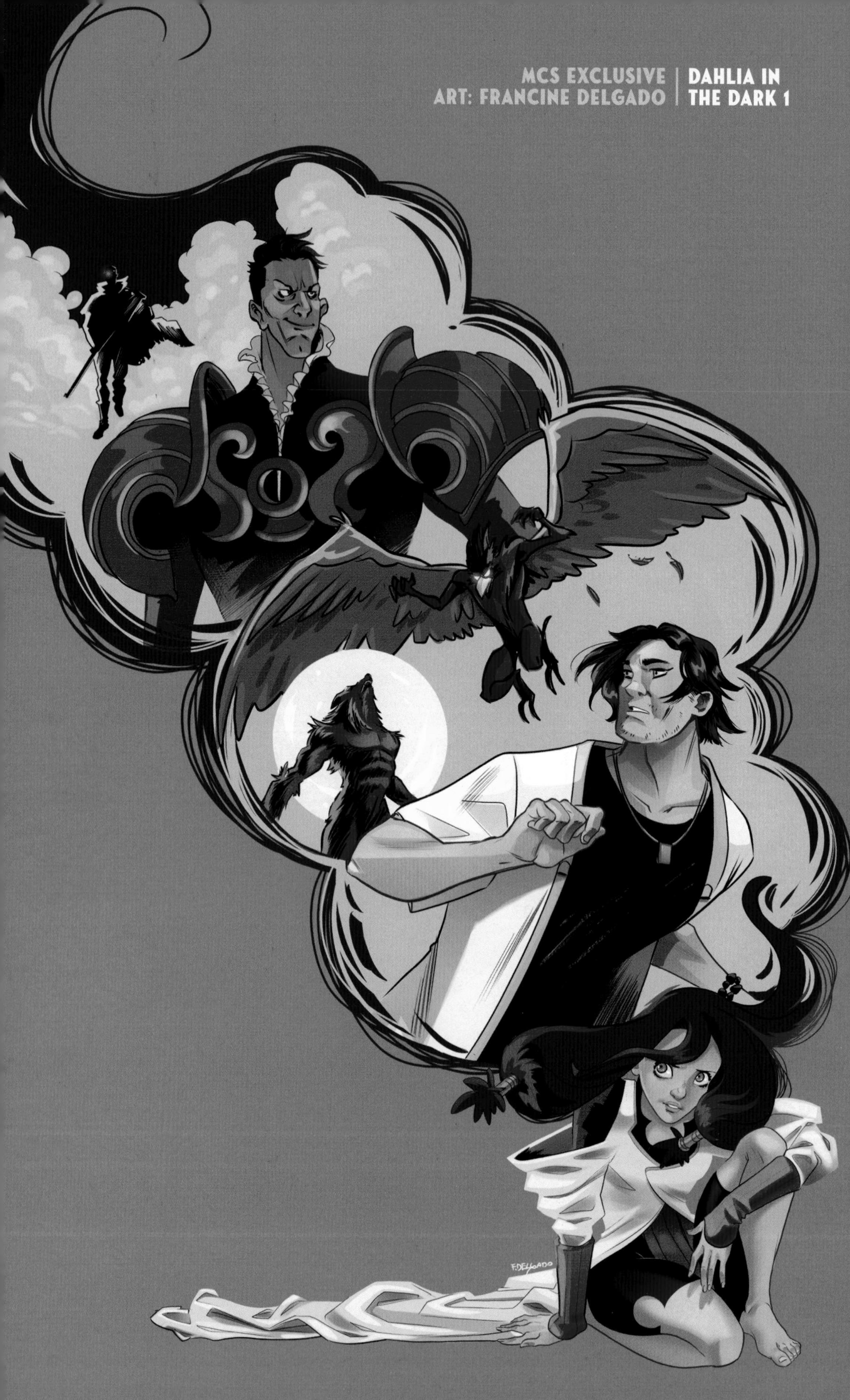
F.DELGADO

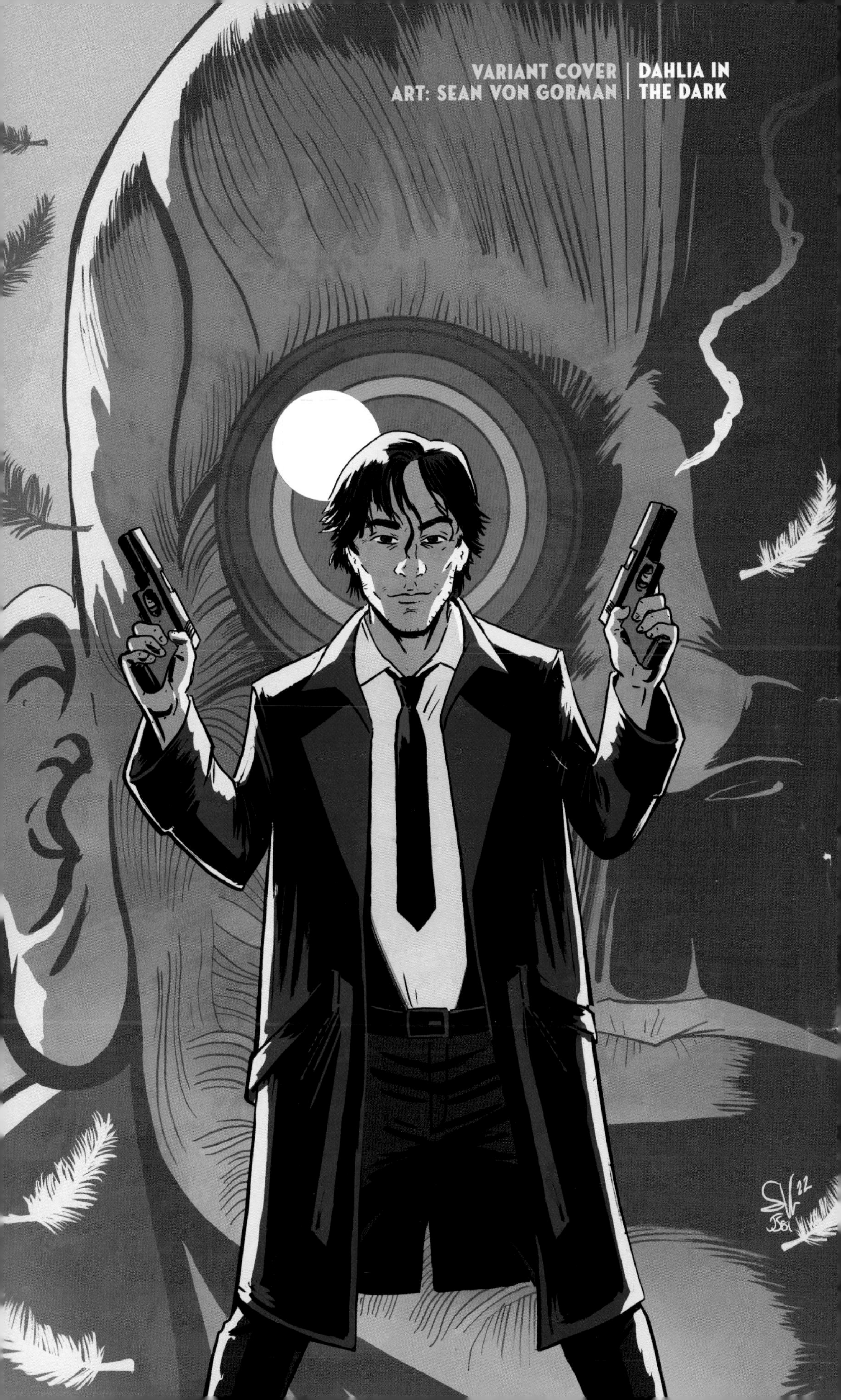

VARIANT COVER | DAHLIA IN THE DARK
ART: SEAN VON GORMAN

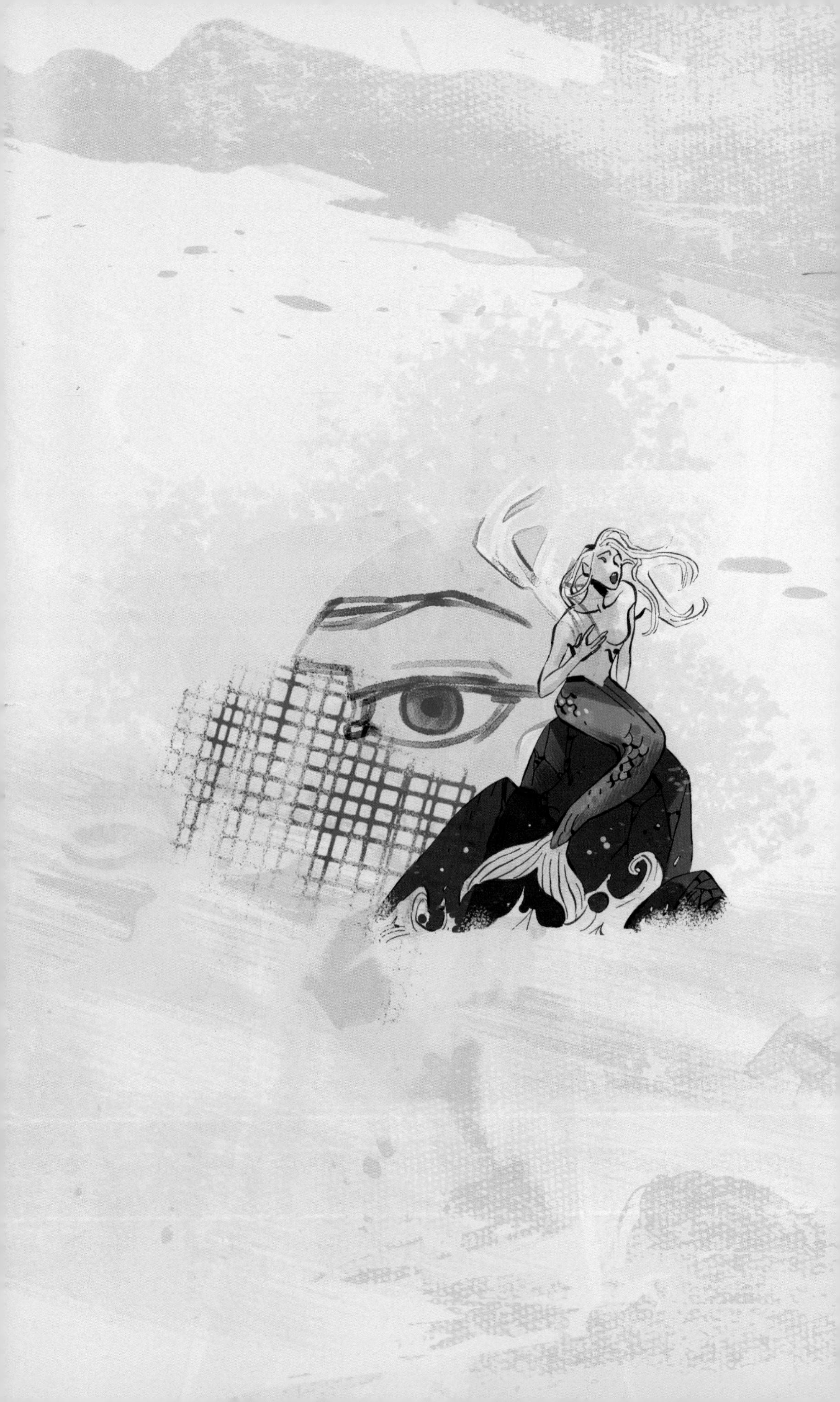